Chambers

# Dedication

For Dad, a crafty old ...

# LOST CRAFTS

### REDISCOVERING
### TRADITIONAL SKILLS
### UNA McGOVERN

Chambers

CHAMBERS
An imprint of Chambers Harrap Publishers Ltd
7 Hopetoun Crescent, Edinburgh, EH7 4AY

Chambers Harrap is an Hachette Livre UK company

© Una McGovern under licence to Chambers Harrap Publishers Limited 2008

Chambers® is a registered trademark of Chambers Harrap Publishers Ltd

This edition published by Chambers Harrap Publishers Ltd 2009
Hardback edition published 2008

Every reasonable effort has been made by the author and the publishers to trace the copyright
holders of material quoted in this book. Any errors or omissions should be notified in writing to
the publishers, who will endeavour to rectify the situation for any reprints and future editions.

Extract p110 from *Liquid Pleasures*, p113; extract p115 from *Liquid Pleasures*, p156; extract
p126 from *Liquid Pleasures*, p99. *Liquid Pleasures* by John Burnett (Routledge, 1999). Used
by permission. Extract p113 from *Home Brewed Beers and Stouts* by CJJ Berry (1963,
© Amateur Winemaker Books 2002). Used by permission. Extract p131 from *The Complete
Guide to Country Living* by Suzanne Beedell and Barbara Hargreaves (David and Charles,
1979). Used by permission. Extract p143 from *Food for Free* by Richard Mabey © Richard
Mabey 1972. Reprinted by permission of HarperCollins Publishers Ltd. Extract p330 from
*Country Crafts Today* by JE Manners (David and Charles, 1974). Used by permission.

All internet addresses were correct at the time of going to print. The author and Chambers
Harrap Publishers Ltd are not responsible for the content of external websites.

www.chambers.co.uk

Designed by Mark Blackadder
Typeset in Golden Cockerel and Lamar Pen by Chambers Harrap Publishers Ltd, Edinburgh
Printed and bound in India

# Contents

## FARMING

## HUNTING AND GATHERING

## FOOD AND DRINK

# Contents

## HOME AND GARDEN

## PRACTICAL CRAFTS

## DECORATIVE CRAFTS

# *Introduction*

Once upon a time an ordinary day might have started with milking the house cow and sweeping down your front step with a besom broom. After making a trip to the wheelwright for a quick repair, you might have visited a nearby copse, under horsepower, to pick up and deliver a cartload of bodged chair legs, tied down with handmade rope. A lunch of homemade cheese, jam and pickles, and honey from your own bees, might have preceded a sneaky visit to the river for some illicit trout guddling. Failing that, you could have skinned and cooked a rabbit to supplement the harvest from your kitchen garden. Twilight might have found you sitting with a friend outside a local inn, whittling and drinking a pint of ale (brewed on the premises and poured from a wooden cask made last year) while the rushlights burned low.

In the modern world, however, life is very different. Where would you turn if you needed fire but had no means of ignition? Would you be able to build a house from mud and straw? Could you feed your family if it wasn't possible simply to visit a shop? Few of us today can honestly say that we possess the skills required for the production of the basic necessities (or even the traditional niceties). Before the industrial revolution, for centuries, or even millennia, the societies of the western world were built upon such skills. Everything from the smallest rural community to international trade relied upon simple, practical knowledge – some common, some shared, some specialist, but all potentially accessible. The raw materials were drawn directly from farming, forest management or nature, and the patterns of work (often meaning the difference between success and starvation) were usually dependent upon the seasons or the weather.

The advent of large-scale production-line manufacturing, increasingly powered by fossil fuels, brought this long tradition to an abrupt end. Within two centuries, most of the skills had all but disappeared, to be replaced by mass production and a 'disposable' society. It is only within the last 40 years or so that people have begun to think seriously about preserving and reviving these crafts before they are lost forever.

In an age of wind-farm debates, biofuels, 'exotic' plastic-wrapped organic foods and carbon credits, these once-threatened crafts can still teach us a great deal about sustainable living – and many are great fun to boot. Browse, daydream, be inspired and maybe even have a go yourself!

*Una McGovern*
*Devon, May 2008*

# About the Author

Una McGovern studied English Language and Literature at the University of Sheffield, before completing an MA in Lexicography at the University of Exeter. She has worked in reference publishing for a number of years and is currently a freelance editor and writer, with books on a wide range of subjects to her name.

Among other titles, she has edited *Chambers Biographical Dictionary* (2002), *Chambers Dictionary of Literary Characters* (2004) and *Chambers Dictionary of Quotations* (2005), and recently compiled, edited and wrote for *Chambers Dictionary of the Unexplained* (2007) – something of an interesting deviation from the mainstream. Elsewhere, she has copy-edited and contributed to other projects, including fiction titles and adult education materials.

She spent many years making regular forays from Edinburgh to the Highlands and Islands of Scotland, before a return to rural Devon brought with it the opportunity to develop an organic kitchen garden, complete with traditional breed chickens. She now lives with her partner in a small Dartmoor town.

# Other Contributors

*Copy Editor*: Stuart Fortey
*Picture Research*: Sharon McTeir, Creative Publishing Services
*Additional Picture Research*: Hazel Norris
*Additional Illustrations*: Andrew Butterworth
*Editorial Assistance*: Katie Brooks
*Design*: Mark Blackadder
*Prepress*: Becky Pickard
*Cover*: Rob Ryan
*Publishing Manager*: Hazel Norris

The publishers would like to thank Camilla Rockwood for her original idea and for her involvement in the initial stages of this book's development. They would also like to thank all those who suggested possible skills, crafts and activities for inclusion.

# Farming

# Dry-stone Walling

## DRY-STONE WALLS OR DYKES

Dry-stone walls, or dykes as they are often called in Scotland, are walls built without mortar. They are held together by their own weight and by the careful positioning of each stone. A well-built dry-stone wall can last for decades before it needs any maintenance, and even then it can be simply rebuilt from its original stones.

## LONG HISTORY

The old techniques of dry-stone walling, very little different from those of today, can be found in such ancient structures as the Neolithic village of Skara Brae on Orkney. Perhaps even more impressive are the Scottish brochs, predominant on Orkney, on Shetland and in the Western Isles. A number of these huge round towers, formed from two concentric dry-stone walls, still stand 2,000 years after they were built, demonstrating the skill of the dry-stone waller as well as the durability of this style of walling.

The majority of the dry-stone walls that can be seen in the landscape today are field walls. While some of these are ancient, probably built up between boundary stones, most were constructed in response to the Enclosure Acts. Much of Northumberland and Wales would have been walled in the 16th century, while many other walls were built during another period of enclosure from the 18th century onwards. The walls have a number of practical purposes: they divide fields and contain livestock, and the leeward side of a dry-stone wall provides shelter for the animals. Building dry-stone walls was also a way of clearing land of rocks and boulders (the resulting wall being known as a clearance wall). Most were built by gangs of itinerant professional wallers and dykers, who travelled the country doing this backbreaking work.

## STONY GROUND

Dry-stone walls are mostly found in upland areas, where hedging might not be suitable, and where usable stones occur. The style of wall building and its colour and appearance vary in different parts of the British Isles, reflecting the geography and geology of the area. Almost any stones can be used, from thin pieces of slate to neat brick-like pieces of sandstone. For field walls a minimal amount of dressing is required – stones are generally used as they are, a good waller having the skill to choose automatically a stone that will fit. Walls can be either single or double. The majority of stones in a single-thickness wall are the full width of that wall. Single walls are often built where a lower wall is needed – up to around 1.2 metres (4 feet) high. Higher walls are made from a double thickness. Two more or less separate walls are built, with a central area, known as the heart, filled with small pieces of rock, sometimes known as heartings. Long 'through stones', which span the width of the completed wall, are set in at intervals to bind the two outer faces together. The wall is finished with a row of cope stones or toppings (also known as cams). These put an edge to the top of the wall, bind the two faces together and protect the wall from damage from determined sheep who decide to scramble over it.

## SMOOTS AND SQUEEZES

Dry-stone walls are sometimes built with a hole at ground level, called a smoot. When a new wall is erected on a nature reserve, smoots are included to let animals such as rabbits and hares pass easily between fields or different areas of land. In the past they have sometimes been used for a rather different purpose – a pit dug below a smoot and fitted with a trap would catch an unsuspecting rabbit for the dinner table. Ground-level holes were left in walls for other reasons too: water smoots allowed water to pass through the wall; and hogg holes (also known as cripple holes and sheep smooses, among other names) allowed sheep to pass between fields. Another interesting feature of some walls is the 'bee bole'. This is a flat-bottomed niche built in a south-facing wall, often near a farmhouse, to take a 'skep' – a simple type of beehive made of straw.

Two types of stile are common to allow humans, but not livestock, to cross a dry-stone wall easily. A step stile is, obviously, a series of steps which can be climbed – either just a few extra-long through stones placed to form a diagonal series of steps, or a staircase formed from a series of long blocks of stone. A squeeze is another type of stile – a V-shaped gap in the wall designed to allow humans to squeeze through, but too narrow for livestock.

## DEVON BANKS AND CORNISH HEDGES

These large solid walls, peculiar to the south-west of England, are of quite a different construction from most dry-stone walls. They are made from two faces of large stones, with the middle section filled with earth. Trees grow from the tops of them, the roots apparently binding them together rather than forcing them apart, as many that line the narrow lanes of Devon and Cornwall are of considerable age.

## NEVER PICK A STONE UP TWICE

A skilled waller will 'never pick a stone up twice'; in other words, they won't waste time picking up lots of different stones, then discarding them, but will choose a stone and use it. This is often the greatest stumbling-block for a beginner, until they have developed the knack of choosing a stone that will be a good fit in the wall.

Some general principles only are mentioned here for the construction of a double-thickness wall. The first task is to collect your stone, either from your own land (backbreaking but free) or from a local quarry. Always collect more than you think you will need. Dig down to create

*Construction of a new dry-stone wall, Grassington, Yorkshire Dales*
© *Ashley Cooper / Alamy*

a level foundation trench, then lay stones into it. Use your largest stones first, as this will create a solid base to the wall and you won't want to lift your larger stones up later on. Once the foundation level is laid, you can start creating two facings, with small filling stones in the middle. Some wallers use a frame and strings to guide the shaping of the wall, which tapers inwards towards the top. You will need to consult expert help to know how many through stones you should use, and where to place them, as this depends on the size of your structure.

## MORE WALLS

If you are interested in dry-stone walling, there are a number of organizations which will be able to help you. These include the Dry Stone Walling Association of Great Britain (www.dswa.org.uk), which has a number of regional branches and provides courses and training. The National Stone Centre in Derbyshire (www.nationalstonecentre.org.uk) also runs dry-stone walling courses, which include a visit to their Millennium Wall. Built in 2000 by members of the Dry Stone Walling Association, this includes 19 different types of walling executed in the appropriate regional stone for each style. There has been a deserved increase in interest in dry-stone walls in recent years. They are long-lasting and environmentally friendly structures that use only one local material and host a variety of wildlife in their nooks and crevices.

# Stone Fencing

## STONE FENCES

A variation on the dry-stone wall is the stone fence, also known as the flag fence or flag wall. Sometimes referred to (somewhat evocatively) as tombstone walls, such fences consist of a single row of large flat slabs, set on end.

## CONSTRUCTION

To construct a stone fence, a narrow trench is dug, up to 60 centimetres (24 inches) deep, into which the stones are placed on their ends. The trench is then gradually filled back in, a layer of soil at a time, with each layer compacted to keep the stones upright and stable. The top of the fence is kept level by burying shorter slabs less deeply than their taller neighbours. While handling very large flags is difficult, stone fences are much quicker to build than dry-stone walls, although when the fence begins to collapse, or lean drunkenly, all the slabs must be removed and reburied.

## MATERIALS

As with dry-stone walls, stone fences use locally quarried materials. Caithness in Scotland has the greatest concentration of stone fences in Britain. Here, the stones are red sandstone, and the style of construction is of flags overlapping by around 12–15 centimetres (5–6 inches), with the top of the fence kept remarkably level.

In the Lake District in England, stone fences are constructed from local slate. The earliest Lake District fences show that great care was sometimes taken to dress the flags so that they interlocked to form a very strong wall, while later walls use a slight overlap – a far simpler method.

## VACCARY WALLS

One particular type of stone fence is known as the vaccary wall. Vaccary was the name given to early cattle enclosures in hilly or moorland districts. Essentially, these were early cattle ranches, used for breeding cattle or oxen. Vaccary walls, erected to contain the livestock, were constructed in the same way as other stone fences, but often used thicker slabs. They were most common in Yorkshire and Lancashire, where a number still survive.

# Making Wattle Hurdles

## WATTLE HURDLES

Wattle hurdles are an ancient form of lightweight fencing, made from coppiced hazel or willow. Split and round rods are closely woven around a number of uprights, which have sharpened feet for sticking into the ground. Wattle hurdles are usually associated with the medieval period, when they were used primarily as portable fencing panels for building temporary sheepfolds. However, hurdle-makers still craft wattle hurdles today, using the same techniques as in the past, although their products are now found as decorative fences in gardens, having been replaced by electric fencing and sheds on the sheep farm.

## THE GOLDEN HOOF

The wool trade of the Middle Ages did much to make England wealthy, but sheep were valued (although perhaps to a lesser degree) for another role as well. Before the advent of nitrogen fertilizers, it was essential that arable land was manured before it could be successfully used to raise cereal crops. This was most easily achieved by letting sheep manure it directly (under the feudal system, tenants were required to fold their sheep on the Lord of the Manor's land for a certain part of the year in order to keep his land in good condition). The sheep did not roam free, but were kept enclosed in folds created from wattle hurdles, and were moved on when their job was done. Because of their nitrogen-rich manure sheep became known as 'the golden hoof'.

## TWILLY HOLES

A small gap would be left in the weave of the hurdle, known as a twilly hole, through which a stick could be passed so that the hurdles could be hoisted onto the back. A shepherd could carry four hurdles with him, each measuring 1.8 metres (6 feet) long and 1 metre (3½ feet) high. They had a number of uses (for example, as temporary gates for controlling sheep when they were being sheared) and also provided some protection from the elements, especially at lambing time.

*The same Excess of Winds blow also in some dry, large, open Fields, and the more, where the Land lies on Hills: In both which Situations, the close Hazel-rodded Hurdles are now much in Use; and, indeed are an excellent Sort to break off the cold*

*bleak Winds, and other Weather, from the Sheep, as they lie confined all Night in a Fold; for, indeed it is enough for the poor Creatures to endure the Chill of the Earth, and not to suffer besides, the Violence of Winds, Rain, Snow, and Hail.*

William Ellis,
*A compleat system of experienced improvements, made on sheep, grass-lambs, and house-lambs* (1749)

*Large wattle hurdles*
© www.wattlehurdles.com

## WATTLE WEAVING

The first task in wattle weaving is preparing the materials. Straight hazel or willow rods, around 30 millimetres (1¼ inches) in diameter, are used for the uprights, which are known as zales or sails. The two zales for the ends of the hurdle are left round, while the rest of the zales are split (or 'cleaved') in two using a billhook. There are ten zales in a completed traditional hurdle (although regional variations in this and other elements of hurdle making, such as the pattern of the weave, do exist). The zales are sharpened and placed in a frame, sometimes known as a gallows. This holds the zales upright so that smaller rods, around 20 millimetres (¾ inch) in diameter, can be woven around them. A key part of this weaving comes with taking the rod around an end zale before weaving it back along the hurdle. To manage this without snapping the rod, it must be twisted so that its fibres separate and it becomes more flexible.

A number of courses in traditional hurdle making are available, and details of many of these can be found by searching online. The very keen enthusiast should take a course in coppicing first, in order to learn how the hurdle-maker's materials are grown.

# *Coppicing*

## COPPICING

Coppicing is an ancient method of woodland management. When certain trees are felled (and these include most native British broad-leaved species), rather than dying they grow several new shoots very rapidly from the base of the remaining stump. After a number of years, depending on the species of tree and the use the wood will be put to, these shoots can be harvested. Further shoots will then grow, allowing the process to be repeated some years later. This can go on for hundreds of years, making coppicing an extremely effective and sustainable way of getting the most out of woodland – indeed, coppiced trees will usually live much longer than trees that have never been cut.

*New shoots on a coppiced hazel tree*
*© Agripicture Images / Alamy*

## HOW IT WORKS

When a pine tree is cut down, it will die, but when a broad-leaved tree is felled, it will coppice. This means that, as long as the stump and roots are left intact, the tree will put its energy into regrowing by sending out new shoots. Much of the work of coppicing, traditionally carried out using hand tools such as billhooks, takes place during the winter. The cutting is followed by vigorous regrowth in the new season. In species such as hazel, ash and oak, the new shoots (called 'spring') come from the sides of the stump, which then becomes known as a 'stool'. In other species such as cherry, the new shoots are suckers sent up from the roots. Each of these will grow to be an individual tree, while the original stump gradually rots away. In either case, the new shoots grow extremely vigorously, as they are supported by a root system that was big enough to feed a large tree. They also grow very straight, up to the light, producing extremely useful poles in a relatively short space of time. These can be harvested when they reach the appropriate size for their purpose, and the process will begin again, with the stool producing more shoots. The length of time between cuttings is known as the 'rotation'.

A similar method is used in 'pollarding' – essentially, coppicing a tree but further up its unfelled trunk. A pollard (as such a tree is known) is cut around 2.4 metres (8 feet) above the ground, and new shoots will grow from this point. While the resultant poles are not as straight as those produced by coppicing, pollarding was a useful way of growing firewood in grazed areas, as the new shoots formed above grazing height. Pollards were also sometimes used to mark the boundaries of woods.

## ANCIENT WOODSMANSHIP

The Neolithic wattle trackways laid in the Somerset Levels, and made from straight rods of wood, are often cited as evidence that the craft of coppicing in Britain can be traced back to around 4000 BC, although it cannot be known whether coppicing was carried out in any systematic way. It is thought that coppicing was practised during the Bronze Age and the Roman and Saxon periods, but the craft was perhaps perfected in medieval times, when the majority of woodland was heavily managed, either as coppice or as woodland pasture. From medieval times onwards, all wood obtained from coppicing was put to some use: for example, it was burnt as fuel; made into charcoal; used in house building; woven into hurdles; used in basketry; made into besom brooms; used as handles for tools; made into hedge stakes; used as kindling; made into faggots for burning; and used as pea-sticks (sticks placed in the ground to support pea plants). It was during this period that the practice of including 'standards' (trees, often oak, that were allowed to mature naturally in order to provide larger pieces of timber) among coppiced trees became widespread. The coppiced trees growing below the standards were known as 'underwood'.

## DECLINE AND RISE OF COPPICE CRAFT

Coppicing went into decline from the 18th century onwards, as the trend for plantations of larger timber trees set in. These plantations consisted

of trees of a single variety, rather than the mixed species found in coppice areas, where the different woods were valued for their variety of uses. From the mid-19th century many of the traditional uses of coppiced wood died out – in particular, coal and coke became the favoured fuels instead of firewood and charcoal. However, a limited amount of commercial coppicing did survive, and there has been a revival of interest in the craft in recent years; partly because it is now understood to be an important way of maintaining traditional woodland, and partly because demand for such things as sustainable barbecue charcoal has opened up new markets for coppice-wood products. There are now a number of regional coppicing associations which promote and support the craft, and a number of organizations, such as the British Trust for Conservation Volunteers (www2.btcv.org.uk), run courses in coppicing.

# Hedge Laying

## HEDGEROWS

Essentially, a hedgerow is a line of shrubs, with or without trees, that forms a boundary. Some British hedges date back to Roman times, others were planted in the medieval period to mark parish and other boundaries, while the majority of historical hedges that can still be found in today's landscape were laid as a result of the Enclosure Acts of the 18th and 19th centuries. It has been estimated that in the 20th century some 200,000 miles of Britain's hedges were grubbed up in a bid to make bigger fields which could be farmed more easily with large machinery. More recently there has been a drive to lay new hedges, and 'important' hedgerows (those of a significant age and exhibiting a variety of species) have been protected to some degree by an Act of Parliament. Hedges are excellent windbreaks, sheltering both livestock and crops. They also help to prevent soil erosion, and are very important for wildlife, both as habitats in themselves and as wildlife corridors, allowing movement between other habitats.

## QUICKSET OR QUICKTHORN HEDGES

The quickset hedge is a common manner of hedging – 'quick' meaning alive, as hedges are a living and growing barrier – made by planting thornbushes. Various styles of hedge are found in different parts of Britain, depending on location and usage. Rather than referring to a hedge of a particular style, the following is a more universal guide, showing some of the general principles.

## Planting a hedge

The first job in creating a new hedge is to grow or buy your thorn seedlings. The common hawthorn (*Crataegus monogyna*), also known as whitethorn or may, is often used. If the seedlings are planted in their final position when they are still small, they need to be protected from grazing animals for four years. The craft of hedge laying comes once the thorns are established. For a hedge to be maintained, it must be checked every few years and relaid when necessary.

## Laying your hedge

*Newly-laid hedge,
winter*
© *Iain Cooper / Alamy*

The hedge-layer's equipment consists of a billhook, a long-handled slasher (a heavy-duty tool consisting of a sharp blade on a long handle, used to cut back very overgrown hedges), perhaps an axe, and leather gloves for protection from the thorns. The job is done during the winter months, when the hedge is free from leaves.

The first task is to clear the bottom of the hedge of brambles and undergrowth. Then stakes are cut from the hedge that will be used in laying it. These should be cut so as to leave strongly growing bushes at fairly regular intervals along the length of the hedge. Next, working uphill, a downward cut is made halfway through the first main stem in the hedge, using a billhook. This cut is vital – it must be made close to the ground and go through enough of the stem to allow it to be bent, but not go so far as to kill the plant. The half-cut stem is then forced downwards to nearly horizontal. This process is repeated along the length of the hedge so that all the large stems are bent over at as near the same angle as possible. The stakes that were cut earlier are driven into the hedge, interwoven with the hedge material, to help keep it secure (in some styles these stakes are upright, whereas in other styles they lean at right angles to the bent stems). Finally, the tops of the stakes are often intertwined with pliable material such as long willow or hazel rods, although this binding does not appear in some styles. The stakes and binding material will eventually rot away, but by that time the hedge will be secure.

## DATING A HEDGE

While few of us will have the opportunity to try our hand at hedge laying, it is possible to try hedge dating on almost any country stroll. Hedges often display a wide variety of species, even if they were originally planted only with thorn. Over time plants such as oak, holly, hazel, bramble and honeysuckle, as well as many wild flowers, become established in the hedge through natural means, their seeds having been blown there by the wind or carried there by birds or other animals. Naturalist Dr Max Hooper was the first to suggest that the age of a hedge could be calculated by counting the variety of species in it. 'Hooper's hedge hypothesis' was first published in 1974, and while it has never claimed to give precise results or to be accurate in all circumstances, it is still a very useful rule of thumb. According to the hypothesis, the number of different woody species in a stretch of hedge approximately 30 metres (30 yards) long is equal to the age of that hedge in centuries. To try hedge dating, use the length of your pace to measure out approximately 30 metres of hedge and, with the help of a field guide if necessary, try to count the number of different woody species that are present there.

## MORE HEDGEROWS

Should you want to know more about hedges and the craft of hedge laying, further information can be obtained from the following societies and groups: the National Hedgelaying Society (www.hedgelaying.org.uk); the British Trust for Conservation Volunteers (www2.btcv.org.uk); and the Farming and Wildlife Advisory Group (www.fwag.org.uk).

# *Tree Felling*

## FELLING TREES

Trees have been felled for as long as man has wanted to use their timber for shelter or fuel, or to cultivate the land on which they stand for farming. The basic principles of safely felling a tree by hand, be it with a sharpened stone or a purpose-made axe, have remained the same since ancient times, although on a commercial scale the axe has been replaced by the 'tree-harvester', a machine which can fell, debranch and chop up a substantial tree in seconds.

## THE INFLUENCE OF THE MOON

*With the moon's wedel [waning] 'tis good to begin the hewing of wood.*
Calendar printed by Hupfuff in Strasbourg (1511)

In some places it was once believed that the best time for tree felling was when the moon was waning, and that wood cut when the moon was waxing was no good as it was full of moisture (making it of no use for the carpenter or as fuel). The idea behind this belief was perhaps linked to the effect of the moon on the tides – the sap in the trees decreased or at least flowed downwards, making the wood drier, as the visible portion of the moon decreased. However, folklorists have discovered that quite opposite beliefs were held in different parts of the world; so while, for example, many French foresters did their felling as the moon waned, some German woodsmen would only do it as the moon waxed. While gardening by the phases of the moon is still popular among a minority of horticulturalists, tree felling by the moon seems to have died out.

## THE THREAT OF THE AXE

Should you have a fruit tree that it no longer seems worthwhile to keep because it never rewards you with any fruit, you should perhaps consider threatening it with an axe before taking the irrevocable step of actually cutting it down:

*To make a Barren Tree bear Fruit*
*Having girt and tucked up your clothes, and having taken an axe or hatchet,*
*approach the tree with resentment, wishing to cut it down: but when any body comes*
*to you, and deprecates the cutting of it, as if responsible for a future crop, seem to be*
*persuaded, and to spare the tree, and it will bear fruit well in future.*
Thomas Owen, *Agricultural Pursuits* (a translation of *Geoponika*, 1805–6)

## I'M A LUMBERJACK

Safety has to be the prime consideration in felling a tree, and it is not a craft to practise lightly. The following description relates to felling a tree with an axe and a crosscut saw, rather than a chainsaw (the use of which requires training and specialist protective clothing).

The first task when felling a tree involves looking at it and deciding which way it is likely to fall. A tree will naturally lean in one direction, and to make the job simpler you should cut it down so that it falls in that direction – as long as its path to the ground and the ground itself is clear for the entire length of the trunk, and the felled tree won't land on anything it shouldn't. If you think the tree will naturally fall where you don't want it to, felling it will be a more complicated operation, and not for the beginner (neither are very large trees nor trees in tricky situations). Also, think about what the tree is likely to do when it hits the ground – uneven ground might make it bounce, or on steep ground it might roll. Next, check to see if the branches of the tree are tangled up in any way, for example with the branches of another tree, as these will need to be removed first. Think about which areas will be safe while you are felling the tree and make sure everyone knows which way they should run if anything goes wrong. Check the trunk to see if there is any obvious rot, and if there is, cut above it rather than into it, as the rot would make the movement of the tree unpredictable.

The first cut should be made using an axe. It should be made horizontally into the trunk on the side where you want the tree to fall. It should go no more than a third of the way into the trunk. The second cut is a down-angled cut, which, together with your first cut, will remove a wedge-shaped piece of wood from the tree. Then move to the opposite side of the tree, and together with a willing friend, and making a final check that anyone nearby knows what is going on, use a two-handled crosscut saw to slice horizontally into the tree just above the level of your 'wedge' cut. This is the cut that will fell the tree. You will hear a crack before you have cut all the way through. Move away, and the tree will fall. For added safety, you can tie a rope securely to the trunk before you start, and strong volunteers can hold it taut while you are working, guiding the tree in a safe direction. Remember that the rope *must* be longer than the height of the tree to avoid flattening your helpers.

A very small tree – with a trunk of less than around 12 centimetres (5 inches) in diameter – can be felled with an axe alone, by chopping into the trunk and then giving it a push.

## USES OF THE FELLED TREE

Every part of the felled tree can be used in some way. The wood has the most obvious uses – when seasoned it can be used as fuel or in carpentry. But don't forget the bark, which has long been used in tanning leather and as a natural dye (beech bark can be used to make a pinky-red dye, for example), or which can be chipped and used as garden mulch.

# Milking a Cow

## MILKING

Animals have been milked for thousands of years. The first mammals exploited for their milk were sheep and goats, but by the 16th century the cow had become the predominant dairy animal. All milking was done by hand until the beginning of the 20th century, when milking machines were gradually introduced. Many farmers continued to milk by hand because of the expense of the equipment, but today hand-milking is only really carried out by smallholders who keep a very limited number of stock (perhaps one dairy cow and one goat).

## HOW TO MILK YOUR COW

*To prevent Cows from contracting Bad Habits while Milking.*—*Cows should always be treated with great gentleness, and soothed by mild usage, especially when young and ticklish, or when the paps are tender, in which case the udder ought to be fomented with warm water before milking, and touched with the greatest tenderness, otherwise the cow will be in danger of contracting bad habits, becoming stubborn and unruly, and retaining her milk ever after. A cow never lets down her milk pleasantly to the person she dreads or dislikes.*

Sarah Hale, *The New Household Receipt-Book* (1854)

Cows need to be milked twice a day, ideally with a twelve-hour interval between the two milkings. Clean equipment and clean hands are essential. You will need a low milking stool and a pail. First, give the cow some feed to keep her happy and quiet. Next, wash the cow's udder and teats with warmish water – the massaging action of cleaning her will actually make milking easier, as it will help relax the udder and release the milk. Sit down next to the cow, facing her tail, with your pail gripped between your knees at an angle (as a beginner, you may find the cow becomes a bit restless, and if she accidentally kicks the bucket you are less likely to lose the milk if you are holding on to it).

Take hold of two of the teats gently but firmly. Keeping the top of each hand at the top of each teat (so the hand is slightly pressed against the udder), milk by squeezing with each finger in sequence – first squeeze with the thumb and forefinger (this stops the milk from going back up into the udder), then bring in the second finger, then the third and finally the little finger, until milk has been expelled and you are left gently gripping the teat with all your fingers. Alternate this squeezing with each hand until all the milk has been forced out, then move on to the final two teats. Never pull on the teats – this will hurt the cow and you won't get any milk. Practise on a dummy teat if possible (perhaps made from a rubber glove) until you are sure of keeping the motion rhythmic, as you don't want to upset your cow. Ideally, find a docile cow that is accustomed to being milked by hand (a startled cow and a nervous milker don't go very well together). Goats and sheep are milked in the same way – they have only two teats, but this certainly doesn't make them easier to milk.

# Shearing a Sheep

## SHEARING SHEEP

Wool has been collected from sheep for thousands of years. The earliest sheep did not need to be shorn, as they naturally moulted each summer, and the farmer could either collect the wool from the ground where it fell, or pluck it from the sheep by hand at moulting time (a process known as 'rooing' in Orkney and Shetland). As sheep breeds with improved wool were developed, moulting diminished and shearing became the norm, with fleeces cut off in one piece using hand-held shears. Shears were used for hundreds of years, and although the first mechanical shearing machines were introduced in the 1880s, it was not until the mid-20th century that hand-shearing became something of a rarity and electric clippers became widespread.

## FIRST WASH YOUR SHEEP

*Wash sheep (for the better,) where water doth run,*
*And let him go cleanly, and dry in the sun:*
*Then shear him, and spare not, at two days an end,*
*The sooner the better, his corps will amend.*
Thomas Tusser, *Five Hundred Points of Good Husbandry* (1557)

In the past, the first part of the shearing process was washing the sheep. This was often done by herding them into a suitable stream, where they would swim and hence their fleeces would become cleaner. The names of two Devon villages reflect this tradition: Washbourne refers to the stream once used for washing sheep, and Sheepwash means 'place where sheep are dipped'. Several days were left between washing and shearing for the fleece to dry and for the natural grease, known as 'yolk', to recoat the fibres of the wool. Initially, each farmer would shear his own sheep, but as flocks became larger shearing was taken over by gangs of itinerant shearers, who would travel between farms from late May to August. Although they now use electric clippers, gangs from New Zealand and Australia still travel the world shearing sheep.

## THE WOOLSACK

The wool trade once formed one of the most important sectors of the English economy. The Woolsack, a square cushion of wool on which the Speaker of the House of Lords sits, reflects this. It was introduced during the reign of Edward III (1327–77), and symbolized the wealth of the country and the source of this wealth. Originally stuffed with English wool, it is now filled with wool from around the Commonwealth.

*Traditional sheep-shearing*
© *Highland Folk Museum*
*Licensor www.scran.ac.uk*

## GETTING YOUR SHEEP SHORN

While methods vary (and always have done), the shearer generally throws the sheep on its back (in which position it is least troublesome) and grips it between his legs, leaving both hands free for the work of shearing. One hand holds the fleece taut, while the other clips it away in one complete piece. The aim is to clip as close to the sheep as possible without nicking it. In the past, accidental injuries to the sheep were treated with Stockholm tar to prevent infections – hence the saying 'spoil the ship for a hap'orth of tar' (in which 'ship' is a dialect version of 'sheep'). Sheepshearing is a true craft, involving a great deal of skill as well as hard physical work. An agricultural show can be one of the best places to learn more about traditional

# Shearing a Sheep

sheepshearing, as the programme will often include a hand-shearing demonstration or competition. While most shearers are men, women do compete as well. It is an impressive sight to see a sometimes feisty sheep being expertly shorn in around ten minutes, although the competitions are not simply against the clock – both fleeces and sheep are checked to see that a good job has been done.

# Beekeeping

## BEES

Bees are kept for honey and for beeswax (and they are also highly beneficial in pollinating crops). Our ancient ancestors no doubt knew how to steal honeycombs from wild bees, but bees have also been kept for thousands of years and modern beekeepers, or apiarists, continue this tradition.

*Making bee skeps, the Cotswolds*
*© Paul Felix Photography / Alamy*

## WAX AND HONEY

The heyday of British beekeeping was perhaps during the thousand years before the Reformation, when beekeeping prospered as a result of the enormous demand for church candles (made from pure beeswax, and quite unlike the smelly, smoky tallow candles used by 'ordinary' people). Every monastery kept an apiary for the wax (although the honey was not wasted either – it was either eaten or used in making the alcoholic drink mead), as did the houses of the nobility. Each farm would have had its bees, and swarms would have been more common than they are today.

The bees were caught when they were swarming in late spring, and kept in simple straw hives called skeps (these had replaced dome-shaped hives made of wattle and daub, which themselves had replaced hollow logs, the earliest form of 'hive'). The skep was made from straw plaited into rope. The rope was twisted round and sewn to the previous coil, until a conical basket was formed, with holes left for the bees to enter and leave by. The skep was then placed in a 'bee bole', a flat-bottomed niche built into a wall. This afforded the skep some protection from the wind and rain. In autumn the skeps were checked, and the heaviest were taken for their honey. This generally meant destroying the bees by burning a piece of sulphur under the skep. The honeycomb was then dug out, and crushed and strained to release the honey. From the 17th century onwards, this bee-killing method became less popular, and some preferred to place an empty skep on top of a full one, with a hole made between the two, so that the bees could move to the empty skep and survive the honey harvest. Various hive designs appeared in an attempt to overcome some of the problems of the skep. These had removable frames to hold the honeycombs, but each failed to some extent as the frames would become unmovable when the bees plastered them into place with a resin called propolis or by building honeycomb. The beekeeping breakthrough did not come until 1851, when an American beekeeper called Reverend Lorenzo Langstroth discovered what he called the bee space (the exact space that should be used between frames in a hive). It was discovered through observation that if the space in a hive is too small for a bee to pass through comfortably the bee will block it with propolis, and if it is much bigger than it needs to be then the bee will construct comb in it. This, together with a number of his other innovations, still forms the basis of the modern craft.

## TELLING THE BEES

*Marriage, birth or buryin',*
*News across the seas,*
*All you're sad or merry in,*
*You must tell the Bees.*
Rudyard Kipling, 'The Bee Boy's Song' from *Puck of Pook's Hill* (1906)

It was once a widespread superstition that any important family news should be shared with the bees. 'Telling the bees' was particularly important if there was a death in the family – if the bees were not told it was thought that they would either die, or swarm and leave their hive forever. Sometimes a set routine was followed: the teller might first knock on the hive with the key to the house, or a set phrase would be used to impart the news, such as 'Bees, bees, your master's dead, and now you must work for your missis'. The hives were often draped in black cloth when there was a death in the family, and the bees were 'invited' to the funeral. At its most extreme, the custom also involved briefly lifting the hives at the same moment as the coffin was lifted to be taken from the house for burial, thus symbolizing the bees' inclusion in the funeral procession. Telling the bees was a commonly observed custom in the 19th century, and while such traditions as draping the hives with mourning cloth date from that century, it is not known how much older the practice of keeping your bees informed of family news might be. Some modern-day beekeepers continue the tradition of politely informing their bees of any changes in the household.

There are a number of other superstitions relating to bees, all of which are characterized by the belief that they are sensitive to human behaviour and quick to take offence. Bees are said not to like bad language, and will not thrive if the family that owns them is quarrelsome. Well into the 20th century, many people believed that bees should not be bought and sold in the normal way because this would offend them. They were most commonly bartered (a swarm in exchange for a small pig, for example). At a push, some beekeepers thought that bees could be exchanged for gold, and while some saw no harm in giving them as a gift, others believed that bad luck would follow this. Bees have also been thought wise and pious, and were once said to hum in their hives at midnight on Christmas Eve to honour the birth of Jesus.

## STARTING UP

It is expensive to set up as a beekeeper, but once you have invested in the necessary equipment the running costs are minimal, and you should be rewarded with delicious honey and extremely useful beeswax. To get started, some of the key things you need are: a hive; some bees; a bee suit (including a veiled hat); a smoker; bee gloves; a feeder; and some expert advice, whether from an experienced beekeeper or a book (or preferably both). There are numerous decisions to make before you start, including what type of hive and bee you want. You also need to consider the responsibilities of beekeeping – winter is fairly quiet, but late spring and early summer is a much busier time, when you need to prevent your bees from swarming (and leaving you). The British Beekeepers Association (www.britishbee.org.uk) provides help and information for the novice beekeeper. It holds introductory courses, can give advice and support, and provides the contact details of the many local beekeeping associations.

*Harvesting*

## HARVESTING GRAIN CROPS BY HAND

The climax of the arable farming year comes with the grain harvest. In many respects very little changed in the craft of harvesting from the time of the Bronze Age farmers until the Victorian period – hand tools were used to cut the crop, which was bundled into sheaves to dry before threshing (knocking the grain from the husks) and winnowing (removing the husks and other chaff). While the tools slowly evolved over the centuries (along with improvements in the crops), the labour-intensive nature of the harvest remained the same until mechanized harvesting methods were developed in the 19th century. Mechanical reapers and the earliest combine harvesters (which combine the tasks of cutting the crop and separating and cleaning the grain) were patented in the 1830s, although their use did not become widespread for many years. In the early 20th century, traditional harvesting methods could still be seen on a few of the smaller farms in Britain, but with the introduction of self-propelled combines in 1940 (the earliest combines had been drawn by horses, then later pulled by tractors) harvesting became an almost entirely mechanical procedure, with one person able to do the work of many in a fraction of the time. However, the craft of traditional harvesting has never been entirely lost.

## SICKLES, REAPING HOOKS AND SCYTHES

The tools used for cutting grain crops prior to mechanization were sickles, reaping hooks and scythes. A sickle is made of a curved blade

out without rotting). A mow was made by standing a circle of sheaves on their ends, with the heads leaning into the middle. Another circle of sheaves was placed on top of this, and so on, but with fewer sheaves in each layer until the top point of the mow consisted of the ears of just a few sheaves. To stop the sheaves from slipping, a handful of stalks from a sheaf in the previous layer could be tucked under the band of a sheaf in the next layer. When rain fell on a mow, it ran down the stalks to the ground. A more weatherproof option was a thatched rick. The sheaves were laid horizontally, ears inwards, layer upon layer from the centre out. Shaped to a roof-like point, the rick could then be thatched and was effectively protected for the winter. As well as keeping water out, stacks and ricks needed to repel rats. Smaller circular corn stacks were sometimes raised off the ground on 'staddle stones', which were shaped to prevent rats from climbing up them. Raising a large rick was a more serious undertaking:

*A stack or rick is laid in Form of a long Square, with its Top in Shape of an old-fashioned House's Roof, for the water to fall quickly off. In this Shape Wheat-sheaves in the Beginning should be laid with their Arses outward all the Way up, to let in the Air to the Ears of Corn, and keep Wets and Vermin from entering. And, the better to prevent Rains hurting our Stacks of Corn, we commonly lay Pease, or Beans, or only straw, on the Top-ridge Part of it, and then timely thatch with Straw over all ... And in this Form it is, that we stack Wheat-sheaves, Barley, Oats, Pease, Beans, Thetches, Clover, St. Foyne, and natural hay. But, to keep any of these Corns the more secure from Accidents, some lay them on a Frame of Joists with fixed Boards over them, supported by Stone, Brick, or oaken Pillars, of two Feet or more high, with square Caps of Stone or Wood upon each, to hinder the Ascent of Rats, Mice, and other Vermin, and prevent the Mischief of Damps and Vapours of the Earth.*

William Ellis, *The Modern Husbandman* (1744)

## THRESHING AND WINNOWING

Once the grain was fully ripened and dried, it was threshed and winnowed. Threshing was a winter occupation, often carried out inside a barn on a threshing floor, sometimes made of wood but often of stone. The untied sheaves were placed on the floor and beaten with a flail – a long hand-held stick joined to a short stick, known as a swipple or swingle, which was hit against the grain. The two parts of a flail were often linked with leather or eel skin, which was tough but flexible and well suited to the task.

Once the grain had been knocked out of its husks, it was winnowed. Traditionally, this was done by gathering the grain into winnowing fans (essentially very shallow baskets, with a handle on either side) or wooden winnowing trays before throwing it up into the air in a strong breeze. All the chaff (the light pieces of husk, broken bits of straw, and so on) would be blown away, and the clean grain, which was heavier, would drop back down, ready to be loaded into sacks and stored, or sent to be milled.

While a modern-day combine will cut and thresh in one go, replacing the many stages of harvesting by hand, there are those who believe a better grain can be had by doing things the slow (and very hard) way.

*Using a winnowing sieve, South Uist, 1936*
© University of Edinburgh
Licensor www.scran.ac.uk

# Haymaking

## MAKING HAY

Hay is grass that has been cut and dried in the sun, and is a vital fodder crop for overwintering livestock. As with the harvesting of grain crops, traditional haymaking methods changed little between the Bronze Age and the 19th century, when mechanization first began to replace hand tools in farming.

## WHILE THE SUN SHINES

*Making hay is an operation simple enough in itself, provided the weather be all that is required, but is variously performed, according to the different means taken against unfavourable weather, and the customs of particular localities. Thus, in some places we may see the grass shaken out immediately after the scythe; in others, left in the swathe till the upper side is dried and browned. In one county, foot-cocks are the fashion; in another, the windrows are collected into heaps of great size; and while in one district forks, in another rakes, in a third the naked unarmed hands of the work-people are chiefly used in tossing and turning the hay.*
*British Farmer's Magazine* (Volume XXVIII, 1855)

In the past, June and July were the busiest haymaking times, although crops of hay could be taken until August. Dry sunny days make for the easiest haymaking, and the best hay comes from grass that has been cut before or just after flowering (but not when the grass has begun to go to seed). Grass is traditionally cut with a scythe, a tool made from a long curving blade attached at a right angle to a long wooden handle, and used since at least ancient Roman times.

Haymaking was a busy part of the farming calendar, as 'winning' a good crop of hay was essential for keeping livestock fed in the winter. Teams of people would work from dawn. First, those with scythes would make their way across the meadow, swinging the scythes to cut the grass. Other workers would follow, and, with different areas favouring slightly different methods, the cut grass would be 'tedded', or spread out, to encourage drying. It would be turned every few hours until it was dry enough to be raked into long narrow rows known as windrows, using a specialized hay rake (a lightweight but durable wooden rake with a long handle and a wide span). From the windrows, the hay would then be forked

*Traditional haystacks*
© *Irishphoto.com / Alamy*

into small domes called cocks, using a simple two-pronged fork. The next day, weather permitting, the hay would be spread again, and turned to keep it drying as much as possible, before being forked back into cocks in the evening. On the third day, if there had been no rain and plenty of warmth and sunshine, it would be ready for stacking. If there had been rain, the hay had to be spread again, and turned and spread until it had properly dried. While a little rain when the hay was in cocks would not be too detrimental, too much rain and, in the worst years, grass that took weeks to dry would make hay that was almost useless, as much of its nutritional value would have been lost.

## HAYSTACKS

When the hay was dry it was forked into piles called stacks. Either the cocks were forked into a number of small stacks in the meadow, or large horse-drawn wagons, or wains, would go around the field collecting the haycocks and taking them elsewhere to be built into giant haystacks.

Smaller haystacks would have ropes, weighted with stones, pulled over them to keep them in place, and were generally only left a month or so before the hay was taken into a barn or other building. Larger haystacks or ricks were built layer by layer with sides that projected slightly outwards, in order to give some protection from rain, and were often placed on a specially constructed platform to keep the hay away from moisture. When the haystack was finished, the top would be thatched with straw for extra protection and stability. The hay was cut from these large stacks as it was needed.

## MODERN HAYMAKING

Modern haymaking is generally done by machine rather than by hand, although smallholders with only a small amount of grass will still use the traditional methods. Haystacks have mostly disappeared from the landscape, replaced by the cylindrical bales produced by baling machines.

*Milling*

## MILLING GRAIN

One of the oldest and simplest methods of milling uses the stone mill, or quern. This is a simple device consisting of two stones, one (which is turned by hand) on top of another (which remains stationary). Grain is fed through a hole in the top stone and ground between the two. While this and later developments in hand-milling were adequate methods for providing flour for one family, the craft of milling came into its own first with the water mill and later with the windmill. These embrace the power of water or wind to mill much larger quantities of grain.

## WATER MILLS

Water mills first appeared in Britain during the Roman period, and the Domesday book mentions over 6,000 water mills in existence in England in 1086.

Probably the most important part of the water mill is the water wheel, turned by the flow of water. Water mills were built next to rivers or streams, and the provision of water to turn the wheel was often improved with the building of weirs, which would raise the level of the water to increase the pressure of its flow. Alternatively, 'leats' were built to channel water from a river to the mill – these were essentially artificial waterways, which could control the flow of water by a series of hatches. Millponds were also constructed, the level of which could be carefully regulated through the judicious use of sluicegates. The control of the supply of water to the wheel was one of the miller's most skilful tasks, as milling could only take place while the wheel turned.

There are three basic designs of water wheel, each adapted to suit the flow of water. In lowland areas, where the course of the river is relatively flat, 'undershot' wheels were most commonly used. These wheels dip into the water, and are turned by the current alone. Where faster-running streams occur in hillier land, the more efficient 'breastshot' and 'overshot' wheels were used. These are essentially turned by weight of water rather than by current. In breastshot wheels the water is fed into the wheel half way up, and in overshot wheels the water comes along a chute and hits the top of the wheel. Water wheels were made of wood – the paddles were often of elm, while the wheel and shaft might be oak. The turning of the wheel would turn a shaft, which would turn a system of cogs and wheels and eventually work the millstones – in pairs, the lower one stationary, the upper one moving; very similar to quernstones, but much larger.

Water mills (and other forms of mill) were originally in the hands of either the Lord of the Manor or the local monastery, and both exercised 'soke rights'. This meant that all tenants on the land were obliged to have their corn ground at the mill, and to pay for the privilege. The payment was made in grain, the average toll, or 'multure', being one sixteenth of the total. Milling at home was forbidden, and the use of a quernstone could result in a fine levied by the manorial court. Millers were treated with some suspicion, and had a reputation for dishonesty. They commonly took a larger share of the grain than was due by pressing their thumb on the scales when the grain was being weighed, thereby increasing the weight and the size of toll – hence the saying, 'every honest miller has a golden thumb'. Some millers were thought to cheat the lord as well as the peasant by passing on less than was due in grain rent. Chaucer's miller had a golden thumb, and was capable of stealing corn and taking three times the toll:

> Wel koude he stelen corn and tollen thries;
> And yet he hadde a thumbe of gold, pardee.
>> Geoffrey Chaucer, General Prologue to *The Canterbury Tales* (1387)

From the 18th century onwards, mills were no longer in the ownership of the church or the landowners, and in 1796 a law was passed under which the miller must be paid with money – a rather clearer undertaking than the earlier toll of grain, especially as a miller could be fined if he did not clearly display his prices.

Millers had to know a variety of skills to successfully run a mill. While many other craftspeople were involved in creating and repairing water mills and their machinery, including carpenters, joiners and blacksmiths, millers had to be able to maintain their mills on a daily basis. They also had to be constantly aware of the flow of water, the turn of the stones and the quality of the flour being produced. Some even dressed their own millstones, although this was often left to a skilled stone dresser, as they had to be cut in just the right way to grind flour satisfactorily, pushing the flour from the centre to the outside of the stones, where it could be collected.

*Right. Water mill: Rossett Mill, Wrexham*
© Alan Novelli / Alamy

*Far right. Post mill: Chillenden Windmill, Kent*
© Chris Laurens / Alamy

## WINDMILLS

The earliest written references to windmills in England date from the 12th century. Wind power is not as reliable as water power, so windmills were generally located in cereal-growing areas which lacked the fast-flowing streams needed to power a water mill – English windmilling developed in the flatlands of East Anglia. Three types of windmill developed over time: the post mill; the smock mill; and the tower mill. Through a system of cogs and wheels, the rotation of the windmill's sails could turn pairs of millstones to grind grain to flour.

The earliest type of windmill was the post mill, so named because the whole body, or 'buck', of the mill (which contained the mill machinery and supported large sails) was balanced on a large upright post. The whole body could then be rotated so that the sails always faced into the wind. This movement was made possible by a long beam, called a tailpole, which protruded from the back of the body. By pushing on the tailpole the miller could rotate his mill.

After post mills came smock mills, probably developed in the 17th century. The invention of the rotatable cap meant that smock mills were a significant improvement on post mills. The wooden body of a smock mill remains stationary, while only the cap, with the sails attached, is moved to catch the wind. Smock mills could be built taller, with larger sails to catch more wind. The body of the mill could also be bigger, accommodating more pairs of millstones and so able to grind more corn.

Tower mills were the final improvement on the smock mills. By replacing the wooden body with a brick tower, tower mills could be even bigger and taller than smock mills, and their brick construction also made them more durable.

*Far left. Smock mill: Herne Windmill, Kent*
© Marco Secchi / Alamy

*Left. Tower mill: Stow Windmill, Norfolk*
© Richard Osbourne/Blue Pearl Photographic / Alamy

## MORE GRIST TO THE MILL

While traditional mills are predominantly associated with milling flour, they had other applications too – for example, water wheels were used to drive machinery for forges, and for driving the hammers to 'full' cloth (beating it to finish it). Even so, mills went into decline with the Industrial Revolution – even though an increased demand for flour for the towns initially kept them busy. Mills were abandoned, and became derelict. Of the mills that have survived, many have been converted to houses, although towards the end of the 20th century there was a move to restore mills to working order where possible. Some mills are run as working museums of rural industry, but there are now a limited number of both windmills and water mills once again producing flour commercially in the traditional way. If you would like to know more about mills and their restoration, the Society for the Protection of Ancient Buildings has a dedicated mills section on its website (www.spabmills.org.uk). The society campaigns for the protection and sympathetic restoration of mills, and organizes an annual National Mills Weekend.

# Hunting and Gathering

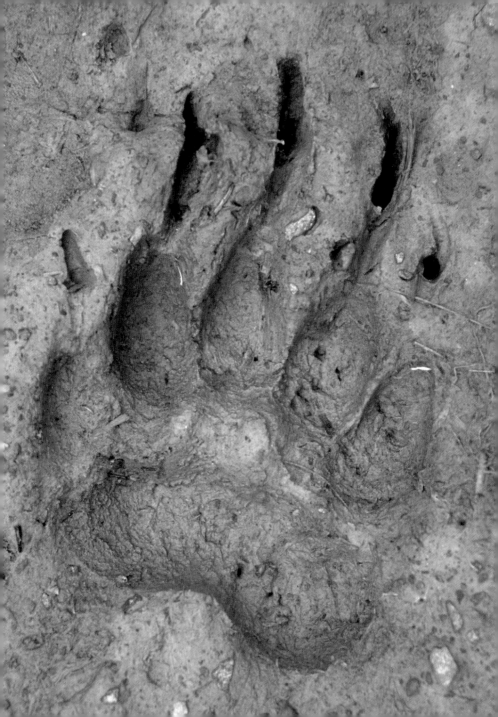

## ANIMAL TRACKING

The most obvious way to track an animal is to follow its actual tracks (ie its 'footprints') in either snow or soft ground. Less obvious methods include identifying an animal's droppings (or 'scats'), or looking for more subtle signs – the telltale damage to vegetation that some animals cause (for example, bark stripped from trees by deer) or the food remains that they leave behind (such as the exceptionally neat, small round holes that dormice leave in discarded hazelnut shells). For our Stone Age ancestors, the ability to track animals was a vital part of hunting for meat, which was essential to survival before the widespread cultivation of crops. Nowadays the craft of animal tracking is more often a hobby, used to identify the wildlife present in an area.

> *Badger print*
> © *Arco Images GmBH/*
> *Alamy*

## FOSSILIZED FOOTPRINTS

Animal tracks are of interest not only to the hunter or the wildlife enthusiast. The fossilized footprints of a number of extinct creatures, including dinosaurs, have been found in various parts of the world. The study of these may not lead to the animal, but can provide information on the size and the gait of the creature and the speed at which it moved (calculated from the distance between prints). The discovery of fossilized footprints in Dumfriesshire in the 19th century caused the geologist (and Dean of Westminster) William Buckland to wax philosophical:

*The historian or the antiquary may have traversed the fields of ancient or of modern battles; and may have pursued the line of march of triumphant conquerors, whose armies trampled down the most mighty kingdoms of the world. The winds and storms have utterly obliterated the ephemeral impressions of their course. Not a track remains of a single foot, or a single hoof, of the countless millions of men and beasts whose progress spread desolation over the earth. But the reptiles that crawled upon the half-finished surface of our infant planet, have left memorials of their passage, enduring and indelible ... Centuries and thousands of years may have rolled away between the time in which those footprints were impressed by tortoises upon the sands of their native Scotland, and the hour when they were laid bare and exposed to our curious eyes. Yet we behold them, stamped upon the rock, distinct as the track of the passing animal upon the recent snow; as if to show that thousands of years are but as nothing amidst eternity—and, as it were, in mockery of the fleeting, perishable course of the mightiest potentates of mankind.*

*Chambers's Edinburgh Journal*, Volume XVII, January–June 1852

## IN THE FIELD

To learn the craft of animal tracking, you really need a guide (be that in the form of an expert or a book), but some basics for getting started are given below.

### Tracks

A good place to start when you are trying to identify the tracks of British animals is to count the toes. The track left by a badger is quite easy to recognize – badgers have five toes, and a large kidney-shaped pad behind them. Otters also have five toes, but the large pad is almost round, and in very soft mud you might be able to distinguish the webbing between the toes. Foxes have four toes, but unfortunately so too do dogs. However, fox prints are more compact. Deer are cloven-hoofed, so their prints show only two toes. Sheep are also cloven-hoofed, but the toes are shorter, making deer prints easy to distinguish.

### Droppings

To help you to confirm the identifications you have made from tracks, the distinguishing features of some British mammal droppings are as follows. Badgers deposit their droppings in specific areas known as latrines – these are communal, and can often be found either near the sett or at the edge of the feeding range used by the group. Badgers dig out a pit for this purpose, but do not cover over the droppings. Otter droppings are called 'spraints', and are often found in a prominent position, such as on top of a rock. They vary in accordance with the otter's diet (as all animal droppings do) but are often black or dark green and have a very distinctive odour, which has been described as being like anything from new-mown hay to lavender. Fox droppings are often left in the same place each night (sometimes somewhere prominent) and are pointed and twisted. Deer droppings can be confused with those of rabbits (which are small and round) but are more oval in shape.

## FURTHER TRACKING

The International Society for Professional Trackers (www.ispt.org) is an organization for anyone interested in tracking, from professionals to those who enjoy it as a hobby. Some 'bushcraft' schools teach courses in tracking (a search on the Internet should reveal some of these), and numerous books are available which will help you to identify tracks and droppings, such as *Animal Tracks and Signs* (2006) by Preben Bang and Preben Dahlstrom.

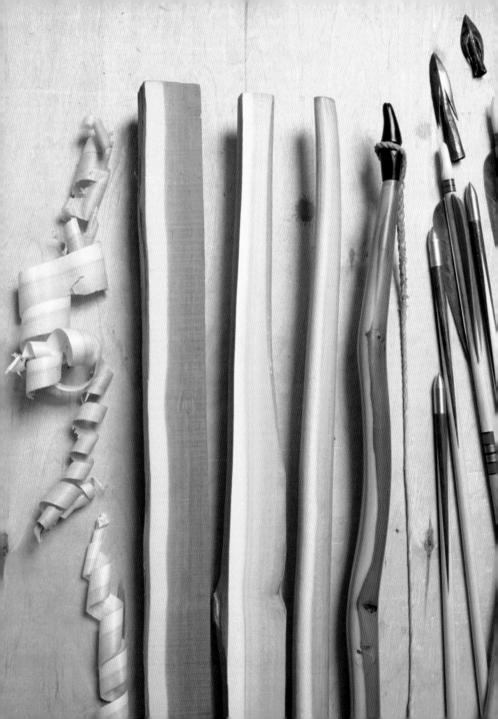

*Making a Bow and Arrows*

## THE BOW AND ARROW

The bow and arrow is an ancient weapon, used for hunting, in warfare, and latterly most often seen in the sport of archery. Different materials have been used for the components of the bow, which is used to shoot the arrows, but it generally consists of a piece of flexible wood bent into a curve by a string that is attached to both ends. The arrows themselves are traditionally made from a shaft of wood tipped with a sharpened piece of flint, bone, antler or metal. Fletches (traditionally made from feathers) are added to the other end of the arrow shaft to aid flight.

## HUNTING

Stone Age man was hunting with the bow and arrow in the late Palaeolithic era, and prehistoric cave paintings in France and Spain depict hunting with a bow and arrow. This was an important development – the bow and arrow allowed man to kill his prey, or his enemy, from a distance, making hunting safer. Bows of various designs developed and were used in almost every part of the world at different times, but the bow and arrow is now often associated with Native American peoples:

*The implements used in hunting by the Clatsops, Chinnooks, and other neighbouring nations, are the gun, bow and arrow, deadfall, pits, snares, and spears or gigs ... The most common weapon is the bow and arrow, with which every man is provided, even though he may carry a gun, and which is used in every kind of hunting. The bow is extremely neat, and, being very thin and flat, possesses great elasticity. It is made of*

*the heart of the white cedar, about two feet and a half in length, and two inches wide*
*in the centre, whence it tapers to the width of half an inch at the extremities.*

*History of the Expedition Under the Command of*
*Captains Lewis and Clarke* (1842)

It is thought that the bow and arrow was widespread in North America by c.500, replacing the atlatl (a throwing stick, used to give a spear greater propulsion). It remained a popular weapon even after the introduction of firearms, and is still used in hunting by traditional cultures in various parts of the world.

## ARCHERS AT WAR

The bow and arrow was the principal weapon of the armies of ancient Egypt, and was still being used in warfare in Europe in the 14th century. The firepower of the English archers at the Battle of Crécy in 1346 is often said to have been the decisive factor in the English victory over the larger French army. The English archers had such a reputation for deadly accuracy that at one time it was said (presumably in England rather than Scotland) that 'each English archer carries twelve Scotsmen under his girdle', referring both to their reputation and to the twelve arrows each carried in his belt. At Crécy the archers were equipped with longbows. Made of yew and as tall as the men using them, the longbows outranged the crossbows of the Genoese, fighting with the French, and the archers could have their next arrow ready (each carried 48 in total) before a crossbow could be reloaded.

## WILLIAM TELL

Perhaps the most famous feat with a bow and arrow is that of the legendary archer and Swiss hero William Tell. The story is generally told that on 18 November 1307 a yeoman farmer called William Tell was in the town of Altdorf in the Swiss canton of Uri with his young son. He walked through the town square, straight past a pole that was erected there. Either through ignorance or political motivation, Tell had committed a crime in walking past that pole, because the cruel Austrian bailiff Hermann Gessler had placed his hat at the top of it, and required all those who walked there to bow to it, as a means of showing his authority. Gessler had Tell arrested, and devised a devious punishment. Either Tell had to accept the challenge of shooting an apple placed on his son's head (taking the risk of killing his son) or both would be killed anyway. Tell accepted the challenge, preparing two arrows for his crossbow, and succeeded with the first shot. Asked why he had been prepared to make two shots, Tell replied that had he killed his son he would then have killed Gessler. After imprisonment and escape, the story concludes with the hero Tell finally assassinating the oppressor Gessler.

The legend of William Tell was not the first to tell of a father forced to shoot an apple from the head of his son. In the Scandinavian Saga of Thidrek, an archer called Egil is commanded by King Nidung to perform the same task. Egil also prepares two arrows, but succeeds with the first, and is asked why he had been ready to make a second shot. Egil's response that should he have killed his son, he would then have killed King Nidung does not lead to punishment in this story – King Nidung commends Egil for his honesty.

## MORE THAN ONE STRING TO YOUR BOW

In the past, archers literally had more than one string to their bows, as they would often carry a spare for emergencies. A bowyer is the traditional name for the maker of bows, and those who made arrows were called fletchers. Both of these were highly skilled professions, carried out by true craftsmen. The following method makes only a very crude bow and arrow, but is an interesting place to start. You will need a knot-free length of springy wood, ideally ash or elm, around 1 metre (3 feet) long (yew is the traditional choice, but the wood is poisonous and probably best avoided); a penknife; some straight, dry sticks (for arrows); sharpened flint (for arrowheads); strong, thin string (hemp string is very good); feathers; strong thread; sandpaper; and glue.

*William Tell*
© *Classic Image / Alamy*

## The bow

First you need to shape your bow. Take your length of springy wood, and use your penknife to taper the ends of the wood. Remember that where you scrape wood away will eventually be on the inside of the curve of the bow, as this will make it much stronger and less likely to break on your first attempt at firing it. To do the tapering safely, lay the length of wood on the ground and carefully scrape away from you with the knife. The central

part of the bow needs to be strongest, so no wood should be whittled from this. You will be left with a piece of wood that is strongest and thickest in the middle portion of its length, with ends that are more flexible. Carve two notches around 5 centimetres (2 inches) in from each end of the bow, where you will later attach the string. In the past, bowstrings were made of any suitable material, including sinew, linen or hemp, and in an emergency a bootlace or twisted plant fibres can be used. Take the string that you are using (something strong rather than stretchy) and attach it to one end of the bow, sliding it into the notches you made earlier and tying it securely. Bend the bow, then attach the string to the other end (this will be trickier because of the pressure of the bent bow, so you might want to tie a loop that you can slip over the end, to be held by the notches). If the string is not taut enough, release one end and tie it tighter.

## The arrows

Trim and sand the sticks you are using for arrows, making them as smooth and straight as possible (for completely straight arrows, and much less effort, buy some dowelling and simply cut this into lengths instead). For an authentic early arrowhead you will need a sharp shard of flint (for more detailed information, see the section on flint knapping on p59). Take a good-sized piece of flint and bring it down sharply onto another piece (wear goggles for safety). The flint should break into shards. Select one that most resembles an arrowhead – it needs to be flat, and long enough to be securely attached to the shaft of the arrow. If it needs further shaping (which it will, unless you are lucky) do this carefully, nicking away at the edge of the flint with the screwdriver tool on your penknife. You may need to have quite a few goes before you come up with an arrowhead you are satisfied with.

Use your penknife to make a shallow notch in one end of your arrow (the bowstring will slot into this when you are preparing to fire), then cut a slit into the other end. Push the end of the flint arrowhead into this slit. To keep the arrowhead in place, wrap some strong thread around the shaft for the length of the slit, and tie it securely. The next job is to fletch your arrow. If possible, use feathers for this, but if you cannot find any, paper will do. Cut fletches from the feathers (in the shape of shallow parallelograms), leaving a little of the central spine attached to hold the fletch together. Three fletches should be glued to the shaft of each arrow, with equal spacing between them. Leave some bare wood at the very end of the arrow, as you will need to grip this with your fingers as you draw your bow.

## ARCHERY

*Of all things in the world, health is the most important. I fear our little girls do not take sufficient exercise in the open air ... Ladies usually shoot at a distance of about fifty yards: two targets are placed opposite each other, and the archers shoot from one to the other: that is, when all the party have shot at one target, they walk up to it, gather their arrows, and shoot back to the one they came from, to which they again return when their arrows are expended ... so that, not merely the arm, but the whole frame, enjoys the benefit of salutary exercise in the open air.*

Mrs Child and Mrs Leslie, *The Little Girl's Own Book* (1847)

Should you successfully make your own bow and arrow, you will want to test it. Set up some targets in a garden, and enjoy what you have made, but remember that the bow and arrow is still a weapon and needs to be used carefully – don't shoot at or near anyone, and beware of inflicting damage on yourself when you are learning to draw.

## PURSUING THE CRAFT

If you want to take the craft further, there are a number of books available on the topic, which contain more of the true craftsmanship of the subject, including *The Traditional Bowyer's Bible*, by Jim Hamm et al (4 volumes, 1992–2008). Various organizations run bow-making courses (an Internet search should help you find one), and these will introduce you to some of the skills of traditional bow making.

*Flint Knapping*

## FLINT KNAPPING

Flint knapping, also known as flint working, is the craft of shaping flint by using tools to apply pressure to the stone, thus causing flakes of flint to fall away. Today, most flint-knappers are hobbyists, whereas for Stone Age man working with flint was a necessary skill.

## PREHISTORIC FLINT WORK

Prehistoric man shaped flint to make weapons and tools. A certain amount of flint can be picked up from the ground, but archaeological evidence shows that in Neolithic times flint was already being mined. This suggests that flint-knappers learned very early on that better-quality and larger pieces of flint could be had through mining, flint found above ground being smaller and often fractured because of frost. Once a large piece of flint had been mined, it would be struck – typically with a hammerstone, the earliest versions of which were simply a worn pebble of a material such as granite or quartzite – to break it into pieces small enough to be worked. To knap flint successfully, the knapper must be able to break it in a predictable way, a skill which is developed through practice.

Three techniques are used to shape flint: percussion flaking; pressure flaking; and indirect percussion flaking. In percussion flaking, the edge of the piece that is being worked, known as the core, is struck a sharp blow. The earliest tools for doing this were the hammerstone or a piece of deer antler. In pressure flaking, flakes of flint are detached by exerting downward and outward pressure on the edge of the core using a relatively sharp tool – originally an antler tine, or a sharpened piece of bone or hardwood. Two tools are used in indirect pressure flaking: a punch-like piece of bone or antler is held against the edge of the core and gently struck with a hammer. Through shaping pieces of flint Stone Age man was able to create a range of tools and weapons, including arrowheads, axe-heads, daggers and scraping tools for preparing animal skins. Many of the surviving pieces of Stone Age knapped flint show a high level of skill, although in practice flint knapping can be a hit-or-miss affair, with many pieces having to be discarded before a satisfactory finish is achieved.

## STRIKE A LIGHT

*Flint-knapping equipment*
© National Museums Scotland Licensor
www.scran.ac.uk

The spread of metal extraction and working brought about the end of flint-tool making. However, flint did not drop out of use. Flint forms sparks when struck against other materials, and its fire-starting properties continued to be exploited long after the Stone Age. Before the invention of the safety match in 1827, a tinderbox containing a piece of flint and a specially shaped piece of metal to strike it against provided a reasonably portable means of ignition. This arrangement was known as a strike-a-light. The sparks produced by flints were similarly employed in the flintlock action added to firearms from the 17th century onwards. Just as sparks were made by striking flint against the metal bar of the strike-a-light, they were also created when the flint in the spring-loaded arm of a gun was released against the steel lid of the flashpan, and they were sent into the gunpowder below. For a time, knapping became an important skill again, needed for making the shaped flints for the gunmakers. Steel tools were employed, but the principles were the same as those used by the knappers' prehistoric ancestors.

## LEARNING TO KNAP

A number of courses and workshops are available that teach flint-knapping techniques, and a quick search online should reveal one near you. Should you wish to have a go for yourself (especially easy if you live in southern Britain, where you are more likely to pick up some flint to practise on), make sure that you wear safety goggles and keep people and animals at a distance, as flying shards of razor-sharp flint can be dangerous.

# Making a Fire Without Matches

## FIRE

We cannot know when man first discovered how to make a fire, but fire has always existed – started, for example, when lightning strikes a tree, or in the vegetation at the edge of a lava flow. Archaeologists have found burnt sediment and charcoal at sites in Kenya dating back around 1.4 million years, perhaps showing the controlled use of fire, although it is generally thought that if fire was being used at this time it would have been 'borrowed' from naturally occurring fires rather than started. Fire is a source of warmth and protection and provides the means for cooking, essential for the survival of modern man, and as the safety match was not invented until 1827, a number of methods existed for making a fire without matches.

*Making fire with a magnifying glass*
© Niall Benvie / Alamy

## PLAYING WITH FIRE

Fire can, obviously, be dangerous. If you want to try one of the methods for starting a fire described below, do it in sensible surroundings (ie outdoors), and perhaps keep a bucket of sand or water handy in case your attempts at the craft of fire making are a bit too successful (especially important if the weather has been dry, which can make a fire spread rapidly). Keep the fire small, and always make sure it is out before leaving it (douse it with water if necessary). Ideally, try the craft on your own bonfire site in the garden, or at least do it somewhere that fires have been lit before (so you aren't adding to the damage to wild vegetation).

## NO SMOKE WITHOUT FIRE

*The most obvious source of igneous action with which mankind has always been familiar, is undoubtedly the orb from whence our earth is indebted for light and heat. It is not, indeed, probable that the earliest fires kindled by the progenitors of the human race were derived immediately from this luminary – as they could not be acquainted with the method of collecting its rays by the burning glass, nor of concentrating them by concave mirror: it is now, however, well known, that in some parts of the world vegetable and other matters may be in a state of dryness and inflammability, sufficient to allow them to become ignited by the mere action of the solar heat upon them.*

John Holland, *History and Description of Fossil Fuels, the Collieries, and Coal Trade in Great Britain* (1835)

On a sunny day, it is possible to start a fire by focusing the sun through a magnifying glass, or similar, onto dry tinder. Unfortunately, in so far as sunny days are not reliable, neither is this method of making a fire without matches.

## DRILL METHODS

*I have certainly made a thousand fires with rubbing sticks, and I have made at least five hundred different experiments. So far as I can learn, my own record of thirty-one seconds from taking the sticks to having the fire ablaze is the world's record.*

Ernest Thompson Seton, *Woodcraft and Indian Lore* (1912)

Some of the oldest, but most reliable, methods of starting a fire without matches rely on friction. Perhaps the best of these is the bow-and-drill method, said to be efficient even in bad weather.

In this method, the drill (a spindle of wood) is held upright under the palm of one hand. A bearing block (a piece of wood with a notch in it into which the drill comfortably fits) protects the palm from the drill. The base of the drill is pressed into a board of wood (sometimes referred to as the hearth) which has a notch cut out of it (drill a shallow hole, then cut a notch in this before you start drilling to make the fire). The notch allows dust created by the friction to collect and form an ember (which can be transferred most easily by placing a piece of bark or the blade of a knife under the notch before you start). The final piece of equipment is the bow. The string of the bow is twisted once around the drill, and with one hand pressing down on the drill and the hearth held in place by a foot, the other hand is free to move the bow backwards and forwards, causing the drill to bore into the hearth.

Once you have a good ember you should transfer it to a grapefruit-sized bundle of tinder (dry combustible material such as dry grasses or fine wood shavings). Place the ember in the bundle (without squashing it and putting it out), and blow on it gently (but carefully) to encourage the tinder to burn. Once it is burning, place the tinder among some kindling (small dry pieces of wood). Once the kindling is burning, you can gradually add pieces of firewood (collect this in advance, selecting wood that is dead and dry). It is said that for the most reliable results you should make your drill and hearth from the same wood, which should ideally be dead and dry (ie seasoned and not rotten). For maximum efficiency, shape your drill into a broad point at the bottom (where you want most friction) and a narrower point at the top (where you want least).

The hand-drill method is similar to the bow-and-drill method, but requires fewer pieces of equipment (no bow or bearing block), and is somewhat less dependable. Again, the foot holds the hearth in place, but the drill is twisted backwards and forwards between the palms of the hands, rather than with a bow.

## FIRE, FIRE

If your appetite is whetted for the ancient craft of making a fire without matches, then further techniques and details can be found in such books as *Essential Bushcraft* (2003) by Ray Mears, who has collected fire-making techniques from around the world.

*Making fire with a bow drill*
© Adam Hart-Davis / SPL

# *Catching Eels*

## EELS

Eels have often been regarded as somewhat enigmatic creatures. Their life cycle in particular was long shrouded in mystery – Aristotle believed they sprang from mud, and Pliny thought that when an eel rubbed itself against a rock, the pieces of flesh that came away turned into new eels. It was many centuries before this and other theories of spontaneous generation were conclusively disproved, and not until 1922 that the spawning grounds in the Sargasso Sea were identified. Despite this, eels have been an important source of food for thousands of years, trapped or caught in a variety of ways.

## EATING EELS

While the eating of eels is now most often associated with the jellied eels of London's East End, they once graced the tables of kings. It is said that when Henry III celebrated St Edward's Day in 1257, 15,000 eels were prepared for the feast. For many years eels were the staple fare of those who lived along the Thames or Severn, on the Somerset Levels or in the East Anglian Fens, and they were eaten throughout the country. However, from the mid-18th century the middle and upper classes lost their taste for eels. Dishes such as 'elver cakes', prepared from the young eels caught making their way upriver in spring, remained popular among the poorer classes, but by the mid-20th century eels were only eaten infrequently outside London (where even eel pie and mash, another favourite of the East End, went into decline). In other parts of Europe eels were not so ignored as in Britain, where a recent vogue in fashionable restaurants for smoked eel has still caused only a small upturn in the consumption of this fish.

## TRAPPING

The traditional trap for catching eels is made from willow. The basic shape is that of a long tube, tapering to a closed point at one end, with a funnel-shaped basket inserted into the entrance that has a hole small enough to allow the eel to enter the trap. The funnel shape guides the eel into the trap, but once inside it finds it much more difficult to locate the hole and escape. Some people used to add sticks or spikes to the inside of the funnel to further discourage the eel from escaping. These traps were baited (often with chicken or sheep guts), weighted and placed in the water in the evening and lifted the next morning, preferably full of eels. The basic design, with local variations, seems to have changed little over thousands of years.

Later eel-trappers working on a stretch of fairly slow water would often construct a wooden framework from which to suspend a row of basket eel traps, which could then be winched in and out of the water. Medieval monks on

*Eel trap, East Lothian*
*© East Lothian Museums*
*Service Licensor*
*www.scran.ac.uk*

the River Bann, in Northern Ireland, created a large eel trap by driving posts into the river bed and constructing wickerwork fencing between these posts to channel the eels into a net-filled gap. Water-powered mills often had a fixed eel trap, constructed of stone or logs, providing the miller with food and with an extra source of income.

Fyke nets are another popular method of trapping eels, although unfortunately these can also drown otters. The nets are similar to a keep net, but have two 'wings' at the opening to guide the eels in.

## SNIGGLING, STITCHERING AND SPEARING

*Sniggling for eels is another remarkable method of taking them, and is only to be practised on a warm day when the waters are low. This requires a long line of silk, and a small hook, baited with a lob-worm. Put the line into the cleft of a stick, about a foot and a half from the bait, and then thrust it into such holes or places, before mentioned, where he is supposed to lurk; and if there be one, it is great odds that he takes your bait. Some put the part of the line next the hook into the cleft; but whichever way it is managed, it ought to be so contrived that the line be disengaged from the stick, without checking the eel when he takes the bait. When he does swallow it, he is not to be drawn out hastily, nor until he is pretty well tired with pulling, when you may make him an easy prey.*

William Pitt Lennox, *Pictures of Sporting Life and Character* (1860)

'Sniggling' was once a popular pastime. The hook described above was more often replaced with a stout needle, such as a darning needle, and the equipment was easily assembled. How likely you were to succeed with such a method is not recorded, although it must certainly have been more reliable than 'stitchering'. This was apparently once favoured in the drainage ditches of Hampshire, and involved attaching an old sickle to a long pole, then using this weapon to flip eels out of the ditch onto the bank. Both sniggering and stitchering offered the eel a rather more sporting chance than spearing, another method of catching them during daylight. Long since outlawed, eel spears were gruesome weapons, their four barbed prongs thrust into the river until an eel was caught on them.

## BOBBING OR BABBING

A further method for catching eels is known as bobbing or babbing. The bob, or bab, is made by threading worms on to worsted or wool. This is then tied on to some string (which is attached to a stick) in such a way that loops of baited wool fall from a central part, where a weight can be fixed. This mop-like construction is then lowered to the bottom of a muddy stream, and the theory goes that within a few minutes you will be able to draw it back up, teeming with eels.

*You must provide a large quantity of well scoured lob-worms, and then with a long needle pass a thread through them from head to tail until you have strung about a pound. Tie both ends of the thread together, and then make them up into about a dozen or twenty links. The common way is to wrap them about a dozen times round the hand, and then tying them all together in one place, makes the links very readily ... You must angle in muddy water, or in the deeps or side of streams, and you will*

*soon find the eels run readily at your bait. When you have a bite, draw them gently*
*up towards the top of the water, and then suddenly hoist them in the shore, or in your*
*boat; by this means you may take three or four at a time.*

*The Sportsman's Dictionary; or, the Gentleman's Companion for Town*
*and Country* (1785)

## CATCHING AND SKINNING YOUR EELS

Many people are somewhat squeamish about eels. They are rather snake-like in appearance, and they do wriggle a lot and take a long time to die. Also, while they can be found in almost every river and canal in Britain, and in gravel pits, lakes, ponds and reservoirs too, they have undergone a dramatic decline in numbers in recent years, and some feel that they should no longer be caught. If you decide to try to catch an eel by one of the traditional methods, or simply with a fishing rod, check first whether the method you have selected is legal, and if so what licence or permit you might need. The eel season runs from approximately May to October. It is in October that the mature eels can be caught as they make their way to the sea and the long journey to the spawning grounds.

Skinning an eel is very straightforward. Simply slit the skin all around the base of the head, lift up the skin slightly, attach some pliers, and with a very firm grip on the head (some nail it to a board for this job), pull.

# Trout Guddling or Trout Tickling

## CATCHING TROUT BY HAND

The art of catching trout by hand, with no other equipment or tackle, is variously known as trout guddling or trout tickling. It is an ancient craft, but its practice is, strictly speaking, illegal in the UK.

## INTO THE POACHER'S POCKET

*It is a liberty taken by poachers with the little brook running through Castle Coombe, to catch trout by tickling. I instance the practice there because I have there witnessed it, although it prevails in other places. The person employed wades into the stream, puts his bare arms into the hole where trout resort, slides his fingers under the fish, feels its position, commences tickling, and the trout falls gradually into his hand, and is thrown upon the grass. This is a successful snare, destructive to the abundance of trout, and the angler's patient pleasure. The lovers of the 'hook and eye' system oppose these ticklish practices, and the ticklers, when caught, are 'punished according to the law,' while the patrons of the rod and line escape.*

William Hone, *The Table Book* (1827)

Trout guddling has been particularly associated with poachers, as it removes the need for cumbersome rods and tackle, making it easier for the poacher to flee from the gamekeeper. It has to be said, though, that compared to other methods of fishing it is time-consuming, and in previous centuries the craft was practised more from the need to eat than for profit. The penalties for poaching were steep, but many men resorted to it in times of rural poverty, particularly in the 18th century when the enclosure movement forced many small farmers off their land (their source of food). In more recent times, and certainly during the first half of the 20th century, trout streams were more often poached by boys, simply guddling for fun.

## LITERARY TICKLING

Much literary trout tickling is aimed at men, rather than fish.

> *What dost thou think I fish without a bait wench?*
> *I bob for fools? he is mine own, I have him,*
> *I told thee what would tickle him like a trout,*
> *And as I cast it so I caught him daintily,*
> *And all he has I have 'stowed at my devotion.*
> John Fletcher, *Rule a Wife and Have a Wife* (1624)

In John Fletcher's comedy, Estifiana refers to catching a man in terms of tickling for trout, and Shakespeare's pompous Malvolio is described as 'the trout that must be caught with tickling' in *Twelfth Night* (1601).

## NOODLING FOR CATFISH

Noodling (or grabbling) for catfish is an American version of fishing by hand, legal on certain rivers in certain states. It is a rather more extreme sport than guddling for trout. In noodling, a 'noodler' climbs into a river, finds a likely-looking hole in the riverbank, and wriggles his fingers (or toes) in the entrance to it in an attempt to lure out the catfish that might be inside, before grabbing the fish and wrestling it onto the bank. Obviously, using your own body as bait does have its dangers – catfish have rows of tiny teeth, and can grow to a maximum size of 1.5 metres (5 feet) long. Fingers, toes and even lives have been lost.

## THEORY OF THE CRAFT

Because of its legal status, the theory of trout guddling is given for interest only.

When a trout is startled by a movement on the bank of a stream it will swim for shelter, often hiding under the bank or a nearby rock. The theory of guddling tells you to watch out for that movement, making a quick mental note of the last place that the trout was seen before disappearing, then quickly head for that place. The trick then is to place your hands gently in the water, bring them slowly together around where you think the trout lies (it is, obviously, out of sight at this stage), then try to stroke the belly of the fish. It is said that this stroking (or tickling) will cause the fish to enter a trance-like state, enabling you to tighten your grip enough to lift it from the water. Trout guddlers of the past must have been well practised in their art – any sharp movements when you first place your hands in the water and the trout will dart rapidly away, and locating the underbelly of a fish that you cannot see is also a considerable skill. But for many, the thought of guddling takes them back to simpler, sunnier days:

*We, and the friend of our bosom, now a thriving colonist in New Zealand, went forth, nothing dismayed, to spy the capabilities of the land, and provide against the imminent famine. First of all we came to a burn, which we 'guddled'*—Anglice, *we groped for trout: and, in a trice, some dozen of speckled beauties were walloping on the sod.*

Blackwood's Edinburgh
Magazine, June 1852

*Fishing with Creels*

## CREELS AND OTHER LOBSTER POTS

There is one basic principle behind all creels and other lobster pots –
bait entices the lobster, or other crustacean, into the container through
funnel-like entrances that prevent its subsequent escape. It is thought that
the earliest traps were woven from willow, and such lobster pots were
made and used well into the 20th century, when they were finally replaced
by mass-produced pots made of wood or steel and nylon.

## TRADITIONAL TRAPS

*What are called* Lobster pots, or creels, *which are used for catching these
crustaceans, are made of osier rods, or basket-work; they are constructed on the same
principle as the wire mousetraps, so that when sunk to the bottom of the sea by the
weight of stones attached to them, the Lobsters, which crawl in after the bait, cannot
get out again; great numbers are caught in this way, with their relatives, crabs,
prawns, and shrimps, which, sharing in their fondness for raw flesh, share likewise in
their captivity, and ultimate death.*
Henry Gardiner Adams, *The Sea-Side Lesson Book* (1856)

The simplest lobster pot is a round, flat-bottomed basket with an entrance
at the top. This design, later called an inkwell pot, remained popular after
traditional materials were replaced with steel and nylon mesh. The pots
were woven by the fishermen in the winter, to be ready for the late spring
and summer lobster season. Willow, also known as osier, was the most
common material used. It is said that a skilled man would take only two

hours to weave a new pot, which would then last for several seasons. In preparation for use, the pots were weighted with stones and baited – lobsters were said to be attracted by old salted fish, rotten fish heads or even cormorant flesh.

The half-cylinder, or D-shaped, Scottish creel is perhaps the most recognizable of any lobster pot. This was originally constructed from a wooden frame, covered with netting. It often had an entrance at each end, on opposite sides, and was baited and weighted in the same way as inkwell pots. Wooden creels may still be seen in use, alongside modern synthetic alternatives.

The size of the entrance is the key in creel and lobster-pot making. If the entrance is too small, only undersized lobsters will be caught, while a much wider entrance allows larger lobsters into the pot, but also makes escape easier for smaller lobsters. Lobster fishing can be carried out with a single pot, heavily weighted and with a float attached (in the past these were made of cork) to identify the location and owner of the pot. More often a string of pots is used. In the past the craft was often practised by two men. A dozen pots would be taken out aboard a small boat, and placed in the sea according to the lobstermen's local knowledge of where the most lobsters could be found.

## LOBSTER LORE

Lobsters are now regarded as a luxury food, but, as with oysters, they used to be eaten by rich and poor alike. Once abundant, their slow growth (even a relatively small lobster will be several years old) make them likely victims of overfishing, although the decline in their population is now being redressed through the work of organizations such as the National Lobster Hatchery and campaigns for more sustainable fishing. Some individuals continue to make and use their own traditional creels, setting them in the inshore waters that the commercial operations now spurn.

# Making Fishing Nets

## FISHING NETS

The craft of making fishing nets is an ancient one. By knotting cord (made from natural fibres such as flax or hemp) early hunter-gatherers could make nets to catch fish either from rivers or from the sea. Different nets developed for different catches: drift nets are long nets, weighted at the bottom and with floats attached at the top (the fish are caught when their gills become entangled in the meshes – these nets are also known as gill nets); trammel nets are also set vertically in the water, and are made from a layer of fine mesh sandwiched between two layers of looser mesh; drag nets are dragged along the bottom of water; and trawl nets are shaped like a long tapering bag, with the mouth of the bag held open as the net is hauled through the sea behind a trawler. Until the early 19th century, when factories opened which made fishing nets by machine, net making was predominantly a cottage industry. A fisherman and his family would make and mend the nets he needed, and at one time many women were employed in making nets. Supplied by local rope yards, these women 'braided' nets at home.

## LASTING TRADITION

*Nets of every description are now made by machinery in London, and sold at a considerably reduced rate; they are however, in many instances, very inferior to such as are made by experienced fishermen.*

S F Every, *The Art of Netting* (1845)

Although net-making machinery was already in use at the time, the huge trawl nets used by the Grimsby herring fisheries in the early part of the 20th century were still knotted by hand, using twine made from natural fibres. However, the work was done in net factories rather than fishermen's cottages. In Great Yarmouth net-menders (known as beatsters) still mended nets by hand until the 1950s. The job was generally done by women, who stood patiently mending miles of nets.

Few nets are now made by hand, and most are made from artificial fibres. The craft of net mending has fared better, and survives among some small-boat fishermen, who still dextrously mend their nets on the harbourside. However, concerns that even this skill was dying out recently led the Cornwall Fisheries Resource Centre to offer net-mending courses.

## KNOTTING YOUR NET

*It is a very easy thing to net, when shown the method by any one who is expert at the practice of the art; but by no means easy to write an account of the different movements, in such a way, that beginners may be enabled to execute what they wish, from simply reading a description of the right method.*

S F Every, *The Art of Netting* (1845)

Net making by hand is not difficult, and requires little equipment. What it does require is patience – just think how many knots there are in a large fishing net.

If you want to try your hand at knotting a net, you will need some twine; some light rope; a mesh stick to keep the size of your mesh consistent; and a netting needle. The mesh stick can be made quite easily from a flat piece of wood – cut it to the width that you want your finished mesh to be, sand it and round the corners. A netting needle can be bought online – originally made of wood or bone, it is shuttle-like and has the twine wound on to it.

A plain diamond mesh is the easiest to master. Two knots are used – the clove hitch and the sheet bend (see the section on knots, p316, for instructions on how to tie these). First, tie a light rope between two fixed points – this will form the top line, or foundation, of your net, and needs to be taut. Working from left to right with your netting needle, tie the twine to the rope using a clove hitch. Then place your mesh stick parallel to your foundation rope (and below the first knot) and take the twine down in front of the stick and up behind it to the foundation rope, and tie another clove hitch. Repeat until you have the desired width. This creates a row of half-meshes, with equal spaces between the knots, and equal lengths of twine hanging down in each loop.

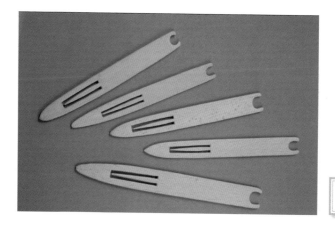

Net making is always done in one direction only (left to right is generally favoured by the right-handed), so next, and at the end of every row, turn the work over (or walk to the other side of it, if you are starting big). Hold your mesh stick below the last loop you made, bring the needle and twine around it, from front to back, and then, starting by going through the back of the loop above, tie a sheet bend. Continue along the row, tying a sheet bend in each loop. At the end of the row, turn the work, and do the same again.

# Making Fishing-rods

## FISHING-RODS

While sustenance fishing generally involves the use of nets, fishing-rods have also been used to catch fish for thousands of years. Figures are depicted fishing with rods in ancient Egyptian art, and the descriptions of angling left by Roman writer Claudius Aelianus (c.170–c.235 AD) reveal an activity very similar to modern fly-fishing. A simple fishing-rod (perhaps properly called a fishing-pole) is a long, flexible pole with a line attached to one end, to which a baited hook can be added. While few anglers now make their own rods, early anglers had to learn the craft of rod making before they could learn to catch their fish.

## AN EARLY ENGLISH TREATISE

*A Treatyse of Fysshynge wyth an Angle* (1496) is not the earliest English work on angling, but it is one of the most famous. It is often attributed to the English prioress Juliana Berners, but its authorship is a subject of some dispute. It is thought the author had a practical knowledge of fishing, and it certainly shows that at the end of the 15th century the angler made his or her own equipment.

*And howe you shall make your rod craftely, here I shall teache you, ye shall cut betweene Michelmas & Candelmas a fayre staffe of a fadome and a halfe longe and arme great of hasyll, wyllowe or aspe, and breath hym in a hote ouen, and set hym euen.*

A Treatyse of Fysshynge wyth an Angle (1496)

Juliana (or some unknown author) recommended a rod made from two parts – a 'staffe' or butt, and a top part called a 'croppe'. The butt should be cut from hazel, willow or ash during the winter, and straightened and dried before being hollowed out. The top part of the rod has two sections – first, a piece of green hazel is inserted through the butt, then a final piece of blackthorn, crab tree, medlar or juniper is added. A great many processes are involved in finishing the rod, including straightening, drying, hole-burning and binding, but the final product 'wyll be very lyght & nymble to fyshe with at your pleasure' (but extremely heavy and cumbersome compared to modern rods). The rod described in the *Treatyse* does not use a reel (not known in Britain until perhaps the early 17th century). Fishing lines are explained. These were painstakingly made by hand from twisted or braided horsehair, with varying thicknesses employed depending on the fish you were hoping to catch (the author of the treatise even colour-codes them). How many rods were made to these specifications is not known, but until rods and tackle were first sold in shops a century later, every angler needed to know these or similar crafts.

## A ROD OF YOUR OWN

Rods. *These are made to great perfection, and may be had of every variety from the professional makers, but as they are generally expensive for a boy, with a little trouble and skill, he will be able to make one that will answer his purpose as well as the most costly. For the very young angler a hazel stick will make a good rod for fishing for small fish, such as sticklebacks, minnows, &c. Having selected as straight a one as possible a common knife is all that is required to polish it into shape. The next best rod that a boy may make for himself is formed of two pieces—the bottom of ash, and the top of lance-wood; these if properly tapered, and not too heavy, will be found to have an equal and regular spring; and the two pieces can be firmly bound together, by splicing the two ends and binding them together tightly with waxed or small string. The best rods however, are made of bamboo cane with tops of various lengths: twelve feet will be found a convenient length, but they are sometimes made to fourteen and even sixteen feet long.*

Ebenezer Landells, The Boy's Own Toy-Maker (1858)

To make a very simple fishing-pole, simply attach some fishing line to the end of a reasonably straight hazel stick, add a hook and some bait, and try your luck (having sought the appropriate permits and licences, of course).

To make something a little more sophisticated, find a long, straight stick or bamboo cane. This needs to be taller than you are, and the wood should be green so that it is flexible, rather than dead and dry, when it will soon snap. It should also taper naturally. Cut away any twigs or shoots and use sandpaper to smooth the rod. Add three or four screw eyes along the length of the rod to hold the line, and buy or borrow a cheap second-hand reel to complete it.

# *Making Coracles*

## CORACLES

A coracle is an ancient one-person rowing boat, originally made from wickerwork and animal skins. It is highly manoeuvrable on water, and its lightweight design means that it can easily be carried by its pilot on land.

## HALF A WALNUT SHELL

*The coracle is a small boat constructed with willow twigs in the manner of basket work, or with split slips of elastic wood, both the form and the material varying in different counties. In the neighbourhood of Shrewsbury, the framework is covered with canvass and painted; in Cardiganshire it is covered with flannel, and afterwards with a coating of tar. The boat is something less than six feet long, and about four feet wide, with a seat across the middle. The form of paddle with which this little boat is impelled and guided along is also varied: in the Severn, the blade is square, but a more elongated blade is the form in use on the Dee. The boat, which in appearance is not unlike half of a walnut-shell, is so light and portable that the fisherman carries it to and from the water on his back. These coracles ... are of great antiquity: they were known in Caesar's time, and are described by Lucan to be very nearly the same as in our own days.*

> *'With twisted osiers the first boats were made,*
> *O'er which the skins of slaughter'd beasts were laid;*
> *With these the Britons on the oceans row,*
> *And the Venetians on the swelling Po.'*

William Yarrell, *A History of British Fishes* (1841)

Coracles of different styles and designs have been used for thousands of years in many different parts of the world. Even within Britain slightly different forms of coracle developed, the Ironbridge coracle and the River Teifi coracle being two of the types most commonly made today. The great versatility of the coracle comes from its lightweight construction, allowing it to be carried by one person. All coracles are essentially either a wickerwork or latticework basket, covered with some waterproof material. The earliest coracles were covered with animal skins, while later ones used tarred fabric, often canvas or calico. Most recently, bitumastic paint has been used as a waterproofer. Even though it is lightweight and relatively cheap and simple to make, a coracle can last for several years, any tears or holes in the fabric being repaired with patches. The construction of a coracle includes a seat, usually a plank, to which a carrying handle is attached. They are propelled by a single paddle.

## FISHING AND FERRYING

In Britain, coracle use is now often associated with salmon and sea-trout fishing on the rivers of Wales, which still persists to some degree, and with crossing the Severn at Ironbridge, near where traditional coracles are still made. Welsh coracle fishermen still work on the Teifi, the Towy and the Taf, although they must now be licensed and their numbers are very small. The fishermen work in pairs, holding a net between them and drifting with the current to catch salmon and sea trout. Near Ironbridge, coracles were used by locals as a means of crossing the River Severn as there were few bridges over the river there. When the Iron Bridge opened in 1781 Severnsiders resented having to pay a toll to cross it, so families would keep a coracle to row themselves across the river.

*Coracle construction*
© *Celtic Knotworks*
*Experimental Archaeology*
*Group Licensor*
*www.scran.ac.uk*

## CURRACHS

Currachs (or curraghs) are Irish boats, often associated with coracles. They too are made from a wooden frame – originally covered with animal skins, but now made from waterproofed fabric – but are a more conventional boat shape. Still relatively lightweight, they are carried and rowed by more than one person, and have long been used on sea-going journeys. They are still built and raced by enthusiasts on the west coast of Ireland.

## LEARNING MORE

There are a number of organizations that can help you to learn more about coracles. The Green Wood Centre (www.greenwoodcentre.org.uk) near Ironbridge is part of the national woodland charity, the Small Woods Association. They teach coracle making, among many other woodland-related crafts. The National Coracle Centre (www.coracle-centre.co.uk) in Wales has a collection of coracles from around the world, as well as information on how coracles are made and used. A number of coracle regattas are held during the year – opportunities for enthusiasts to race their craft or for beginners to learn more about coracles.

# Building Wooden Boats

## WOODEN-BOAT BUILDING

Building boats from wood is a truly ancient craft. Thousands of years ago, simple 'canoes' were hewn from single tree trunks, and relatively soon techniques were developed for joining planks of timber together.

## CLINKER AND CARVEL

Wooden boats are either clinker-built or carvel-built. In clinker-built boats, the planks, or 'strakes', overlap, while in carvel-built boats, the planks are laid edge to edge. Clinker construction, also known as lapstrake, is thought to have originated with the Vikings, while the carvel style seems to have originated in the Mediterranean. Carvel-building is a slower, more labour-intensive process, as each plank must be carefully matched to the next, and carvel-built boats tend to be stronger than those that use the clinker technique. Clinker-building is cheaper, but produces a slightly more flexible structure. For these reasons, clinker-building was often favoured for smaller, lower-cost vessels, with carvel-building reserved for larger boats and ships.

Over time, different parts of the British coastline developed boats of an individual style, suited to local conditions and uses. Boat building is a skilled craft, and numerous small yards provided boats for local needs. While the techniques of boat building are too many to be covered here, some of the traditional inland and inshore British clinker-built and carvel-built boats, and their uses, are mentioned below.

## PORTLAND LERRETS

Lerrets are unique to Chesil Beach in Dorset. They are clinker-built 'double-enders' – that is, they have a bow at each end. Up to 5.2 metres (17 feet) long, and 1.8 metres (6 feet) wide, lerrets have fairly flat bottoms. Their shape was designed specifically to cope with the conditions of Chesil Bank – steep, shifting shingle on the beach and often turbulent seas – and with the task of mackerel fishing with seine nets. One end of the seine net was left on the shore with a team of men, while the boat was launched directly from the beach. Lerrets were generally propelled by four or six oars, each pulled by an oarsman. The boat was pushed into the sea at an appropriate moment, with the strong arms of the oarsmen immediately taking on the waves. As they rowed in a wide semicircle back to the beach, the seine net would be dropped over the side. When the boat reached the shore again, most of the crew would jump out to help gradually haul the ends of the nets in and bring the catch ashore. The lerret was then left in the charge of one man or boy, whose job was to check that nothing went wrong with the net. This task was made easier by the double-ended nature of the boat, allowing it to be rowed in either direction. This last man or boy was brought ashore once the catch had been safely landed – he could simply throw a line to the rest of his crew and be hauled in onto the beach. The oars of the boat were then greased and placed on the beach to be used as rollers to haul the lerret away. Portlanders were also known for launching their lerrets (which could be put out in any conditions) to help when shipwrecks occurred nearby.

## NORFOLK WHERRIES

Traditional Norfolk wherries were clinker-built of oak in a wide, shallow shape. They were first used on the Norfolk Broads, where they transported freight under a distinctive black sail, although wherries were also adopted elsewhere. They worked the Broads for more than 200 years, carrying goods for export or import to and from the coast, as well as supplying villages along the way. When their useful life was over, Norfolk wherries were simply sunk. Enthusiasts have raised and restored a small number of these traditional boats.

## NOBBIES

The nobby was born on the north-west coast of Britain in the late 1800s, although the popular design of this carvel-built boat led to its wider use around the coast of Britain. The most famous nobby was the Morecambe Bay prawner, used for trawling for shrimps. Single-masted and thought elegant when sailing, they inspired a number of yacht designs, and fared better than many of the other traditional craft mentioned here. Nobbies are still sailed, having been converted to pleasure craft when they were superseded as fishing vessels.

## FLATNERS

A flatner is another double-ender with a flat bottom. Either clinker-built or constructed from flat elm boards, flatners are particularly associated with Somerset, where different styles and sizes of flatner were used for fishing and transporting goods. Turf boats and withy boats were both types of flatner, 5–6 metres (16–20 feet) long, and used on the Somerset Levels for transporting peat and willow to market respectively. The 'Parrett flatner', named after the river of that name, was used for fishing in the river and the estuary. It was around 6 metres (20 feet) long, and had a specially curved bottom that allowed it to be launched down the muddy banks of the river. Parrett flatners were rowed upstream with the tide, and the

*Nobby, constructed*
*1910*
*© fstop2 / Alamy*

salmon which were caught with a dip-net provided a useful extra income for local farmers. The 'Watchet flatner', or 'flattie', also used for fishing, had a double-planked bottom for launching from the rocky shores of Watchet Bay, while the largest flatners were those of Weston-super-Mare – 7 metres (23 feet) long, they were used for fishing during the winter and pleasure trips during the summer.

## COBLES

*COBLE, a peculiar kind of boat, very sharp and wedge-shaped in the bow, and flat bottomed and square at the stern. It has only one mast, stepped close forward, on which a lug-sail is set. Cobles are used on the North-East coast of England, from the Tweed to the Humber, by the pilots and fishermen, who are extremely expert in their management. They are excellent sea boats, and for their size, carry a large sail.*
John Trotter Brockett, *A Glossary of North Country Words* (1846)

Cobles were inshore fishing boats, used off north-east England and Scotland from the Humber to the Tweed. Clinker-built and flat-bottomed, they worked from the beach, and in the past each village had its own fleet of cobles. The large square lug-sail of the coble led it to be likened to Viking longships, although a popular belief that cobles are the direct descendants of these is unproven. Cobles are built around a distinctive keel plank, or 'ram', around 6.7–7.3 metres (22–24 feet) long.

## DECLINE OF TRADITIONAL CRAFT

There are various reasons for the decline of the traditional boats mentioned here. Some were superseded by boats made of different materials, while others, such as the Norfolk wherries, were essentially replaced by rail and road. Traditional wooden-boat builders still exist, although their numbers are small and much of the work they do is on high-end leisure craft. However, enthusiasts, working individually or in groups, preserve some of the traditions, if not the practice, of this working craft.

# Skinning a Rabbit

## RABBITS

Among previous generations knowledge of the craft of skinning a rabbit would have been a given. Few people cook rabbit at home now, and of those who do only a minority skin the rabbit themselves. If you decide to catch your rabbit yourself, or buy a rabbit from one of the few butchers who still sell them with their coats on, skinning will become an essential art in your repertoire.

## SOFT RABBIT FUR

*Bring out your cony-skins, fair maids, to me,*
*And hold 'em fair, that I may see;*
*Grey, black, and blue: For your smaller skins,*
*I'll give you looking glasses, pins:*
*And for your whole cony, here's ready, ready money.*
*Come, gentle Joan, do thou begin*
*With thy black, black, black cony-skin.*
*And Mary then, and Jane will follow,*
*With their silver-hair'd skins, and their yellow.*
*The white cony-skin I will not lay by,*
*For, though it be faint, 'tis fair to the eye;*
*The grey, it is warm, but yet for my money,*
*Give me the bonny, bonny black cony.*
*Come away, fair maids, your skin will decay:*

*Come, and take money, maids; put your ware away.*
*Cony-skins! cony-skins! Have ye any cony-skins?*

John Fletcher, Philip Massinger and Francis Beaumont,
*Beggar's Bush* (published 1647)

In the past there would have been little waste from your rabbit, and its skin would have been used in any of a number of ways. The fur, for example, was used in hat making and to trim clothes and make mittens and muffs. Some pelts are still used, although many are thrown away.

*Rabbit man,*
*magazine illustration,*
*1823*
© *Mary Evans Picture*
*Library / Alamy*

## THE WAY TO SKIN A RABBIT

While it is said that there is more than one way to skin a cat, there is really only one sensible way to skin a rabbit.

A rabbit should be 'paunched' (or gutted) before it is skinned and soon after it has been killed (if you buy a rabbit from a butcher it will have been paunched, even if it hasn't been skinned). For many beginners this is the most difficult part of preparing a rabbit, but if you eat meat at all it is a necessary part of the journey from field to table. (Just think about the delicious dinner the rabbit will provide you with later.) It can be a messy undertaking, best done in old clothes and out of doors. Using a small, sharp knife, cut a hole in the rabbit's belly, just big enough for you to insert two fingers, and no deeper than around 6 millimetres (¼ inch). Pull the skin apart at the cut and, inserting a finger at either side, pull again, tearing a larger opening which will expose the guts. This may sound unnecessary, but if you use a knife to cut the larger opening, you run the risk of puncturing the stomach and intestines, the contents of which would contaminate the meat. When the guts are exposed, scoop them out. Where they are attached, pull or cut them away, again making sure you don't puncture the stomach or intestines with your knife. Next, look inside the body cavity and you will find a membrane that separates the stomach and intestines from the upper chest. Use a little pressure to break this, then pull out the heart and lungs (and everything else that is in there). This completes the paunching.

To begin skinning your rabbit, cut off all the paws with a sharp knife or good kitchen scissors (be careful if you leave sharp bones sticking out). Starting at the belly, separate the skin and fur from the flesh by gently but firmly gripping one in each hand and pulling – the skin and fur will come away more easily than you think. Work towards the hind legs, and expose these in turn (this is like taking off the sleeve of a jacket). The skin will still be attached at the tail – cut the tail off. Hold the hind legs, and pull the skin away as far as the front legs. Expose the front legs and pull the skin until it is over the rabbit's neck. Now cut off the head. The pelt should come off in one piece. Check for any remaining organs, and cut out the anal canal. Wash the rabbit to remove any sticky bits of fur or blood and pat it dry with a clean tea towel. It is now ready for your favourite rabbit recipe.

# Plucking a Fowl

## PLUCKING

With the exception of some game dealers who still sell pheasants with their feathers on, most birds are now sold oven-ready, and the art of preparing a bird is only known by those who either rear their own poultry or shoot their own game birds. Most 19th-century cookbook writers expected the housewife to know how to pluck and 'draw' (ie gut) a bird without any instructions, while the majority of those of the 21st century expect the home cook never to need to know. It is a useful skill to have for anyone who eats fowl, and a necessary one if you are ever given anything fully feathered to deal with.

## I'M A PHEASANT PLUCKER

Birds that aren't hung, such as chickens, are best plucked as soon as they are killed, as the feathers will come out much more easily when the carcass is still warm. Some people dunk cold fowl in boiling water prior to plucking for the same reason, but this can be tricky, as you can easily start to cook the skin. Always pluck a bird before drawing it.

For many, the plucking is easier than the drawing, although it can be a slow process for the beginner. It is probably best not to start with a duck, as these are notoriously tedious.

If possible, do your plucking in a clean shed, and wear clothes that you don't mind getting messy. Large fowl are more easily tackled if they are hung from a beam or hook, with a bin below to catch most of the feathers (there will be more of these than you think). Work from the tail to the head, and pluck by taking a small bunch of feathers between finger and thumb, and pulling out and away. Never try to take too many feathers at once, as you will tear the skin. Work your way around the bird until it is all done (with the exception of the head). The most troublesome feathers are the large ones in the wings, and if your fingers are getting sore, you can try using pliers on these. You can cut the ends of the wings off before plucking if you prefer – simply find the 'hinge' halfway along the wing and cut with strong kitchen scissors. If necessary, the bird can then be 'singed'. Use a burning taper to remove any remaining hairs or small feathers, but take care not to blacken the skin. Then rub the bird with a clean tea towel.

The next job is to cut the head off. Using a knife, make a slit in the skin from the bottom of the neck up to the head, then cut the head off and throw it away. Peel the skin of the neck away from the neck-bone. Cut through the neck-bone as close to the body as possible and remove it (the neck-bone can be used for making stock), leaving the flap of neck skin attached to the body (you will need this flap of skin later if you are stuffing and roasting the bird). Now you have to remove the feet. Cut around the skin at the drumstick joint, but don't cut too deep as you don't want to cut through the tendons. Use your hands to snap the joint, then, holding the drumstick in one hand, pull hard on the lower leg and foot to pull the tendons out (if you leave these in, the drumsticks will be tough). It is relatively easy to remove the tendons from a smaller bird, but if you are tackling a turkey you will need a fair amount of force (some advocate hanging a turkey up by its feet, then pulling hard on its body until you are left with feet and tendons hanging from a hook and a footless and tendonless bird in your arms).

*Plucking a hen, Orkney*
© *Chick Chalmers Licensor* *www.scran.ac.uk*

The next stage of drawing requires time and care, as you want to extract the gall bladder and intestines intact (otherwise the procedure will become very smelly, and you run the risk of tainting the flesh of the bird). Insert a finger into the hole where you removed the neck-bone, and move it around to loosen and sever the innards. Move to the tail end, and *carefully* cut all the way around the vent (anus) without cutting into the rectum. Draw the vent, with guts attached, out of the bird from this end. After the guts will come other organs, including the gizzard, lungs and heart, although you are unlikely to get all these out at one go on your first attempt at drawing (remember to keep the giblets for stock). Check that the bird is empty, then go back to the neck end and remove the crop (you might well find that this contains undigested food; try not to be put off). Finally, rinse the bird well, and pat it completely dry with a clean cloth. You will then be ready to either truss or joint the bird as your recipe requires.

# Foraging for Wild Food

## WILD FOOD

For hunter-gatherers, knowing which wild foods were edible and beneficial was essential, and this knowledge was passed from generation to generation. As soon as people settled in one place and started to grow crops and farm, such knowledge was gradually lost. Wild plants were cultivated and became the vegetables we know today, while their often unrecognizable antecedents were ignored as weeds. However, this was a slow process. Our Elizabethan ancestors still knew the medicinal values and culinary virtues of many wild plants and herbs, although this widespread knowledge later dwindled with increasing industrialization and urbanization. Pockets of wild food foraging obviously persisted – in Britain obvious sources of wild food, such as brambles covered in blackberries in late August or early September, are still exploited – but with the exception of times of food shortage (during the two World Wars, for example), as a whole foraging for wild food is a craft that has died and has had to be relearnt. It is currently undergoing something of a revival.

## PRINCIPLES OF FORAGING

Most of the principles of foraging are commonsense. Never eat anything that you have not positively identified. Many plants are toxic, and while these are relatively rare, you should always double-check before you eat wild food, especially as a beginner. If this uncertainty makes you nervous, simply stick to very obvious foods until you have built up a knowledge of what is safe to eat. Never pick foods from busy roadsides – these will be too heavily polluted by the passing traffic to be good eating. If you are picking food in an area popular with dog walkers, harvest from above dog level, for obvious reasons. A very important principle of foraging is never to pull up a whole plant, as you want that plant to be there next year, providing you with another harvest (quite apart from the fact that such behaviour is often illegal). Similarly, never harvest too much from one plant or bush; you want to leave it healthy and growing. Finally, forage from your own land and open-access land, but don't forage on private land without permission.

## BERRIES

*Bilberries*
© *mediacolor's / Alamy*

*In country places, besides the ordinary fruits of the garden, many of the wild products of the woods and fields are made use of in the manufacture of preserves. The bilberry or blueberry, the barberry, and above all the bramble, are largely employed for this purpose; while in the Highlands and moorland districts, the cranberry ... and even the harsh and unsavoury berries of the rowan or mountain-ash are made into jam ... Bramble-gathering forms a favourite ploy amid the juvenile members of a Scottish family, and we have a very distinct recollection in connection therewith, of wild brakes where the purple fruit grew luxuriantly, amid ferns, hazel-nuts, and wild raspberry bushes, with the invigorating brightness of a September sun overhead, and the brilliant varieties of a September foliage. Faces stained with livid hues, hands scratched with thorns and briers, and shoes and stockings drenched with ditchwater, are among the reminiscences of the joyous days of bramble-gathering.*
Robert Chambers, *Book of Days* (1869)

Late summer and early autumn, when many berries become ripe, is an important time for the wild food forager (and jam maker). Remember that some berries are poisonous, but with a field guide (or an expert friend) it is very easy to learn to recognize the good from the bad, and some of the more common ones, such as blackberries and wild strawberries, are unmistakeable. Some berries are beautiful eaten straight from the bush, while others need a little work to be palatable

– there really is no other use for the sour sloe (fruit of the blackthorn tree) than in making warming sloe gin. Just two of the many wild berries are described below.

## Blackberries

The prickly blackberry or bramble bush (*Rubus fruticosus*) grows in hedges, woods and on waste ground. Its berries are widespread and abundant, making them the most popular of wild foods. The juicy dark purple fruits are made up of a cluster of drupelets, and are delicious raw or cooked. Avoid those infested with insects. Blackberries can be picked from August to early October, although traditionally you must pick them before Michaelmas, 29 September, as on this date the Devil, or witches, are said to urinate on them. The origins of this piece of folklore might lie in the fact that blackberries become watery and sour after the first frost.

Blackberries
© David Askham / Alamy

## Bilberries

The wild British bilberry (*Vaccinium myrtillus*) is closely related to the North American blueberry, now a popular imported fruit. While the fruit of cultivated blueberries is larger and sweeter, bilberries (also known as whortleberries, whorts, blaeberries, hurtleberries and whimberries) are often undeservedly overlooked. The bushes grow low on heath and moorland, with bright green leaves, and the berries (from July to September) are small and nearly black. If you find the berries too sour, cook them in pies or crumbles or make jam.

# NUTS

## Hazelnuts

*Nutting is the grandest amusement, after all, because you have to go into the great woods to get the prime ones, as it is there that the largest hazels grow, some of them as high as a two-storied house. It is of no use to go a-nutting without having a long hook of some kind or another, as the finest and ripest clusters grow at the tops of the hazels, the branches of which are too slender to be climbed, so must perforce be pulled down by the nut-hook, or you will never taste the richest of the creamy kernels.*

*Games and Sports for Young Boys* (1859)

Hazels (*Corylus avellana*) can be found in woods and hedgerows throughout the British Isles, and hazelnuts (also known as filberts or cobnuts) from August until September – but beware, in August you might find them bland when you pick them green, and if you wait too late into October for them to fully ripen, squirrels will quite probably have got there first. Try to collect them between these times. They hang in clusters of two or three, and are encased in thick green husks. When ripe they will readily drop from the bush. To store them, remove the husks but keep them in their shells until you are ready to eat them. Once shelled, they are delicious roasted in the oven and eaten as a snack.

*Hazelnuts*
© The Garden Picture
Library / Alamy

## Sweet chestnuts

The sweet, or Spanish, chestnut (*Castanea sativa*) is found in woods and parks throughout Britain, although it thrives best in southern England. The trees are tall, and have distinctive leaves with serrated edges. The chestnuts are ready from around October, with two or three small nuts contained in cases which are densely covered with very long spikes (you might want to wear gloves). They can be collected from the ground, or helped on their way down with a well-aimed stick. They are best roasted. Simply make a small nick in the brown shiny case (to prevent the nut from exploding and to make them easier to peel) and place in the oven. Do not confuse the sweet chestnut with the unrelated horse chestnut – conkers are not edible.

## MUSHROOMS

*So many fatal accidents happen every season from the use of poisonous mushrooms,
and it is so difficult to distinguish between the edible kinds and those that are
deleterious, that we would advise our readers either to eat none that they have not
examined for themselves, or to be contented with what are raised in artificial beds,
though the flavour of these is as inferior to that of the wild mushrooms as a coop-fed
chicken is to the heath-cock.*

Mistress Margaret Dods, *The Cook and Housewife's Manual* (1824)

There are thousands of species of fungi growing wild in the British Isles,
but extreme care must be taken before any of them are enjoyed as a meal.
Some are deadly poisonous – there
is no antidote to the toxins of the
death cap (*Amanita phalloides*), for
example; you might feel fine for
up to a day after you have eaten
it, but within a week you will be
dead – and many of the poisonous
varieties closely resemble some
of the tasty edible ones. In France
you can enlist the help of a local
pharmacist in identifying your
finds (although some are obviously
more helpful than others), but if
you are without expert help you

Sweet chestnuts
© Penny Tweedie / Alamy

should never eat anything you are even slightly unsure of. Buy a very good
guide that shows a lot of detail, and always collect the whole mushroom
(don't just cut off the top) as you will need all of it to make a proper
identification – the best way to pick a mushroom is to twist it gently until
it comes away in your hand. If at all possible, you should attend a course
on mushroom identification before you begin collecting your own, and
start by learning to identify the deadly varieties so you know what to
avoid. Also, remember that you may be intolerant to certain mushrooms
even if they aren't poisonous. The mushrooms described below have not
been chosen simply for flavour, but because they are among the safer
ones for the beginner to forage for, as they each possess a combination of
features which makes them more readily distinguishable from poisonous

or inedible forms. However, great care should still be taken, as there is not space here to provide all the details necessary for safe identification.

There are some general rules for mushrooming: try to avoid wet days, when the mushrooms will have soaked up a lot of water; avoid anything that has started to decay; remember where you picked the different specimens you collect, as knowledge of habitat will help with identification; avoid immature fungi, as these will be more difficult to identify; collect your mushrooms in an open basket (they will keep better this way); if you are unsure about some of the fungi you collect, keep the species separate (don't mix poisonous and edible up together, as the poisonous ones might contaminate the edible ones); don't handle the specimens too much, as any damage will hinder identification; go through the mushrooms carefully before you cook them, double-checking in your guide that they are good to eat; and clean your mushrooms by wiping them with a cloth rather than washing them.

## Giant puffball

The giant puffball (*Langermannia gigantea*) is one of the most easily identified species of edible fungi. It is large, spherical, white, and around the same size as a football. It grows in fields, gardens and woods, and can be found from summer to autumn. Only firm white specimens

Giant puffball
© imagebroker / Alamy

should be picked. When sliced, the inside of the giant puffball should be firm, smooth and creamy white (if this is not the case, discard it). Giant puffballs can be cooked very simply – slice one into 'steaks' and fry the steaks in butter.

## Cep

The cep (*Boletus edulis*), also known as the penny bun (because of its brown cap) or by its Italian name, porcini, is a highly prized wild mushroom. It is found in any type of woodland from summer to late autumn. It has a brown cap, 8–20 centimetres (3–8 inches) across, which is glossy in wet weather. The stem is thick and bulging towards the base, and cream or beige in colour. Rather than gills, the cep has a spongy layer under its cap, made up of tiny tubes. When cut, the flesh should be firm and white (other *Boletus* fungi change colour when cut, but not *Boletus edulis*). Commercially, cep are often dried, as this intensifies the flavour, and they are frequently used in 'wild' mushroom soup.

*Cep mushroom*
© *Holmes Garden Photos /
Alamy*

## Parasol mushroom

The parasol (*Lepiota procera*) is a distinctive species, easier to spot than many other mushrooms as it grows on open pastures and has a tall stalk and frilly cap. It is not common, but has an excellent flavour. Its cap is 10–25 centimetres (4–10 inches) across, and is pale with darker shaggy scales. It starts off egg-shaped before expanding to an open parasol shape (some people say parasol mushrooms are best picked between these two stages, before they are fully opened). The stem is tall, slender, and slightly bulbous at the base, with snake-like markings and a double 'ring' which will slide up and down the stem. To cook, remove the stems and either slice and fry or leave the caps whole and stuff them and bake them. The shaggy parasol (*Lepiota rhacodes*) is also edible, but is known to cause stomach upsets in some people. It is smaller than the parasol and easy to distinguish, as its flesh becomes red when it is cut.

## FURTHER FORAYS INTO FORAGING

There are simply too many wild foods to mention here, so whole groups have had to be overlooked – edible roots (including wild parsnips), free salads (including watercress) and herbs (such as wild angelica), to name a few. Richard Mabey's *Food for Free* (1972) is a classic book for anyone interested in the subject, and field courses (perhaps the best way to taste and learn) are offered by a number of organizations (you can find a number of options online).

*Parasol mushroom*
© WoodyStock / Alamy

Food and Drink

# *Brewing Beer*

## HOME-BREWED BEER

Brewing beer at home is now thought of as a hobby as well as a craft. It typically involves the brewing of beer on a small scale, with the resultant beverages being consumed at home, entered into amateur beer-making competitions or distributed for free among willing (or not so willing) friends.

## THE STORY OF BEER

Beer is one of the oldest drinks made by man. It is generally agreed that beer was being brewed in Mesopotamia by 6000 BC, although its history may be much longer than that. Brewing activity in Britain dates back to Neolithic times, although the earliest fermented drinks made in Britain would not have been beer. While 'beer' and 'ale' are now used synonymously, at one time 'ale' was used to refer to an alcoholic drink made by fermentation from malted barley, while 'beer' was essentially the same drink but flavoured with hops.

In the past, weak beer was made for everyday consumption. This weak beer was also known as 'small beer' (although 'small beer' is also used to refer to lightly fermented drinks such as dandelion and burdock, and ginger beer). At one time, Britons consumed vast quantities of home-brewed weak beer:

*In private households [beer] was often brewed in great quantities ... since water was often unsafe to drink and tea and coffee not yet available. Beer was therefore consumed*

at every meal and, in stronger forms, in the evening and for entertaining, and was
not despised by the royal court and aristocracy. Elizabeth I normally drank beer at
breakfast, while the Earl of Northumberland's Household Book of 1512 specified for his
and his lady's breakfast a quart (2 pints) of beer and of wine; their two young sons were
allowed 2 quarts of beer but no wine, while two children still in the nursery received
1 quart. Such allowances seem generous, yet Lady Lucy, a Maid of Honour in Henry
VIII's court, received a gallon (8 pints) of ale at breakfast, dinner and supper each day.
Though it is unlikely that such quantities were actually consumed, beer was considered
a very healthy and nutritious drink, the eminent Dr Andrew Boorde writing in his
Dyetary of Helth (1542), 'I myself, which am a physician, cannot away with water,
wherefore I do leave all water and do take myself to good ale, and otherwise for ale I do
take good Gascon wine, but I will not drink strong wines.'

John Burnett, Liquid Pleasures (1999)

While small beer was taken every day, stronger brews were made for
celebrations. The Saxons had 'wassail', meaning 'be healthy', a warmed,
spiced drink shared at winter festivals. Other strong, celebratory ales
included 'church-ales', consumed at drunken festivals of the same name,
which raised money for the church; 'bride-ale', the drink and drinking
at a wedding (from which the word 'bridal' is derived); 'lamb-ale', the
merrymaking hosted by the farmer when the lambing was over, and the
special ale provided for this; and 'audit ale', a strong drink provided at
some Oxford and Cambridge colleges on audit day, when students had to
pay their college bills.

In the 14th century, officers were appointed to assess the quality of
beer produced for sale. These officers were known as ale-conners, a title
which still exists in some boroughs. According to legend, an ale-conner
would enter an ale-house and demand some ale. He would then pour
some of the ale onto a wooden bench and, wearing the leather breeches
his role demanded, sit in the pool of beer. After a time, the ale-conner
would try to stand up – if he did not stick the beer was good, but if he
did stick the beer was of inferior quality and unfit to drink. Ale-conners
certainly existed, and it was in their power to decide whether beer was fit
for human consumption, and later to set its price (where price reflected
strength). They would certainly have tasted many ales, but how much
time, if any, they really spent sitting on beer is not known.

The famous Kentish hop-fields were first planted in around 1520,
and hopped ale, or beer, was made and eventually exceeded traditional

unhopped ale in popularity. The flowers of the hop, *Humulus lupulus* (of the same family as the cannabis plant), provide what is now the accepted flavour of beer, and also act as a stabilizer.

## LAST ORDERS

*In former times, to set about to show to Englishmen that it was good for them to brew beer in their houses would have been as impertinent as gravely to insist, that they ought to endeavour not to lose their breath; for in those times (only forty years ago), to have a* house *and not to brew was a rare thing indeed. Mr. Ellman, an old man and a large farmer, in Sussex, has recently given in Evidence, before a Committee of the House of Commons, this fact: that,* forty years ago, *there was not a labourer in his parish that did not* brew his own beer; *and that now, there is* not one that does it, *except by chance the malt be given him. The causes of this change have been the lowering of the wages of labour, compared with the price of provisions … the enormous tax upon the barley when made into* malt, *and the increased tax upon* hops. *These have quite changed the customs of the English people as to their drink. They still drink* beer, *but, in general, it is the brewing of* common brewers, *and in public houses, of which the common brewers have become the owners, and have thus … obtained a* monopoly *in the supplying of the great body of the people with one of those things, which to the hard-working man, is almost a necessary of life.*

William Cobbett, *Cottage Economy* (1826)

Traditional brewing equipment
© Falkirk Museums Licensor
www.scran.ac.uk

As William Cobbett observed in 1826, home brewing had, by then, already gone into serious decline. In 1880, those home brewers that were left were dealt a serious blow when the Inland Revenue Act decreed that they must buy a licence if they wished to continue their hobby. It was not until 1963 that the restrictions on making your own beer were removed, and there was some hope that the craft would be revived. Amateur winemakers were the first to take up the cause and modern home brewing was born. At around the same time, the first campaigns were launched for a return by 'common brewers' to more traditional brewing methods and more natural ingredients – many small breweries had disappeared, and it was felt that traditional British beer drinking was under threat from the fizzy kegs of the big brewers and the importation of lagers from the continent. The Society for the Preservation of Beers from the Wood was formed in 1963, followed by the Campaign for the Revitalization of Ale in 1971 (swiftly renamed the Campaign for Real Ale). Good beer has made something of a comeback in pubs, and dedicated home brewers have relearnt the brewing craft, although Mr Cobbett would be dismayed by how few produce their own 'necessary of life'.

*Home-brewing equipment*
*© Mike Booth / Alamy*

## BREWING UP

While many people decry the craft of home brewing – and which of us have managed to entirely avoid enthusiastically given but terrible-tasting offerings from home-brewing friends? – it is possible, with the right ingredients and equipment, to create a delicious range of beers at home.

Principally, beer is made from malt, hops, water and yeast. Malt is barley that has been steeped in water, allowed to sprout, dried in a kiln and finally cracked in a mill. This process converts the starch in the grain to sugar and is essential, as it is the sugar that will become alcohol through the action of yeast. To be self-sufficient in beer you would need the equipment of a maltster and enough suitable land to grow your own hops, but as this is beyond the means of most, there are simpler ways of going about it.

The very simplest way to brew your own beer is to buy a brewing kit, which generally comes with full instructions. Often, all you need add is water, although you will also need some other items of equipment (a fermenting bucket, thermometer, hydrometer and siphon tubing are the basics). Some specialist retailers sell kits containing everything the beginner needs. Once you are sure home brewing is for you, you can branch out from kits and source ingredients to make your own brew.

While there isn't room here to go into the full details of brewing, a rough outline of the basic steps involved follows. Always use clean, preferably sterilized, equipment.

First, boil 23 litres (5 gallons) of water, then let it cool to 66°C (150°F). Pour half of the water into your brewing vessel (also known as a mash-tun or mash-tub, this should have a tap near the bottom and an open top), add 12.5 kilograms (27 1/2 pounds) of malt, then the other half of the water, and stir. Cover the vessel with a blanket and leave overnight. By the next morning you will be able to drain off the liquid, which is now 'wort', and 'sparge' (which just means sprinkle) the spent malt that is left behind with fresh boiling water until you have collected your full 23 litres of wort. The spent malt is now referred to as 'mash', and has traditionally been fed to cows.

Pour the wort into a home-brew boiler with a thermostat, or use a large, strong saucepan on the stove. Place 225 grams (1/2 pound) of hops into a muslin bag or similar (a clean pillowcase will do) and add this to the wort. If you are using sugar, stir it in at this point. Boil the wort for a good hour. Next, carefully remove the bag of hops and one jugful of the wort, before transferring the rest of the wort into a clean brewing vessel. Cool the jugful as rapidly as you can (perhaps by plunging it into a bucket of ice) until it reaches 16°C (60°F), and add a packet of brewer's yeast. This will make your 'starter', the yeasty mixture that will turn your wort into beer. Cool the rest of the wort to the same temperature, add the starter, and cover the vessel with a blanket again (this will keep vinegar flies away).

After a few days, skim off the thick foam that will have formed – this is a mixture of yeast and wort called 'barm', and if kept covered in a cool place it can be used in place of yeast in your next batch of beer. After around a week, fermentation will have finished, and the beer can be 'racked', or siphoned off into clean containers without disturbing the sediment. The beer is now ready to be tasted!

*Finally, excellent brewing principles to remember are:*

1   *The more malt, the more body and strength.*
2   *The more body, the more hops needed.*
3   *The more hops, the greater the bitterness.*
4   *The more sugar, the greater the strength.*
5   *The sooner bottled, the greater the head (and risk!)*

C J J Berry, *Home Brewed Beers and Stouts* (1963)

## MORE BEER PLEASE

The Craft Brewing Association (www.craftbrewing.org.uk) is a national home-brewing organization. They publish a journal, *Brewer's Contact*, provide information for home brewers and hold get-togethers and festivals. The National Association of Wine and Beermakers (www.nawb.org.uk) hold an annual show and publish a newsletter. There are many local clubs and federations dedicated to home brewing, as well as dozens of online forums where the art can be discussed. Equipment and ingredients are available online and in local specialist shops.

A number of books on home brewing are also available, including the classic guide *Home Brewed Beers and Stouts* by C J J Berry. Originally published in 1963, it was 'the first modern book on home brewing'.

# Making Cider

## CIDER

Cider is an alcoholic drink made by fermenting the juice of apples. Home-made cider is generally a flat, cloudy and very dry beverage, unlike many of the commercially produced ciders, which are generally clear and sparkling, and sometimes very sweet.

## 'THE ENGLISH WINE'

*In several areas of England, especially but not only the western and south-western counties, the alternative to beer was home-produced cider made from fermented apple juice. Although Celtic origins of cider-making have been suggested, it is generally accepted that it was introduced to England from Normandy in the twelfth century, and that production on any scale dates from the thirteenth, when new varieties of bitter apples began to be cultivated, and cider-making spread on manors and monastic estates. Two types of drink were made – 'cyder', made entirely of apple juice, as strong as much imported French claret and regarded as 'the English wine', and 'cider', which was either cider 'stretched' with water or the product of a second or third pressing of the same apples to produce a much less alcoholic drink for labourers. True 'cyder' was highly esteemed, drunk in royal and noble households and sipped like wine: many writers in the sixteenth and seventeenth centuries extolled its virtues and health benefits while criticizing cider as thin, sour stuff, fit only for the poor.*

John Burnett, *Liquid Pleasures* (1999)

In the past most farms would have had an orchard, and kept the equipment needed for the annual cider making. The apples were crushed in a granite trough, or 'chase', then cut into 'cheeses' or blocks, with a wooden cider-cheese cutter. The cheeses were placed between planks in a press, and all the juice squeezed out and collected, the residue being used as animal feed. The apple juice was then fermented in casks. It is widely believed that these old cider makers often threw dead livestock in with the juice, and that this gave the cider its flavour. It is true that the addition of an old rooster would have aided fermentation, making the yeasts act more quickly, but it would not have been done for flavour. Some believe that these stories are apocryphal in any case, especially when rats are mentioned, stripped to the skeleton when fermentation is finished, but you can still hear cider making discussed in rural West Country pubs, and generally find someone who claims they have witnessed this practice.

## WHERE HAS ALL THE CIDER GONE?

Many orchards were grubbed up in the second half of the 20th century – a problem not limited to Britain, as many orchards in the USA and elsewhere have also been lost. Hard-working enthusiasts have done a great deal of work in maintaining those orchards that are left and creating new orchards with traditional varieties, but orchards are still in a relatively precarious state in Great Britain. Without local orchards, local cider cannot be made.

Factory production of cider was established by the end of the 19th century, but for a long time cider retained a reputation of being an unsophisticated, rural drink. In recent years factory cider has undergone a revolution – mass-produced and mass-marketed as a fashionable drink to have over ice. However, for those who make their own cider there is no comparison between the flavour of traditional cider and the fizzy, modern drinks. If you are not able to have a go at cider making, farm ciders (often advertised as scrumpy) are available, particularly in the West Country, and 'real' cider is undergoing something of a revival, with small producers using more traditional methods than their larger factory competitors, and local groups making their own.

## FIRST PICK YOUR APPLES

*The true value of cider as a wholesome, health-giving beverage scarcely needs emphasis, its rapidly increasing popularity being a sufficient criterion of its worth.*
*Cider-Making on the Farm*, Devon County Agricultural Committee
leaflet (1934)

The first task in cider making is to pick your apples. Some purists believe that good cider is ideally made from cider apples. These have been developed for their cider-making suitability, and include such evocatively named varieties as the Fair Maid of Devon, Tremlett's Bitter, Fillbarrel, Pig Snout and Hangy Down Clusters. However, for the first-time cider maker it is simply important to use a good mixture of apples, including some that are very sweet and some that are very sour, with a few crab-apples for good measure. The apples should not be picked until they are ripe, and then left for around a week to 'mature' – a few bruised or softened apples won't hurt the cider.

As apples don't produce a consistent volume of juice, only a rough guide can be given as to how much cider you will get from a certain number of apples, but around 5 1/2 kilograms (12 pounds) of apples will make 4 1/2 litres (1 gallon) of cider. The apples need to be roughly chopped before the juice can be extracted. One simple method of achieving this is to place the apples in a sturdy wooden box and chop into them with a clean garden spade. If you are making a very small quantity, you could use a food processor,

*Cider press, Cotehele,*
*Cornwall*
*© NTPL / Andrew Butler*

which is less work but also less fun. If you don't happen to have a crusher (essentially a large old-fashioned mincer, worked by turning a handle) you can then pulp the apples by placing them in a sturdy vessel, and repeatedly hitting them with something heavy.

The next step needs a press. It is possible to use a kitchen juicer, but they tend to struggle with any quantity of apples. To make your own simple press, attach four G-clamps, which can be screwed up and down to tighten and loosen them, to a sandwich of two strong boards (for example, an old kitchen work surface could be used). Place the press over a tray – this needs to be larger than the press so that all the juice will be caught. Wrap some of the apple pulp in cheesecloth, place the parcel between the boards, and use the screws on the clamps to press the boards together and thus squeeze out the juice. Pour your first batch of juice into a clean fermenting bin, and refill the press until all the pulp has been dealt with. It is best if the bin is nearly full. There is no need to add any yeast, as the apple juice will naturally contain plenty. In *Self-Sufficiency* (1976), John Seymour suggests covering the bin with muslin, and leaving it in a sink overnight, as 'in the first day or so there is likely to be a rapid fermentation and you want this to bubble over the sides. This trick means that the bubbles carry with them large quantities of dirt and muck over the edge and down the plughole'.

After a few days the cider can be placed in a clean keg or similar, with the bunghole open, and it will continue to ferment for several weeks. When fermentation stops, place a bung in the bunghole and wait for your cider to mature. Leave the cider for at least eight months before drinking, and beware, it might be fairly strong.

# Using Elderflowers

## ELDERFLOWER CORDIAL, ELDERFLOWER CHAMPAGNE AND ELDERFLOWER WINE

Elderflower cordial is a syrup made from the flowers of the elder (*Sambucus nigra*), a small tree common in many gardens as well as wilder places, made into a refreshing soft drink by diluting with water. Despite its name, elderflower champagne is also a soft drink made from elderflowers, being neither a champagne nor even a wine. It is a naturally sparkling and fragrant beverage, best sipped on a warm summer evening. Elderflower wine is a traditional 'country wine', made for centuries in rural areas all over Europe.

## HERBAL HISTORY

*The flowers of the Elder are to be found included in old herbal recipes, and their delicious flavour added to many drinks and confections. A muslin bag of the dried flowers was boiled with jams and jellies to add a delicate muscatel flavour. A popular children's summer drink can be made by plunging the fresh flowers into a jug of milk or water, and allowing to stand a while before removing. The flowers too make a refreshing tea, and can be added to Indian or China tea to flavour them. As an alternative to aspirin, especially mixed with equal parts of lime-flowers and Chamomile, an infusion of the flowers makes a good headache and cold cure. In Tudor times, this was also claimed to retain one's youth.*

Andy Pittaway & Bernard Scofield, *The Complete Country Bizarre* (1976)

In the past, the elder had a confusingly contradictory reputation. Some thought it evil; no part of it was brought into the house, and to burn its wood would bring death to a family member within a year, or a visit from the Devil. The belief of its being cursed has been linked to a tradition that Judas hanged himself from an elder tree – in the county of Dorset it used to be known as the Judas-tree. Others saw the tree as more beneficial, and said that to plant it near the house offered protection from witchcraft, and to carry some leaves or twigs cured rheumatism. At various times all parts of the tree have been used – some of its many attributed benefits are listed here, though not recommended for trial. In the past, the leaves of the elder were made into poultices and ointments, and were said to heal wounds. Elder bark boiled in milk was thought to be good for jaundice, and a necklace

*Elderflower*
© Nic Murray / Alamy

of elder twigs to end epilepsy. Fever could be cured by burying an elder twig in silence, and if you buried a twig that you had rubbed on a wart that wart would disappear. Elderflower tea or wine was considered good for coughs and colds, and the scent of elder leaves was a natural fly repellent. Various concoctions based on the elder were also used as laxatives, muscle relaxants, and chilblain cures. Nicholas Culpeper included the elder in his famous herbal:

*The first Shoots of the common Elder boyled like Asparagus, & the yong Leavs & Stalks boyled in Fat Broth, doth mightily carry forth Flegm and Choller. The middle or inner Bark boyled in Water, and given to drink worketh much more violently; and the Berries either green or dry, expel the same humors, and is often given with good success to help the Dropsie. The Bark of the Root boyled in Wine, or the Juyce therof drunk, worketh the same effects, but more powerfully than either the Leavs or Fruit. The Juyce of the Root taken doth mightily provoke Vomit, and purgeth the watery Humors of the Dropsie. The Decoction of the Root taken cureth the biting of the Adder, and biting of Mad Dogs ... The distilled Water of the Flowers is of much use to clear the Skin from Sunburning, Freckles, Morphew, or the like; and taketh away Headaches coming of a cold caus, the Head being bathed therwith.*

Nicholas Culpeper, *The English Physitian* (1652)

The herbal use of the elder declined, but it continued to be in favour as a culinary ingredient. Elderflower cordial was popular in Victorian times, and for some the making of this and elderflower champagne is still an annual event. Recently, commercial versions of the cordial have been marketed successfully, as has elderflower pressé, which is similar to elderflower champagne, but for anyone with access to an elder, it is a simple and satisfying process to make the real thing at home. Elderflower wine is not particularly fashionable, but much admired by devotees. One simple caution must be remembered when following elderflower recipes – make sure that you use flowers from the European elder, *Sambucus nigra*, rather than some other variety or species.

## A SHORT PICKING SEASON

Perhaps part of the appeal of elderflowers is that they can only be picked for a few short weeks each year, making the preparation of elderflower drinks something of an annual ritual. The flowers are small, but grow in large heads, and they are generally ready in May or June. Experts say that the flowers are best picked on a warm sunny day, when the flowers are in full bloom and at their best. Don't pick from plants near the roadside, as they will be full of pollution. The flowers should be used as soon as possible after you have gathered them, and shaken to remove any insects or bugs – don't be tempted to wash them, as you will wash away their fragrance and flavour. If any heads are damaged or too full of small creatures, discard them in the composting bin.

### *Elderflower cordial*

To make approximately 1.5 litres (2½ pints) of elderflower cordial you will need 20 heads of elderflowers, 1.5 kilograms (3 pounds) of sugar, 2 unwaxed (preferably organic) lemons, and 1.2 litres (2 pints) of water. Most recipes also call for 75 grams (2½ ounces) of citric acid, which acts as an antioxidant. It can be a bit tricky to find, but some chemists and healthfood shops sell it, as well as home-brew shops. It can also be bought online, but make sure it is food grade.

When you have shaken your elderflowers, place them in a large heatproof bowl. Put the water and sugar in a pan and heat, while stirring, to make a sugar syrup. Pare the zest off the lemons, avoiding the pith, and add that to the elderflowers, then slice the lemons and add those too. Pour the slightly cooled sugar syrup into the bowl, and stir in the citric acid. Cover the bowl with a plate, and leave it to stand until the next day. After 24 hours strain the mixture through muslin (it might be easier to place the muslin in a sieve to do this) then pour your cordial into sterilized bottles. It is ready to drink, diluted with water, and will keep in the fridge for a couple of months. If you want to make a larger batch, the cordial can be frozen.

## Elderflower champagne

To make elderflower champagne, place 12 elderflower heads in a bowl with the juice and zest of an unwaxed (preferably organic) lemon, 0.7 kilograms (1½ pounds) of sugar, 2 tablespoons of white wine vinegar and 4 litres (1 gallon) of cold water, and leave for 24 hours. Then strain through muslin and pour the liquid into sterilized screw-top bottles. Leave the 'champagne' for between ten days and two weeks, then drink it, preferably before the end of the third week has passed. Because the champagne is naturally effervescent, pressure can build up in the bottles, so it is best to store them in a place where you won't mind too much if the tops come flying off.

## Elderflower wine

If you have not made wine before, you will need to invest in some basic equipment – a demijohn, or similar vessel, with a fermentation lock. Pour 4 litres (a gallon) of boiling water over 600 millilitres (1 pint) of elderflowers; to measure your elderflowers remove the stems, place the elderflowers in a measuring jug and gently press them down. Add the juice and rind of 3 unwaxed (preferably organic) lemons, 225 grams (½ pound) of raisins and 1.8 kilograms (4 pounds) of sugar. Allow to cool to around 24°C (75°F) and add a tablespoon of yeast nutrient and a sachet of wine yeast (both available from wine-making shops or online). Cover and leave to ferment in a warm place for around three days. Strain the liquid to remove all the flowers, raisins and lemon rind, and pour the wine into a clean demijohn or other clean vessel with a fermentation lock, and leave to ferment. The wine will slowly clear, and after about eight weeks it should be ready to be siphoned into bottles. Try to wait six months before drinking it. Wine can be made in this way with a number of different flowers, including dandelions, broom flowers and gorse flowers.

## MORE USES OF THE ELDERFLOWER

In *Food for Free* (1972) Richard Mabey comments of the elderflower that it has 'probably more uses than any other single species of blossom'. The flowers are traditionally used with gooseberries to make a delicious jam, and are also added to batter to make elderflower fritters. If you miss the crucial picking season for elderflowers, by late summer there will be a crop of elderberries. These have long been used to make elderberry wine.

# *Making Lemonade*

## LEMONADE

Traditional lemonade is a soft drink made from lemons, water and sugar.

## A RESTORATION HISTORY

*Come, come quickly, take those sweetmeats; bring the great cake and knife, and
napkins, for they have not supped; and, Captain, make some lemonade, and send it
by the boy to my chamber; and do you hear, Jolly, you must stay until we come, for we
must lie with you tonight.*

Thomas Killigrew, *The Parson's Wedding* (c.1640)

In Britain, home-made lemonade depended upon the availability of
affordable lemons from the Mediterranean and sugar from the West
Indies. It was first known in the 17th century, as evidenced by its mention
in Killigrew's Restoration play *The Parson's Wedding*, and was sold in the
coffee houses of the time. It is thought that lemonade has a longer history
in Italy, and arrived in Britain from there, via France. It became more
popular in the 18th century, when lemonade was a fashionable summer
drink in wealthy households. As lemons and sugar became cheaper,
lemonade came within the reach of more households. It has always been
made from the same ingredients – lemons, sugar and water – although by
the 19th century Mrs Beeton suggested that 'the lemonade will be much
improved by having the white of an egg beaten up in it; a little sherry
mixed with it, also, makes this beverage much nicer' (*Beeton's Book of
Household Management*, 1861). By Mrs Beeton's time, refreshment stalls sold

home-made lemonade to quench the thirst of the general public on hot summer days, and not all the customers were wealthy.

## THE DECLINE OF REAL LEMONADE

*London in the 1840s had more than fifty soft drink manufacturers, by now often using proprietary essences and compounds in a sugar syrup rather than natural juices and flavours. In the home the time and trouble of making such drinks could be avoided by simply diluting such products as 'Robinson's Patent Barley' ('eminently pure and nutritious'), Soyer's 'Orange Citron Lemonade' and 'Nectar', Hooper's 'Sarsaparilla' or Crosse and Blackwell's range of syrups.*

John Burnett, *Liquid Pleasures* (1999)

As manufactured lemonade became widely available, home-made lemonade went into decline, although the craft was still kept up by some well into the 20th century, and occasional roadside lemonade stalls can still be found in the USA, as a way for children to increase their pocket money. However, in Britain, the true demise of 'real' lemonade came with the popularity of 'fizzy' lemonade. This had already been available for a long time – Schweppes marketed an aerated lemonade in 1835 – but by the late 20th century most people's expectation of lemonade was of a colourless, fizzy drink, rather light on lemons and heavy on artificial sweeteners and preservatives, and a long way from the original thirst-quenching, flat and cloudy drink.

## TAKE SIX LEMONS

To make around 1.75 litres (3 pints) of lemonade, all you need is 6 unwaxed (preferably organic) lemons, around 150 grams of granulated sugar, and some water. Wash the lemons well, then thinly pare their zest with a vegetable peeler or zester – make sure you remove just the top layer of yellow zest, where the flavoursome oils are, and not the bitter white pith. Place the zest in a large heatproof jug or bowl, then squeeze the juice from the lemons and add that too, as well as the sugar. Finally, pour in 1.4 litres (2 1/2 pints) of boiling water, stir everything together, then cover the jug or bowl with a plate and leave it to stand somewhere cool overnight. Next day, stir the mixture again and taste to check for sweetness, adding a little more sugar if it is still too sharp for you. Once you are happy with it, strain the lemonade through a sieve. It is ready to drink now, but if you want to keep it for longer, pour it into sterilized bottles and store it in the fridge. The lemonade can be served as it is, over ice or diluted with water. If you want some gentle fizz, you can dilute it with sparkling mineral water.

# *Making Butter*

## BUTTER

Butter is made by separating the fat from the milk produced by dairy animals. While cows are by far the most familiar milk producers, butter can also be made from the milk of goats, sheep, and more exotic milking animals such as buffaloes, yaks and horses.

## ANCIENT HISTORY

*About the second century of the Christian era, butter was placed by Galen amongst the useful medical agents; and about a century before him, Dioscorides mentioned that he had noticed that fresh butter, made of ewes' and goats' milk, was served at meals instead of oil, and that it took the place of fat in making pastry. Thus we have undoubted authority that, eighteen hundred years ago, there existed a knowledge of the useful qualities of butter.*

Mrs Isabella Beeton, *Beeton's Book of Household Management* (1861)

Despite its long culinary history, which stretches back thousands of years, the process of butter making has essentially stayed the same, although the methods employed have varied. Cream (skimmed from the top of milk) is shaken, or churned, until its fat content is separated. In the past this might have been done by placing the cream in a bag made from animal skin, the skin then being shaken or rocked until the butter formed. It is also thought that hollow logs would have been used for the same purpose: these could have been tied to a branch and swung backwards and forwards. A more familiar method involves a butter churn. There are numerous designs of churn, one of the simplest, and oldest, being the plunge churn – cream was placed in the bottom of the churn, and a plunger worked up and down in it to keep the cream agitated. Swinging churns were, obviously, swung, and pump-action churns pumped. End-over-end churns were perhaps among the most satisfying and efficient, but were still hard work. Attached to a stand, a barrel was tumbled end over end by turning a handle. After the butter had formed, or 'come', it was washed, and then squeezed so that nothing but butter remained. This was sometimes done on a butter worker – a shallow wooden trough with a fluted roller attached, that would be rolled along the trough until all the liquid had been removed. Salt would then be added. Grooved wooden bats, known as butter pats, butter hands or Scotch hands, would then be used to pat and slap the butter into blocks, and wooden moulds or prints were often used to add decoration to the finished product.

*Butter making using a 'kirn' (churn), Shetland*
© *Shetland Museum Photographic Archive Photographer G Robertson*

In the past, well-salted butter, properly stored, would last indefinitely – at least through the winter, when only a small proportion of a dairy herd was kept in milk. In Ireland, barrels of ancient butter are still found in peat bogs, and similar finds have been unearthed in Finland. It is not known for sure whether these buried barrels were placed in the bog for safekeeping, to hide them from invaders, or to mature and develop in flavour (in the same way that cheese is left to mature). It has been suggested that the practice of burying barrels of butter ceased in Ireland by the late 1700s.

## MASS PRODUCTION

Until the 19th century, almost every household would have made its own butter. But with the rise of butter factories from the 1860s, the craft went into decline. Its revival came to some degree in the 1960s and 1970s among those who wished for a more self-sufficient lifestyle, and more recently with the increasing interest in natural rather than processed food, but there are still few who make their own butter on a regular basis.

# HOW TO PAT A BUTTER PAT – A
# SIMPLE METHOD

*If you have a house cow then some of the milk can be made into butter.*
Suzanne Beedell and Barbara Hargreaves, *The Complete Guide to*
*Country Living* (1979)

Even without a house cow (a cow that provides milk for the household, rather than a cow that lives in the house) it is possible to make your own butter. The very simplest method involves one ingredient, double cream, and one piece of equipment, a jamjar. Make sure the double cream is a few days old (if it is too fresh your work will be much harder) and bring it to room temperature before you start. Pour the cream into the jamjar until it is no more than a third of the way up the sides, as it needs plenty of space. Secure the lid, and prepare yourself to shake the jar continuously until butter is formed. Don't be tempted to stop shaking when the jar fills with whipped cream; this is only the first stage. After up to half an hour of constant agitation, you should notice that your jar contains a lump, sloshing around in a watery liquid. The lump is your butter, and the watery liquid is buttermilk.

Carefully tip the buttermilk out of the jar, keeping it on one side if you wish to use it in another recipe, and rinse the butter clean by pouring cold tap water into the jar and gently swirling the butter around in it, replacing the water until it stays clear. The butter can be very soft at this stage from the heat of all the shaking, so you might want to use very cold water to rinse it. Remove the butter from the jar, and press it with the back of a wooden spoon to remove any last traces of buttermilk. Be patient with this final stage, as it is vital that you squeeze all traces of buttermilk from your butter, or it will be left with a rancid taste. Your butter is now ready to be eaten, moulded into a shape, or simply wrapped in greaseproof paper and put in the fridge. If you prefer your butter salted, which will also make it last longer, you can mix through some salt before you chill it, washing it out again if you find you add too much.

For an even speedier method, some people use a kitchen blender to make butter, but if you wish to make a more significant quantity of butter, or you want to use traditional methods, you might like to invest in a churn, Scotch hands and perhaps even a wooden butter mould or decorative print.

# CHEESE.

1—Gorgonzola.  2—Double Gloucester.  3—Koboko.  4—Parmesan.  5—Dutch.  6—Roquefort.
7—Schabzieger.  8—Dunragit.  9—York Cream.  10—Port du Salut.  11—Cheddar.
12—Pommel.  13—Camembert.  14—Mainzer.  15—Cheshire.  16—Stilton.  17—Cream
Bondon.  18—Gruyère.  19—Wiltshire Loaf.  20—Cheddar Loaf.

# *Making Cheese*

## CHEESE

Cheese is a foodstuff made from the curds of milk separated from the whey (often through the addition of rennet). Cheese making is an ancient craft, and using initial methods which are essentially the same a huge variety of flavours and textures can be achieved.

## THE HISTORY OF CHEESE MAKING

Cheese has been made for thousands of years. It is thought that early nomadic tribes made cheese, and to the ancient Greeks it was a standard form of food (Homer mentions cheese in *The Iliad*). Roman legionaries ate cheese as part of their rations – when the Emperor Hadrian lived as a soldier for a time, he ate 'larido, caseo et posca', or 'bacon fat, cheese and sour wine'.

Cows, sheep and goats, among other mammals, have long been exploited for their milk. However, before refrigeration milk did not keep fresh in summer, and in winter milk output was much diminished (in the past, only a small proportion of a dairy herd would have been kept in milk), so cheese making was a way of keeping milk in a consumable condition for longer. Now it is made and sold for its flavour alone.

It is thought likely that the very earliest cheeses would have been of the acid-curd variety. Raw (rather than pasteurized) milk curdles, especially if it is kept in warm temperatures, naturally separating into curds and whey through the action of lactic acid on casein (the most abundant protein in milk). The curds can then be eaten as cheese but must be eaten fresh, as they will not ripen or keep. Many fresh acid-curd cheeses are flavoured with fresh herbs.

Cheeses which keep are rennet-curd cheeses, rather than acid-curd. Legend has it that the rennet-curd process was accidentally invented when a nomad filled his saddlebag (made from a sheep's stomach) with milk before a long journey. After many miles he went to drink from this bag only to find that it contained solid lumps in liquid – again, curds and whey. The stomachs of young mammals contain a chemical called rennet, which coagulates protein in milk. Whether or not this is truly the manner in which this type of cheese was discovered, rennet has been used in cheese making for thousands of years (although vegetarian alternatives are now used in some varieties).

## COTTAGE INDUSTRY

Until the 19th century, when the first cheese factories opened, cheese production remained a cottage industry. Cheese was made by individuals or small cooperatives of dairy farmers, often as a necessary part of the diet. It was common for larger dairy farms to have a special room attached to the milking parlour for the preparation of cheeses, and by pooling their milk groups of farmers could make cheese on a slightly bigger scale – famous cheeses such as Gruyère and Emmental from Switzerland are said to have originated with cooperatives, such cheeses often being named after the village or region in which they were made. Even when mass-produced cheese became available, small-scale cheese makers continued their art, although their numbers dwindled until very few were left. Thankfully, an increased interest in high-quality, local food has led to a revival in artisan cheese making.

## FAMOUS CHEESES

Every country has its famous cheeses – although France is perhaps the best-known cheese-making nation (in a speech in 1951, Charles de Gaulle famously said: 'The French will only be united under the threat of danger.

How else can one govern a country that produces 246 types of cheese?'). While new cheeses still appear each year, some varieties have a long history. By the middle of the 17th century, Dutch cheese makers were already exporting 500,000 of their familiar round cheeses from Edam each year; Cheshire cheese is one of the oldest British cheeses, mentioned in the Domesday Book; crowdie is an ancient Scottish cheese, traditionally made without rennet; Italian Gorgonzola is said to have been made since at least the 9th century (although its blue veins of mould were a feature that allegedly arrived through happy accident in the 13th century); and France's oldest cheese is Cantal, reputedly made in the Auvergne for 2,000 years.

## HARD CHEESE

Suffolk cheese, also known as Suffolk bang, was a less successful variety than some of those already mentioned. Pepys complained that his servants would not eat it:

*And so home, where I found my wife vexed at her people for grumbling to eat Suffolk cheese, which I am also vexed at. So to bed.*

Samuel Pepys, diary entry, Friday 4 October 1661

For many years the British navy issued Suffolk cheese to its sailors. It was hard and durable – fine attributes for a sea-bound cheese; unfortunately, it was also practically inedible. The navy stopped buying Suffolk cheese in the mid-18th century, and instead bought smaller quantities of more expensive, and more tasty, varieties. It used to be said that Suffolk cheese was 'so hard that pigs grunt at it, dogs bark at it, but none dare bite it'. It also:

*Mocks the weak effort of the bending blade;*
*Or in the hog-trough rests in perfect spite,*
*Too big to swallow, and too hard to bite.*

Robert Bloomfield, *The Farmer's Boy* (published 1800)

Suffolk cheese seems no longer to be made.

## MOULDY CHEESE

Cheese can be hard or soft (and in either case can also be blue, with veins of mould running through it), pasteurized or unpasteurized, and is commonly made from ewe's milk, cow's milk or goat's milk (or, famously in the case of mozzarella, buffalo's milk). Many cheeses are aged for anything from weeks to years. The variety in texture and flavour between different types of cheese is arrived at through different methods of preparation. Flavour is influenced by the type of milk used (which itself is influenced by the type of pasture grazed), as well as by the specific technique employed to separate the curds and whey. Then the treatment of the curds varies (the way in which they are cut, drained and pressed in a cheese press), as do the conditions and length of ripening (generally, the harder the cheese the more rigorously it will have been pressed to remove the maximum amount of whey, and the longer it will have been left to mature). Cheese made on a small scale in two different areas can taste different even if the same recipe is followed. It is a natural product, and making it relies on the careful management of specific bacteria and moulds.

*Cheese—It is well known that some persons like cheese in a state of decay, and even 'alive'. There is no accounting for tastes, and it may be hard to show why mould, which is vegetation, should not be eaten as well as salad, or maggots as well as eels. But, generally speaking, decomposing bodies are not wholesome eating, and the line must be drawn somewhere.*

Mrs Isabella Beeton, *Beeton's Book of Household Management* (1861)

## ADVICE FOR THE CHEESEMAKER

*A Lesson for Dairy-Maid Cisley*

*Gehazi his sickness was whitish and dry,*
*Such cheeses, good Cisley, ye floted too nigh.*

*Leave Lot with her pillar, good Cisley, alone,*
*Much saltness in white-meat is ill for the stone.*

*If cheeses in dairy have Argus's eyes,*
*Tell Cisley the fault in her huswifery lies.*

*Tom Piper hath hoven and puffed up cheeks,*
*If cheese be so hoven, make Ciss to seek creeks.*

*Poor cobbler he tuggeth his leatherly trash,*
*If cheese abide tugging, tug Cisley a crash.*

*If Lazar so loathsome, in cheese be espied,*
*Let baies amend Cisley, or shift her aside.*

*Rough Esau was hairy, from top to the foot,*
*If cheese so appeareth, call Cisley a slut.*

*As Maudlin wept, so would Cisley be drest,*
*For whey in her cheeses not half enough prest.*

*If gentils be scrawling, call maggot the pye,*
*If cheeses have gentils, at Ciss by and by.*

*Bless Cisley, (good mistress,) that bishop doth ban,*
*For burning the milk of her cheese to the pan.*

Thomas Tusser, *Five Hundred Points of Good Husbandry* (1573)

Tusser's advice means, in plainer terms, that cheese should not be white and dry (like the leper Gehazi); nor too salty (like Lot's wife); nor full of eyes (like Argus); nor puffed out with air (like the cheeks of a piper); nor leathery; nor corrupted or rotten; nor hairy (like Esau); nor full of whey or 'weeping' (like Mary Magdalene); nor full of maggots; nor burnt.

## CURDS AND WHEY

### Note on pasteurization and hygiene

In order to make many cheeses, milk must be soured. Raw milk naturally contains bacteria which cause souring if milk is kept in warm conditions. Pasteurization kills most of these bacteria, so a special culture of bacteria (called a 'starter') is often added to pasteurized milk at the start of cheese making. Never simply leave pasteurized milk out of the fridge in the expectation you will get cheese, as it no longer contains the right bacteria. If you are making cheese for the first time, you should probably use pasteurized milk (and – if the recipe demands it – a starter), as it is recommended that pregnant women, the elderly and the very young avoid raw or unpasteurized dairy products. Also, make sure everything is scrupulously clean. It is best to sterilize all your equipment when making cheese.

### A simple acid-curd cheese, with a hint of lemon

This is probably the simplest cheese you can make at home. The ingredients are milk and a lemon, and the equipment (perhaps with the exception of the muslin and thermometer) can be found in most kitchens. Heat 575

millilitres (1 pint) of milk to 38°C (100°F) by placing it in a bowl standing in a pan of simmering water – check the temperature either with a special dairy thermometer or a sugar thermometer. When it reaches temperature, remove the bowl from the saucepan and add the juice of a lemon. Stir, then leave to stand for 15 minutes – you should immediately see curds and whey forming. Line a sieve or colander with a piece of clean muslin, then carefully ladle the contents of the bowl into it. Gather the corners of the muslin together, tie with string, and hang it over a bowl for an hour until the whey has drained away. After this time, your cheese will be ready. Scrape it off the muslin, add salt or chopped herbs if desired (or some freshly cracked black pepper) and eat immediately, spread on crackers or fresh crusty bread.

### A simple rennet-curd soft cheese

You will need the same equipment for this as for the lemon cheese. Rennet is available from some chemists and health-food shops, or online. Place 1 litre (1¾ pints) of milk in a bowl and add a pinch of salt. Stand the bowl in a pan of simmering water and heat the milk to 38°C (100°F). Remove the bowl from the heat and stir in two teaspoons of rennet. Leave to stand for 15 minutes, during which time the milk will separate into curds and whey (the curds form at the top and the whey below). Line a sieve or colander with muslin, ladle the curds into it, then tie up the muslin and hang it over a bowl. Leave for around two to three hours, then take the cheese from the muslin and place in a bowl. It should be kept in the fridge, and is best eaten within two to three days. This cheese

*Making cheese*
*© Elphinstone Institute,*
*University of Aberdeen*
*Licensor www.scran.ac.uk*

is fairly bland, and has a lovely smooth texture. It can be used as you would use ricotta, or you can place it in small moulds, then coat it with herbs or oatmeal. If you are intrigued to find out what 'curds and whey' taste like, put some of the cheese in a bowl with the whey, pour over some cream, sprinkle on some sugar, then grate a little nutmeg over the top.

## MORE CHEESE MAKING

To commit further to cheese making, you will need to invest in more equipment (including a press) and start learning more about starters. There is a lot of information online about cheese making, and there are a number of books devoted to the subject, including *Cheesemaking and Dairying* (2003) by Katie Thear.

# Making Jam and Marmalade

## JAM AND MARMALADE

Jam and marmalade are both types of preserve made by boiling fruit with sugar. While marmalade is generally considered a breakfast treat, jam is associated more with scones and afternoon tea.

## STICKY HISTORY

Jam has been made since Roman times, and quite possibly even longer. The Roman cookery book *De re coquinaria* ('On Cookery') by Marcus Gavius Apicius included instructions on preserving fruit in honey, and it was this desire to preserve fruit that led to the development of jam as we know it. It is also thought that jam was popular in the Middle East. Some say that the Crusaders brought the taste for it back to Europe, where the first recipes for jam are said to have been published in the late 1600s.

*This manufacture of jam and jelly may now be said to form an undertaking of some importance in every Scottish household, occupying a position in the social scale above the humblest. In South Britain, the process is also carried on, but not with the universality or earnestness of purpose observable in the north. To purchase their preserves at the confectioner's, or to present to their guests sweetmeats, stored in those mendacious pots, which belie so egregiously the expectations entertained of them at last sight, in regard cubic contents, would in the eyes of the generality of Scottish lathes (those of the old school at least), be held to indicate a sad lack of good housewifeship. Even when the household store was exhausted, as very frequently happens about the months of May or June, we have seen the proposal to remedy the deficiency by purchasing a supply from a shop rejected with scorn.*

Robert Chambers, *Book of Days* (1869)

It is generally accepted that the word 'marmalade' comes from the Portuguese *marmelada*, a sugary concoction of quinces exported to Britain in medieval times. This was a solid sweetmeat consisting of quinces cooked down with sugar, quite unlike the orange marmalade we are familiar with today. A number of legends are attached to the invention of orange marmalade. Some claim that it was invented for Catherine of Aragon (1485– 1536). The story goes that when Catherine married Henry VIII, she missed her sunny home in Spain and also missed Spanish oranges. As shipping at that time took too long for the oranges to remain fresh, marmalade was developed to preserve them for the journey.

Keiller's marmalade
© Douglas MacKenzie
Licensor www.scran.ac.uk

A claim for the invention of modern marmalade relates to one Janet Keiller, an inhabitant of the Scottish town of Dundee in the 1790s. Janet's husband procured a cheap box of Seville oranges from a boat in the harbour, and she was left to work out what to do with these bitter fruits. Janet saved her energy by chopping the peel of the fruit into shreds rather than painstakingly pulping the fruit, as was the usual way, and made the preserve more profitable by leaving it runnier than the norm, through less boiling down, thus filling more pots for sale. Perhaps due in part to Janet's canny nature, modern marmalade was born. While there is no evidence to support this story, the Keiller family did build a marmalade factory in Dundee in 1797, and Dundee is still thought of as the home of marmalade. It is also associated with a particular style of marmalade – lighter and more jelly-like around the shreds than the dark Oxford marmalade. Captain Scott apparently preferred the Oxford variety, as he took a tin of Frank Cooper's Oxford Marmalade to Antarctica. It was rediscovered there in 1980 and, when opened, was said to be in excellent condition.

## FIRE BURN, AND CAULDRON BUBBLE

Jam is made from fruit, sugar and water. Traditional marmalade is made from Seville oranges, sugar and water, although it can be made from any citrus fruits. Both are very simple and satisfying to make and eat, particularly if you are making jam from organic fruit you have grown or picked yourself. The key in preserve making is achieving the correct consistency:

*Jellys and jams form because of a chemical reaction between a substance called pectin, present in the fruit, and sugar. The pectin (and the fruits acids, which also play a part in the reaction) tend to be most concentrated when the fruit is under-ripe. But then of course the flavour is only partly developed. So the optimum time for picking fruit for jelly is when it is just ripe.*

Richard Mabey, *Food for Free* (1972)

Pectin levels in fruit vary according to the type of fruit and its ripeness. For example, blackcurrants, redcurrants, damsons, apples and gooseberries are high in pectin, whereas strawberries, blackberries and medlars are low. As a general rule, the less pectin the less sugar you need to add, and the more pectin the more sugar. Some people prefer to buy pectin to ensure they get the right 'set', whereas others simply adjust the sugar, or include some of the high pectin fruits in all their recipes. Generally, you need 450 grams (1 pound) of sugar to 450 grams (1 pound) of fruit.

Your equipment list for making jam is: a preserving pan or other large, heavy-based saucepan; jamjars; lids for the jamjars, or waxed paper discs and cellophane; and a wooden spoon with a long handle. For marmalade you will also need some muslin. Jamjars should always be sterilized – wash them in soapy water, rinse them and place them in a cool oven for 15 to 20 minutes, then take them straight from the oven when you are ready to fill them with your jam.

Granulated sugar is the most economical type to use, but it does produce more foamy scum than preserving sugar; this scum needs to be skimmed off when the jam starts to boil. Preserving sugar also dissolves faster, but good results can be had with either. To speed the dissolving process up, some people prefer to warm the sugar by pouring it into a baking tray and placing it in a cool oven. Home-made jam is generally prepared according to which fruits are in season, although frozen fruit can also be used. Traditional marmalade made from Seville oranges must be made between December and February, when Seville oranges are in season. Fruit should always be cleaned, with any damaged areas cut out, and hulled or prepared as necessary.

## Strawberry jam

To make six jars of strawberry jam you will need 2 kilograms (4 pounds) of strawberries, the juice of one lemon and 1¾ kilograms (3½ pounds) of sugar. Hull the strawberries, and chop any very large ones into chunks. Place the strawberries and the lemon juice in the pan (you probably won't need to add any water, as strawberries are naturally high in this) and heat very gently until the strawberries are tender (gentle heating will lead to a more efficient release of pectin). Add the sugar, stir it in well until it has dissolved, then bring the pan to the boil. Skim off any scum. Now you need to test the jam to see if it has set. If you prefer scientific methods and have a jam thermometer, you can test the temperature of the jam – it should be 105°C (222°F). Otherwise, test the jam regularly, as follows, until it has reached its setting point. Carefully put a little bit of the hot jam on a saucer, and place it in the fridge for a few minutes. Then push the jam with your finger – if it wrinkles it is ready; if it doesn't, boil it for a little longer. Another test is to watch how the jam falls from a wooden spoon – if the jam forms into blobs before it falls it is ready. Allow the jam to stand for 15 minutes, then fill the hot jamjars, seal and label. If properly covered and stored somewhere cool and dry, jam will keep for many months.

*Yet ... we may allude to the difference of opinion prevalent among those versed in jam-lore, as to the proper time which should be allowed for the syrup remaining on the fire, after having reached the point of ebullition. Some recommend the space of twenty minutes, others half-an-hour, whilst a few, determined that the preserves shall be thoroughly subjected to the action of Vulcan, keep the pan bubbling away for three-quarters or even an entire hour. An esteemed relative of our own always insisted on this last period being allowed, with the result, it must be stated, sometimes of the jam becoming a veritable decoction, in which the original shape of the fruit could scarcely be recognized, whilst the substance itself became, after having cooled, so indurated as to be almost impracticable for any other use than as a lollipop. As her old servant was wont to declare, 'she boiled the very judgment out o't!'*

Robert Chambers, *Book of Days* (1869)

## Seville orange marmalade

To make six jars of marmalade you will need 1 kilogram (2 pounds) of Seville oranges, the juice of a lemon, 2 kilograms (4 pounds) of sugar and 2 1/4 litres (4 pints) of water. Cut the oranges and the lemon in half, and squeeze out the juice. Keep back any pips and pith. Place the juice and the water in the pan, slice the orange peel into strips (this will take a while, unless you have an marvellous old-fashioned marmalade cutter, but the flavour will be worth it in the end) and add that too. Wrap the pith and pips in muslin, and place that in the pan (the pips are a good source of pectin). Simmer the liquid for around two hours, uncovered, until the peel is soft. Remove the muslin bag of pith and pips. Add the sugar and continue to heat gently, stirring until it has dissolved. Bring to a rapid boil, remove any scum and after 15 minutes do your first test for the 'set', as described above. When it has reached the setting point, leave the marmalade to stand for 15 minutes, stir it to ensure that the shreds are evenly distributed so that you will get some in every jar, then pot it up.

# Candying Peel

## CANDIED PEEL

Candied peel is made from the peel of citrus fruit. The peel is cooked, then impregnated with sugar, which preserves it. Candied peel is now most commonly used as an ingredient in fruit cake and Christmas puddings, but the home-made variety also makes a delicious sweet all on its own.

## SWEET HISTORY

Peel has been candied for centuries. By candying the peel of citrus fruit, very little of the fruit is wasted. The sugar also acts as a preservative, keeping this part of the fruit edible for much longer than would otherwise be the case – important in the days before imported fruit could be bought out of season. Candied peel was a popular sweetmeat in the courts of medieval Europe, and in the past any home cook worth her salt would have made her own candied peel. The decline in the art of candying came with the industrialization of food production, as factory candied peel became cheap and readily available. But in recent years there has been a revival of interest in this culinary craft with the realization that, at its worst, the tough, unpleasant shop-bought peel can easily be beaten by the succulent home-made alternative.

## CHINA CHIPS

*To make China Chips.*

*Cut the Rind of* China *Oranges in long Chips, but very thin, and with none of the*

*White; boil them in water 'till they are very tender; then drain them, and put them into a very thick cold Syrup of clarify'd Sugar; let them lye a day or two; then scald them, and when they are cold lay them to dry on Earthen Plates in a Stove. Sevil oranges will do the same Way, if you like them with a little sugar, and very bitter.*

Mary Eales, *Mrs Mary Eales's Receipts* (1718)

Mrs Eales's 18th-century 'China chips' receipt might sound strange, but it is essentially a recipe for candied orange peel – the China oranges she refers to are simply sweet oranges known by that name because they were originally brought from China. It is interesting to note that Mrs Eales referred to herself as 'Confectioner to her late Majesty Queen Anne', though on whose authority she did this (and it was possibly just her own) is not known.

## HOW TO CANDY

The only ingredients you will need to make candied peel are the citrus fruits of your choice (preferably organic, definitely unwaxed), sugar and water. The only equipment required is a saucepan, kitchen scales, a tray lined with non-stick paper (reusable silicone paper is good) and an airtight container to keep your candied peel in. The following notes refer to candied grapefruit peel, but lemon, orange or a mixture can be substituted as preferred.

First, cut four grapefruits into quarters, then carefully pull the flesh away from the peel so the peel stays in large pieces. Boil the peel until it is tender, then boil it again, in fresh water, for 20 minutes (it might seem a bother, but the peel does need the second boiling). Drain the peel, and make your sugar syrup. Place 450 grams (1 pound) of sugar in a pan with 225 millilitres (8 fluid ounces) of water. Heat gently, and stir until the sugar has dissolved. Once the syrup boils, add the peel, and cook at a gentle simmer until most of the syrup has disappeared (this may take a while). Carefully take the peel out of the pan, one piece at a time, and spread the pieces on your lined baking tray. Leave the tray somewhere dry for a few days, turning the pieces occasionally until they are dry. The peel can be left as it is and chopped when you need it in a cake recipe, or cut into bite-size pieces and either sprinkled with caster sugar or dipped in melted chocolate to be eaten as a sweet. In either case, store it in an airtight container.

## SWEETS

Traditional boiled sweets have a long history. They are made of boiled sugar, flavouring and now often colouring.

## STICKY HISTORY

Early sweetmeats were made using fruit and honey, but the sugary sweets we know today are more closely related to those found in a 17th-century apothecary's shop. The notion that sugar had medicinal benefits had come down from Arab physicians, and was established in Britain in the 13th century. Early pharmaceutical treatises included recipes we would associate with a confectioner. At one time it was thought that sugar could cure headaches and stomach ulcers and was good for the chest, lungs and throat – although as early as the 16th century the writer Tabernaemontanus had made the link between sugar and tooth decay – and the saying 'like an apothecary without sugar' referred to something absurd or useless.

Barley sugars are one of the oldest sweets that we still recognize today, and have been made since at least the 17th century. Many say that this traditional amber-coloured sweet was invented by French nuns in 1638. The sweet-making Benedictine nuns founded the Priory of Our Lady of Angels in the medieval town of Moret-sur-Loing in that year, and the sisters made barley sugar (or *sucre d'orge*) there, for a time with great success. The nuns' barley sugars are said to have been popular at the court of Louis XIV, and were thought to have throat-soothing properties (continuing the connection between confectionery and medicine).

However, after the French Revolution it was feared that the secret recipe had been lost; moreover, the nuns had dispersed. Eventually, a nun who knew the recipe returned to Moret and passed it on to a friend, who in turn passed it on to the nuns who came to re-establish a convent there, and the sweets again became popular. When the last sister left Moret in the 1970s, she entrusted the recipe to a local confectioner. Barley sugar is still made in the town – in sticks and in heart-shaped lozenges bearing a cross and the letters R and M (for *Religieuses de Moret*, or Nuns of Moret). The town also boasts a museum of barley sugar, the Musée du Sucre d'Orge des Religieuses de Moret.

## SWEETIE WIVES

*The country folks came in dressed in their best, the schools got the play, and a long rank of sweety-wives and their stands, covered with the wonted dainties of the occasion, occupied the sunny side of the High Street; while the shady side was, in like manner, taken possession of by the packmen, who, in their booths, made a marvellous display of goods of an inferior quality, with laces and ribands of all colours, hanging down in front, and twirling like pinnets in the wind.*

John Galt, *The Provost* (1822)

By the early 1800s, sugar was a cheap commodity, and in Scotland it was common for women to make sweets at home, then sell them on the streets. Such women were known as sweetie, or sweety, wives. Unfortunately for them, from the 1860s confectionery became mass-produced. Specialized machines could produce hundreds of sweets in a short space of time, and these sweets could then be sold very cheaply. Mechanization brought with it a wider variety of sweets, and fewer people saw the need to make sweets at home or buy from the sweetie wives, whose stock was obviously more limited than that of the sweet factories.

## BOILING UP

*The technicalities by which confectioners distinguish the different degrees of sugar-boiling, seem to us calculated rather to puzzle than to assist the reader; and we shall therefore, confine ourselves to such plain English terms as may suffice, we hope, to explain them.*

Eliza Acton, *Modern Cookery, in All its Branches* (1845)

All boiled sweets are made in essentially the same way. Sugar and water is boiled, then, when it has cooled enough, it is poured onto a flat heatproof surface to be worked (it is rather like thick, molten sugar at this stage, and has started to solidify). Colour and flavouring are then added, and the mixture is kneaded to ensure that these are evenly distributed. It can then be shaped into sweets. Blackpool rock is made by assembling fat stripes of different coloured mixtures. They are placed together, then 'stretched' on specially designed machines to make the thin sticks of lettered rock that we all know.

### Barley sugar

Barley sugars are so named because they were originally made from a decoction of barley. Modern barley sugars rarely contain barley, indeed even Mrs Beeton's barley sugar recipe used plain water rather than barley water, but if you want to try the real thing, the process is not a complicated one, although reliable recipes are difficult to come by. Be warned though, boiling sugar mixtures should be treated with extreme caution.

First you will need to make barley water. Place 100 grams (4 ounces) of pearl barley in a pan with 900 millilitres (32 fluid ounces) of water. Bring to the boil, cover and simmer for a couple of hours, then take off the heat and leave to stand for a few hours more. The barley water will eventually settle, and when you can see a clear top layer, spoon out around 225 millilitres (8 fluid ounces) without disturbing the pearl barley and sediment below. Place this, with 500 grams (1 pound) of granulated sugar, in a heavy-based saucepan and add a pinch of cream of tartar. Bring to the boil and cook without stirring until the mixture reaches the 'hard-crack' stage – the syrup will reach a temperature of 149°C–154°C (300°F–310°F). You will need a special sugar thermometer to check this, and if you drop some of the syrup into cold water, it will solidify into brittle threads. Place the pan in cold water to bring the temperature of the syrup down. To make lozenges, carefully pour the syrup into well-oiled heavy

*Barley sugar seller, magazine illustration, 1891*
© *Mary Evans Picture Library / Alamy*

moulds. To make barley twists, wait until the syrup has cooled enough to be workable, pour it onto an oiled plate (or a more professional marble slab) and cut the syrup into strips, twist them, and leave them somewhere to finish cooling.

Although once it was the barley that was thought to make barley sugars good for travel sickness, the modern barley-free versions are still associated with this.

# *Pickling*

## PICKLES

Pickles are made by preserving raw or cooked foods (most often vegetables) in either vinegar or brine. In the USA, 'pickle' refers specifically to a cucumber preserved in brine, the most popular pickled vegetable there. In Britain, small onions pickled in vinegar, which grace every pub-served ploughman's lunch, are the most common pickle.

## FAMOUS FANS

*The ancient Greeks and Romans held their pickles in high estimation. They consisted of flowers, herbs, roots, and vegetables, preserved in vinegar, and which were kept, for a long time, in cylindrical vases with wide mouths. Their cooks prepared pickles with the greatest care, and the various ingredients were macerated in oil, brine and vinegar, with which they were often impregnated drop by drop.*
Mrs Isabella Beeton, *Beeton's Book of Household Management* (1861)

It is thought that vegetables have been pickled for more than 4,000 years – archaeologists believe that the Mesopotamians were pickling cucumbers by around 2000 BC. Apparently, Aristotle praised the pickled cucumber as being beneficial to health, and Cleopatra believed that eating pickles contributed to her beauty. Pliny the Elder and the emperors Julius Caesar and Tiberius are also said to have enjoyed pickles. Amerigo Vespucci, the Italian merchant-turned-explorer after whom America is named, was described by the author Ralph Waldo Emerson as 'the pickle-dealer at Seville', and it does seem that in his capacity as a merchant Vespucci supplied ships with pickles, which reduced the risk of scurvy in sailors on long journeys. American presidents have also been known to be partial to a pickle – George Washington, for example, and Thomas Jefferson, who is said to have remarked that 'On a hot day in Virginia, I know nothing more comforting than a fine spiced pickle, brought up trout-like, from the sparkling depths of the aromatic jar below the stairs of Aunt Sally's cellar.'

Britons have long enjoyed pickles too. Elizabeth I was apparently a fan, and Samuel Pepys (who also mentions pickled oysters in his diaries) dined at least once on brawn and pickled gherkins:

*We did this day cut a brave collar of brawn from Winchcombe which proves very good, and also opened the glass of girkins which Captain Cocke did give my wife the other day, which are rare things.*

Samuel Pepys, diary entry, Sunday 1 December 1661

## WORLDWIDE PURSUIT

Different pickles have developed in different parts of the world – pickled red cabbage, associated with Eastern Europe; fermented cabbage, or sauerkraut, associated with Germany; Japanese umeboshi, pickled ume fruit (related to apricots); and various Korean pickles called kimchi. Indian delights such as lime pickle or aubergine pickle are now known to many in the West. India has a rich tradition of such dishes, although they are relishes or chutneys rather than straightforward pickles, as are the British piccalilli and famous Branston Pickle.

## PICKLING DECLINE

Before canning and freezing, pickling was a way of ensuring that vegetables were preserved for winter. Also, it is in the nature of vegetables to provide a glut rather than a steady supply of produce, and pickling ensured that the surplus did not go to waste. At one time pickling in summer would have been an annual event to ensure good food in the leaner months. The decline in home-pickling came with refrigeration, the industrialization of food and the importation of out-of-season foods from other parts of the world. Now the flavour of pickles is more important than the dose of vitamins they can supply in the winter. However, the craft is enjoying something of a revival now that more people are 'growing their own' and often finding themselves with a backlog of fresh but uneaten vegetables in the summer months. It is satisfying to eat in winter something that was sown, grown and picked in spring and summer, especially as the hard work involved in cultivation is by then largely forgotten. And even if you buy your vegetables, you can still enjoy the results of preserving them in different combinations of spices and vinegars.

## VINEGAR AND BRINE

You can pickle many things, and little equipment is needed. Two key things to remember when you make pickles are: use fresh produce (and wash it carefully), and make sure that the jars you are going to store your pickles in have been sterilized and have good seals and lids that won't rust away.

If you are an enthusiastic pickler, you might want to make your own vinegar, while at the other end of the effort scale you can buy spiced vinegar and ready for pickling. A midway approach is to buy vinegar and then spice it yourself. A description of one spiced vinegar recipe is given below (although you can add any spices you like), as is the method for pickling onions. If you are going to buy vinegar to spice yourself, you will find a wide range to choose from. Wine vinegars are perhaps the best tasting, but they are also the most expensive. Malt vinegar is the most economical, and still produces good results. The only rule is that the vinegar must have a minimum acetic acid content of five per cent.

To make spiced vinegar, you will need:

*Pickles in the dry larder, Lanhydrock, Cornwall*
© NTPL / Andreas von Einsiedel

> 1.1 litres (2 pints) vinegar
> 1 cinnamon stick
> 15 millilitres (1 tablespoon) whole allspice berries
> 15 millilitres (1 tablespoon) blade mace
> 6 cloves
> 6 peppercorns
> 2½ millilitres (½ teaspoon) mustard seeds

To make 'quick' spiced vinegar, place all the ingredients in a saucepan, cover and bring to the boil. Then remove the pan from the heat and leave for around two hours before straining – leave the lid on, as it will preserve the flavours and the smell of hot vinegar is very strong. For a better flavour, the spiced vinegar must be started at least one month before it is needed. Simply add the spices to unheated vinegar and leave for one to two months before straining ready for use.

To use your spiced vinegar for pickled onions you will need pickling onions, salt and water. Dissolve 225 grams (8 ounces) of salt in 2.3 litres (4 pints) of water to make a brine. Put 1.4 kilograms (3 pounds) of pickling onions (unskinned) in a bowl and pour the brine over. Place a plate on top of the onions to keep them submerged (put a weight on the plate if needed). After twelve hours, pour the brine away and skin the onions. Make up a fresh brine and pour this over the onions, covering them with a plate again. Leave for two to three days. Finally, drain and rinse the onions, pack them into your jars, pour over your spiced vinegar and seal. Freshly pickled onions need to be left for at least two months before they are really good to eat.

Different vegetables require different treatments, but recipes for pickles are readily available in general cookery books as well as specialist ones, and online. As a quick guide to some of the most popular pickles: beetroot are cooked, then peeled and sliced and pickled in vinegar, or baby beetroots are cooked, peeled and pickled whole; apples, especially crab-apples (often pickled in the past), also need to be cooked first; red cabbage, cauliflower and gherkins (as with the onions described above) are placed in brine rather than cooked before they are pickled. It is generally said that pickles are best eaten within six months of making them, although some picklers claim they can be kept much longer.

# Smoking

## SMOKED FOOD

Smoking is an ancient method of (originally) preserving, and (later) simply flavouring, meat or fish. Wood smoke is used, and popular smoked foodstuffs today include smoked salmon, Arbroath smokies, kippers and smoked bacon.

## LONG HISTORY

Food has been smoked for thousands of years. To begin with, meat or fish was smoked in order to preserve it, a process which dates back to before recorded history. Even by the Middle Ages in Europe, fish could not be transported far from the port at which it was landed unless it had been heavily salted or smoked. By the mid-19th century, perishable goods could be transported quickly via steamships and railways, and while the need for smoking declined, an appreciation of the flavour of mildly smoked foods remained.

Two forms of smoked fish that we now regard as traditional were allegedly developed just as the need to smoke was on the wane – the kipper and the Yarmouth bloater. The modern-day kipper is said to have been accidentally invented by John Woodger, at Seahouses, Northumberland, in 1843 (the word 'kipper' was in use before this, but was used to refer to smoked salmon, while Woodger's kipper was a herring). The story goes that Woodger left some split and salted herring in a shed where a fire was left burning overnight. At first he thought that the smoke would have ruined the fish, but once cooked it became apparent they were delicious.

The Yarmouth bloater (a herring again, but traditionally left whole and ungutted rather than split) is claimed by some to date back to the 1830s, when it is said to have been invented by a fish-curer who found that a batch of fresh herring had been overlooked – left neither gutted nor cured. He did not want to waste them, so he decided to see what would happen if they were salted and hung in the smokehouse. He went on to perfect the Yarmouth bloater – although the story (and its date) could be a red herring.

Scotland also has a rich fish-smoking heritage, and the Arbroath smokie is another delicacy said to have been discovered by accident. Legend has it that a fire broke out in a cottage in Auchmithie in which

haddock had been hung to dry. The house was ruined, but the haddock were delicious. Later, many people from Auchmithie moved to Arbroath, taking their smoked haddock with them, and the fish became known as the Arbroath smokie. In 2004, the designation 'Arbroath smokie' was recognized as a 'Protected Geographical Indication' by the European Union. Also conferred on such delights as champagne and Parma ham, in the case of the smokie this means that to be called an Arbroath smokie the fish must be haddock, and it must be smoked in the traditional way within 8 kilometres (5 miles) of Arbroath.

*Smoking haddock,*
*Auchmithie*
*© Angus Council (Signal*
*Tower Museum, Arbroath)*
*Licensor www.scran.ac.uk*

## HOT OR COLD

While exact smoking methods vary greatly, there are a few basic principles of smoking that are generally consistent. Fish or meat is first cured, using salt – either salt is rubbed onto the surface of the food or, commonly, the food is left in brine. During curing, moisture is drawn from the meat or fish. This is the first stage in preserving the food. After curing it can then be either hot-smoked or cold-smoked. Hot-smoked foods (such as Arbroath smokies and smoked mackerel) are cooked as well as smoked, so are ready to eat. Some cold-smoked foods (such as cold-smoked salmon) are also ready to eat, but many (including smoked bacon, kippers and Yarmouth bloaters) require cooking. For hot-smoked foods a shorter brining time and a hotter smoking temperature are used. Cold-smoked foods are kept in brine for longer and are also smoked for longer at lower temperatures. The scientific explanation for the effectiveness of smoking lies in the fact that certain extracts in the smoke inhibit the growth of bacteria which would cause the food to spoil.

## SMOKING AT HOME

If you have an open fire, the simplest method of smoking at home is to place your meat or fish high up in the chimney and keep a hardwood log fire burning below – always use wood and never coal, as coal smoke is too toxic to use in food preparation. It is also possible to buy specially designed smokers (which look something like a barbecue), create your own smokehouse (self-sufficiency expert John Seymour used an outside, brick-built lavatory converted to the purpose with a wood-burning stove), or use a barrel, as Mrs Beeton suggested:

*TO SMOKE HAMS AND FISH AT HOME*
*Take an old hogshead, stop up all the crevices, and fix a place to put a cross-stick near the bottom, to hang the articles to be smoked on. Next, in the side, cut a hole near the top, to introduce an iron pan filled with sawdust and small pieces of green wood. Having turned the tub upside down, hang the articles upon the cross-stick, introduce the iron pan in the opening, and place a piece of red-hot iron in the pan, cover it with sawdust, and all will be complete. Let a large ham remain 40 hours, and keep up a good smoke.*
Mrs Isabella Beeton, *Beeton's Book of Household Management* (1861)

Pheasant.

Ptarmigan.

Woodcock.

Hare garnished.

Wild Duck.

Grouse.

Larks on Toast.

Snipe.

Guinea Fowl.

Roast Turkey.

Boiled Fowl.

Boned Capon.

Roast Goose.

Roast Duck.

Roast Fowl.

Boiled Rabbit with Onions.

GAME & POULTRY.

# Preparing Hare, Pigeon and Rabbit the Mrs Beeton Way

## MRS BEETON

Isabella Beeton (1836–65) was not a cook, but in compiling *Beeton's Book of Household Management* (1861) her name became irrevocably linked to the culinary arts, and she is perhaps the most famous British cookery writer of all time. While her book has remained popular, many of the dishes and techniques described in it have not been so fortunate.

## HARE, PIGEON AND RABBIT

Hare, pigeon and rabbit once formed a far larger part of the British diet than they do today, when they might be eaten occasionally, in restaurants, rather than regularly, at home. At one time they were meant to be caught and eaten, not bought and eaten, but even by Mrs Beeton's time there had been a massive shift in the population of Britain from rural to urban, a move which was part of the Industrial Revolution. However, Mrs Beeton did expect the Victorian housewife to know how to deal with the fur and feathers of these three beasts. They were less squeamish times than today, and meat did not come shrink-wrapped in plastic – Mrs Beeton's instructions to 'carefully pluck, draw and wash' your pigeons (with no further information) would not be understood by many home cooks today, and would probably be followed by even fewer. As it isn't necessary to kill and prepare your own game to enjoy eating it, it does seem a shame that wild rabbit is so often overlooked for industrially farmed chicken.

Mrs Beeton includes ten rabbit dishes, four pigeon and six hare – just one for each is given below. If you can't face 'drawing' a bird or 'paunching' a hare (in other words, gutting them and removing the inside bits that you don't want to eat), either buy the game from a butcher who will prepare it for you, or find someone who can. Some basic instructions are given in the sections on plucking, p96, and skinning, p93, but if you can find someone to demonstrate the techniques to you, then so much the better.

## FIRST CATCH YOUR HARE

Hares are hung whole for around five to six days, to improve the flavour, before being skinned and paunched. Only young hare is suitable for roasting. As with rabbits, smooth, sharp claws are a sign of a young hare. Also, the hare-lip is hardly noticeable in very young hares, as this becomes more pronounced only as the hare grows older. Hare is available from September to March, and unlike rabbit is always wild (never farmed). Below are Mrs Beeton's two versions of jugged hare, once a popular dish but now nearly forgotten.

### JUGGED HARE.

*(Very Good.)*

INGREDIENTS – 1 hare, 1½ lb. of gravy beef, ½ lb. of butter, 1 onion, 1 lemon, 6 cloves; pepper, cayenne, and salt to taste; ½ pint of port wine.

*Mode.*—Skin, paunch, and wash the hare, cut it into pieces, dredge them with flour, and fry in boiling butter. Have ready 1½ pint of gravy, made from the above proportion of beef, and thickened with a little flour. Put this into a jar; add the pieces of fried hare, an onion stuck with six cloves, a lemon peeled and cut in half, and a good seasoning of pepper, cayenne, and salt; cover the jar down tightly, put it up to the neck into a stewpan of boiling water, and let it stew until the hare is quite tender, taking care to keep the water boiling. When nearly done, pour in the wine, and add a few forcemeat balls ... these must be fried or baked in the oven for a few minutes before they are put to the gravy. Serve with red-currant jelly.

*Time.*—3½ to 4 hours. If the hare is very old, allow 4½ hours.
*Average cost, 7s.*
*Sufficient for 7 or 8 persons.*
*Seasonable from September to the end of February.*

II.

*(A Quicker and more Economical Way.)*

INGREDIENTS – *1 hare, a bunch of sweet herbs, 2 onions, each stuck with 3 cloves, 6 whole allspice, ¹/₂ teaspoonful of black pepper, a strip of lemon-peel, thickening of butter and flour, 2 tablespoonfuls of mushroom ketchup, ¹/₄ pint of port wine.*

*Mode.*—Wash the hare nicely, cut it up into joints (not too large), and flour and brown them as in the preceding recipe; then put them into a stewpan with the herbs, onions, cloves, allspice, pepper, and lemon-peel; cover with hot water, and when it boils, carefully remove all the scum, and let it simmer gently till tender, which will be in about 1¹/₄ hour, or longer, should the hare be very old. Take out the pieces of hare, thicken the gravy with flour and butter, add the ketchup and port wine, let it boil for about 10 minutes, strain it through a sieve over the hare, and serve. A few fried forcemeat balls should be added at the moment of serving, or instead of frying them, they may be stewed in the gravy, about 10 minutes before the hare is wanted for table. Do not omit to serve red-currant jelly with it.

*Time.*—Altogether 2 hours.
*Average cost, 5s. 6d.*
*Sufficient for 7 or 8 persons.*
*Seasonable from September to the end of February.*

*Note.*—Should there be any left, rewarm it the next day by putting the hare, &c. into a covered jar, and placing this jar in a saucepan of boiling water: this method prevents a great deal of waste.

Unfortunately, the phrase 'first catch your hare' so often quoted as belonging to Mrs Beeton does not appear anywhere in her famous book. Neither was it coined by Hannah Glasse (the standard alternative attribution), whose instructions for roast hare, in her book *The Art of Cookery Made Plain and Easy* (1746), began: 'take your hare when it is cased [skinned]'.

## STOP THE PIGEON

Pigeons require no hanging and are available all year, although it is said they are best between May and October. Fledgling pigeons are called squabs, and you will sometimes find recipes (such as squab pie) which specifically call for these. It is very hard to judge the age of a pigeon, so you will just have to hope that you don't buy anything too old and tough. If you follow Mrs Beeton's recipe for roast pigeon, below, you should allow one bird per person.

INGREDIENTS – *Pigeons, 3 oz. of butter, pepper and salt to taste.*

*Trussing.*—*Pigeons, to be good, should be eaten fresh (if kept a little, the flavour goes off), and they should be drawn as soon as killed. Cut off the heads and necks, truss the wings over the backs, and cut off the toes at the first joint: previous to trussing, they should be carefully cleaned, as no bird requires so much washing.*

*Mode.*—*Wipe the birds very dry, season them inside with pepper and salt, and put about 3/4 oz. of butter into the body of each: this makes them moist. Put them down to a bright fire, and baste them well the whole of the time they are cooking (they will be done enough in from 20 to 30 minutes); garnish with fried parsley, and serve with a tureen of parsley and butter. Bread-sauce and gravy, the same as for roast fowl, are exceedingly nice accompaniments to roast pigeons, as also egg-sauce.*

*Time.*—*From 20 minutes to 1/2 hour.*
*Average cost, 6d. to 9d. each.*
*Seasonable from April to September; but in the greatest perfection from Midsummer to Michaelmas.*

Almost as if to show how much less squeamish the Victorians were, the following instruction is given in the *Book of Household Management*'s version of pigeon pie:

*Clean three of the feet, and place them in a hole made in the crust at the top: this shows what kind of pie it is.*

You may or may not want to follow this advice next time you make a pie.

## RUN RABBIT RUN

*On the farm, ev'ry Friday*
*On the farm, it's rabbit pie day*
*So ev'ry Friday, that ever comes along*
*I get up early, and sing this little song ...*

*Run, rabbit, run, rabbit, run, run, run*
*Run, rabbit, run, rabbit, run, run, run*
*Bang, bang, bang, bang! goes the farmer's gun*
*Run, rabbit, run, rabbit, run, run, run*
Lyrics from the popular wartime song, 'Run rabbit run'

Rabbits are best eaten young and wild – young rabbits are tenderer, and wild rabbits are tastier. They are available all year round. Unlike many other types of game, rabbits aren't hung, and can be prepared for cooking as soon as they have been killed. If you are buying a rabbit that still has its skin on, look for one that has soft ears and good claws; as Mrs Beeton points out, 'choose rabbits with smooth and sharp claws, as that denotes they are young: should these be blunt and rugged, the ears dry and tough, the animal is old'. This is the recipe for rabbit pie from *Beeton's Book of Household Management*:

GAME & POULTRY.

1.—Snipe on Toast.  3.—Larks on Toast.  5.—Roast Pheasant.  8.—Roast Pigeons.
3.—Roast Fowl.  6.—Roast Goose.  7.—Roast Duck.  8.—Boiled Fowl.
9.—Roast Turkey.

*INGREDIENTS – 1 rabbit, a few slices of ham, salt and white pepper to taste, 2 blades of pounded mace, ¹/₂ teaspoonful of grated nutmeg, a few forcemeat balls, 3 hard-boiled eggs, ¹/₂ pint of gravy, puff crust.*

*Mode.—Cut up the rabbit (which should be young), remove the breastbone, and bone the legs. Put the rabbit, slices of ham, forcemeat balls, and hard eggs, by turns, in layers, and season each layer with pepper, salt, pounded mace, and grated nutmeg. Pour in about ¹/₂ pint of water, cover with crust, and bake in a well-heated oven for about 1¹/₂ hour. Should the crust acquire too much colour, place a piece of paper over it to prevent its burning. When done, pour in at the top, by means of the hole in the middle of the crust, a little good gravy, which may be made of the breast- and leg-bones of the rabbit and 2 or 3 shank-bones, flavoured with onion, herbs, and spices.*

*Game and poultry illustration, Beeton's Book of Household Management, 1907 edition*
© *Mary Evans Picture Library / Alamy*

Time.—1¹/₂ hour.
Average cost, from 1s. to 1s. 6d. each.
Sufficient for 5 or 6 persons.
Seasonable from September to February.

Note.—The liver of the rabbit may be boiled, minced, and mixed with the forcemeat
balls, when the flavour is liked.

# Home and Garden

A FEW SKETCHES at THE MANUFACTORY of

# Pears' TRANSPARENT Soap.

"The most refreshing & agreeable of Balms for the skin" — Mr Erasmus Wilson F.R.S

DISTILLING THE OILS

PREPARING THE RAW MATERIAL

LANADRON one of THE FACTORIES AT ISLEWORTH.

LONDON OFFICES Nº 38 Gt RUSSELL STREET

MIXING MACHINERY & REFINING APPARATUS.

BOX MAKING & FILLING ROOMS

PACKING FOR EXPORT

# Making Soap

## SOAP

Soap is a cleansing agent which, chemically speaking, is made of salts of fatty acids. Soaps were originally made from animal fats or vegetable oils mixed with ashes, an alkali which when combined with fat causes the chemical reaction which creates soap.

## SOAP HISTORY

*The word* soap *(sapo) occurs first in Pliny. He informs us that it was an invention of the Gauls, who employed it to render their hair shining; that it was a compound of wood-ashes and tallow, that there were two kinds of it, hard and soft (spissus et liquidus); and that the best kind was made of the ashes of the beech and the fat of goats. Among the Germans it was more employed by the men than the women.*

Thomas Thomson, *The History of Chemistry* (1830)

While Pliny attributed the invention of soap to the Gauls, it is known that soap solutions were used by the Sumerians in 3000 BC. They used a mixture of ash and water to clean raw wool. Ashes are alkaline, and by mixing them with some of the natural grease and oil on the wool, a soap solution was formed, which dissolved the rest of the dirt. Realizing that the grease made the ash solution more effective, the Sumerians made soap solutions by boiling animal fats and oils with plant ashes and water.

Exactly when soap was first made in Britain is not known, but from the Middle Ages onwards soap was made in Northern Europe by boiling animal fat with an extract of plant ashes (lye) and lime, while in

Mediterranean countries the animal fat was replaced by olive oil (as it was in oil lamps). As early as 1192, the English chronicler and monk Richard of Devizes referred to the foul smells which the activities of Bristol soap-makers produced, and other large towns such as Coventry and London also became soap-making centres. Most soap was used in the cloth-making industry, and for centuries soap in the domestic setting was a luxury item, as fat was needed for necessities such as candles and rushlights. Soap was also heavily taxed from an early stage, and the large pans used for boiling the mixture were fitted with padlocks in order to control the amount of soap that was made.

## IMPROVEMENTS

While the chemical process of soap making (boiling fats or oil with alkali to produce soap) did not fundamentally change, a number of improvements were made in the manufacture of soap between the 17th and early 19th centuries. Increasing imports of oils such as olive oil, coconut oil and linseed oil provided a wider choice of raw ingredients; a greater understanding of the chemistry involved in soap production led to a widening variety of fragrant soaps; and an alternative to lye, caustic soda, became cheaply available at the end of the 18th century, when it was produced from salt by the French chemist Nicholas Leblanc. In 1852, the tax on British soap was finally abolished, and a couple of decades later the first cheap mass-produced soap became available. Soap was found in most ordinary households for the first time, commonly used for bathing as well as washing clothes.

## ALTERNATIVES TO SOAP

Nature provides a number of alternatives to soap, exploited by individuals and used as soap substitutes for washing clothes. Soapwort (*Saponaria officinalis*) grows near streams. By boiling the leaves in water a lathery liquid is produced, once commonly used for washing woollen clothes. The roots of red campion (*Silene dioica*) have been used in the same way, and other so-called 'soap' plants have been exploited in various parts of the world at different times.

*Making Soap*

## HOME-MADE LYE

Because lye is an alkaline solution, it loosens grease and dirt in clothes
and linen, and long before the introduction of soap powder many homes
made their own lye. This was done by making water seep through wood
ash. The ash was placed on a cloth in a 'lye dropper' (a wooden bucket with
holes in the bottom). The water was poured onto the ashes, from where
it dripped through the holes into a tub placed below. Washing with lye
solution was known as 'bucking with lye', the procedure taking place in
a large bucket known as a buck. If the lye water was to be used to make
soap, it was concentrated by boiling it down until a fresh egg (in its shell)
would float on the mixture. It was then simmered with melted fat or oil
for a number of hours, before salt was added as the mixture cooled. The
salt hardened the soap, but settled to the bottom of the mixture and was
left behind when the soap was poured into moulds. Herbs could be added
to the moulds to improve the scent of the soap. Lye making was a difficult
procedure, and more unpleasant than it sounds when you consider that
it is caustic.

## SOAPY SUPERSTITION

Everyone knows that soap is slippery, and as such is liable to slip from
the hands. Nevertheless, in the 19th century some people considered this
extremely unlucky, and likely even to lead to death. In this report, a woman
called Kate Elshender goes to a quarry hole in the Scottish Highlands to
wash her clothes. She buys soap from a village shop, but it slips from her
hands. She buys more, but it slips from her hands again:

*She returned for a third half pound of soap. This time the old woman in the shop
was thoroughly frightened, and begged and prayed her not to go back again; but she
would go, in spite of everything that could be said to her. Shortly after the old woman,
being quite unable to rest in her shop, went away to the quarry, she found no one
there, and the clothes lying on the side of the hole. She gave the alarm, and, on search
being made, the said Kate Elshender was discovered, drowned, at the bottom of the
quarry hole.*

*Notes & Queries* (1876)

## MODERN SOAP MAKING

Fat and alkali are still needed to make soap. While in the past fat was obtained from slaughterhouses, soap-makers now use either fat that has been processed into fatty acids or vegetable fats such as olive oil, coconut oil and palm oil. The alkali used is commonly sodium hydroxide (for hard soap) and potassium hydroxide (for soft soap). Additives are used to give the soap colour and scent. Hobbyist soap-makers still make soap on a small scale at home, but generally use ingredients from specialist suppliers rather than saving up animal fat and mixing it with home-made lye. A number of books are available on soap making, and some courses are also taught (search online for a course in your area).

# Making Oil Lamps

## OIL LAMPS

Simple oil lamps have been used since prehistoric times to create light, relying on capillary action to deliver oil or animal fat along a wick to a flame. The earliest oil lamp was probably a stone with a natural depression filled with animal fat, and with a lighted twig laid in the fat as a form of wick. Archaeologists have also found early lamps carved from soft stones such as soapstone or hard stones such as quartz, while early pottery lamps were simply shallow earthenware dishes with a pointed lip on which the wick could rest. A variation on this 'floating wick' style of lamp came with the spout lamp, favoured by the ancient Greeks and Romans. Generally made of clay, a spout lamp has a central reservoir for the oil and a number of spouts, with a wick in each spout. For many centuries these primitive lamps, initially home-made and later crafted by potters and metalworkers, changed very little.

## OILS

Lamps could be fuelled with oils from animals, vegetables or minerals. In the Mediterranean olive oil was generally used, while in Britain only the wealthy could afford such imported oils and rather worse-smelling fish and animal oils would have been burned instead, producing a great deal of smoke. Whale oil became popular in Britain in the mid-18th century – it produced little smell and much less smoke – and was in such demand that the Greenland whale was nearly made extinct. As whales became scarcer and the price of whale oil rose ever higher, vegetable oils such as that extracted from rapeseed became widespread, and remained so until paraffin oil became available in the mid-19th century.

## LATER LAMPS

Some lamps, such as Scottish 'crusies', and the similar Betty lamps, popular with colonists in America, were made of iron, and were similar in design to some of the earliest earthenware lamps. They were often attached to a wall, and burned fish oil. When whale oil became scarce and expensive, lard was burned, and patents were brought out specifically for lard-burning lamps. Later lamps had a wheel to turn that extended the wick,

but the first truly significant development in making oil lamps came in the early 1780s, when a Swiss physicist and chemist called Aimé Argand invented the Argand burner, described in its English patent as 'a lamp so constructed to produce neither smoak [smoke] nor smell and to give considerably more light than any lamp hitherto known'. By using a cylindrical woven wick held between metal tubes, Argand increased the amount of air getting to the flame, thus

*Oil lamps, 1st century BC and 1st century AD © Science Museum / Science and Society*

allowing for full aeration. The burner was placed inside a glass chimney. His lamp produced more light – claimed to be equivalent to ten candles – than any others of the time. Further improvements were made to the Argand design over time, and the introduction of paraffin provided a stable fuel that burned well (and with minimum smell). Oil lamps were still in use in the early 20th century, the trimming of the wick and the cleaning of the chimney part of the daily routine of domestic life.

## RECREATING THE PAST

An ancient Mediterranean oil lamp (using olive oil rather than some of the more noisome northern European alternatives) can be recreated with a shallow, heatproof earthenware dish, a strand from the head of an old-fashioned cotton mop and, of course, some olive oil. Remember that care must be taken when dealing with hot oil and flames. Place some oil in the dish, add the strand from the cotton mop (your wick), wait until your wick has soaked up some oil, and light it. If your dish doesn't have a handy lip for keeping the burning end of the wick out of the oil, use some wire to create one.

# *Making Rushlights*

## RUSHLIGHTS

Rushlights are an ancient form of domestic lighting. Essentially a cheap form of candle, they were made from the partially peeled pith of a rush, dipped in melted animal fat. Once dry and ready for use, a rushlight was placed at an angle in a rushlight holder and lit.

## POOR MAN'S CANDLE

Rushlights are thought to have been in use in Britain since before the Romans arrived. They were initially used by rich and poor alike, although during the Middle Ages the very rich used candles too, while the poor were left with light from the fire and their rushlights alone. Rushlights could be made for free if you had access to animal fat and rushes, but they were in any case cheap to buy. They were seen as the poor man's candle, especially when, from 1709 to 1831, both tallow candles (made from animal fat) and wax candles (superior candles made from beeswax) were taxed, making them too expensive for the poorer and working classes. By the mid-18th century, rushlights were only found in the servants' quarters of the grander houses, but they remained in common use in poorer homes well into the 19th century, and were still being used in some rural areas in the early part of the 20th.

## ART OF MAKING A RUSHLIGHT

*At first a person would find it no easy matter to divest a rush of its peel or rind, so*

*as to leave one regular, narrow, even rib from top to bottom that may support the
pith: but this, like other feats, soon becomes familiar even to children; and we have
seen an old woman, stone-blind, performing this business with great dispatch, and
seldom failing to strip them with the nicest regularity. When these junci are thus far
prepared, they must lie out on the grass to be bleached, and take the dew for some
nights, and afterwards be dried in the sun.*

Gilbert White, The Natural History of Selborne (1789)

Two types of rush can be used for making rushlights: the common
rush (*Juncus conglomeratus*) and the soft rush (*Juncus effusus*). Rushes grow
throughout Britain, and a year's supply used to be gathered in the summer
while the rushes were still green. They were then soaked in water to
prevent shrinking and drying, before being peeled in such a way as to
leave a single strip of the outer skin behind. This was important, as this
strip provided support for the peeled rush.

Once stripped, the peeled rushes were bleached in the sun, before
being dipped in hot melted animal fat. Mutton fat made the best
rushlights, while bacon fat was regularly used but less satisfactory – all
rushlights smoke and smell of burning fat, but some do so more than
others, providing less light at the same time.

Rushlights could be made at no cost by anyone who collected their
own rushes and slaughtered their own animals (retaining some of the
fat for the purpose), and Gilbert White also notes that any 'careful wife'
could obtain her fat for nothing by collecting the 'scummings of a bacon
pot'. Once dipped in the fat, the rushlights were left for the fat to solidify,
before being stored until needed.

A variety of holders were used to take rushlights. The simplest was a
split stick, the rushlight being placed at an angle in the cleft and moved
forward each time it burned down to near the holder. More elaborate
holders were carved from wood or made from metal, with a pincer-like
holder to grip the rushlight, again at an angle, making it easy to move
the rushlight as it burned down. The more affluent often had a rushlight
holder which included a socket for a candle.

## MODERN RUSHLIGHT MAKING

If you want to try making your own rushlights, the following hints might
help. Once you find your rushes, cut them close to the ground, as only the

178

solid pith from the lower section will be usable. Place the cut ends of your rushes in a bucket of water until you are ready to peel them, which can be done (carefully) with a knife, or with a fingernail – with practice you will learn how to leave the single strip of outer skin behind. Next, to cure your peeled pith, place it somewhere warm and airy. The pith will curl as it dries, but can be kept straighter by placing the rushes in a bundle with some wooden dowelling, and gently tying them in several places along their length.

Melt your animal fat in a shallow pan, then draw the dried rushes through it until they are coated. When the fat has solidified and they are dry, they are ready for use. For a simple holder, split a small stick, or attach your rushlight to a stick with a paperclip. The length of time a rushlight will burn for depends on the fat used and the diameter of the pith, but as a very rough guide a rushlight 30 centimetres (12 inches) long will burn for perhaps 20 minutes. Be prepared for the smell of domestic lighting of the past.

# *Making Candles*

## THE CANDLE

A candle is a block or cylinder of wax or tallow surrounding a central wick, which is burned to give light. Candles were traditionally made with tallow (rendered animal fat) or beeswax, while later paraffin wax and stearin wax were the preferred ingredients. The craft of candle making is ancient, although candles did not appear in European homes until the Middle Ages, and even then were a commodity for the rich.

## CHANDLERS

*The Tallow-chandler is a distinct trade from the Wax-chandler: the first claims the pre-eminence, in furnishing an article of general utility; but the purity, convenience, and elegance of a wax-candle, are justly to be preferred to any other.*

*Little Jack of All Trades* (1823)

From the Middle Ages onwards, there were two types of chandler, or candle-maker: the tallow-chandler and the wax-chandler. The tallow-chandler used rendered animal fat, generally from cows and sheep, to make candles (although tallow-chandlers were sometimes soap-makers too, as this was another craft that involved the use of tallow). The candles were very smelly when they burned and also produced a good deal of smoke, but they were cheaper than the beeswax candles produced by the wax-chandler. The wax-chandler's candles (which produced far less smoke and smell) were used by the church and the very rich – the church's preference for superior candles borne out by every monastery's keeping its own bees. Tallow candles were made by a number of methods, but in Britain the most common and earlier type was the dipped candle: a rush wick was dipped into hot fat, drawn out again to cool and harden, then dipped again, the process being repeated until the candle had reached the required thickness. By draping the wicks over a wooden frame, several candles could be dipped at once, and a chandler's workshop would be filled with racks of drying candles at different stages of completion. Another method involved repeatedly pouring melted fat onto suspended wicks, with containers below which caught the excess fat so that it could be reused. Later, tallow candles were also made in moulds – a wick was placed in a mould and hot fat poured into it, the candle then being left to set. Beeswax candles were made by the same methods, although they can also be made by rolling a thin sheet of beeswax around a wick.

## DEVELOPMENTS IN CANDLE MAKING

In the 18th century, rush wicks were replaced by twisted cotton strands, although these had the disadvantage of needing constantly to be trimmed as the candle burned. Plaited and then slightly flattened cotton wicks soon became standard, as these curled over when they burned, and essentially trimmed themselves, causing less smoke. In the late 18th century, spermaceti was first used, a waxy matter from the head of a sperm whale. Like beeswax, this did not smell, and it produced a good bright light. In 1831, the British tax on candles was abolished more than a century after it had first been imposed, and candles became more affordable (up until this time, the poor had commonly lit their homes with rushlights, the 'poor man's candle'). At around the same time, two new candle-making ingredients were introduced – stearin wax, developed when stearic acid was extracted from animal fatty acids, and paraffin wax, distilled from petroleum or shale – and the mass production of moulded candles was introduced.

## SELLING BY THE CANDLE

'Selling by the candle' was once one of the normal ways in which an auction could be organized. At least two variations existed: in one, a pin was stuck into a candle a short distance from the top and the bidding stopped when the candle burned down to the pin and the pin fell out; in another, a short candle was lit and the winning bid was the last one placed before the candle burned down and went out. Samuel Pepys attended at least four candle auctions, which he mentions in his diary, and by the 17th century they were already a long-established practice, reputable enough to be employed by the Admiralty. At one such auction, which Pepys refers to as sales 'by an inch of candle', one bidder revealed to him an apparently foolproof way of securing the winning bid:

*After dinner by water to the office, and there we met and sold the Weymouth, Successe, and Fellowship hulkes, where pleasant to see how backward men are at first to bid; and yet when the candle is going out, how they bawl and dispute afterwards who bid the most first. And here I observed one man cunninger than the rest that was sure to bid the last man, and to carry it; and inquiring the reason, he told me that just as the flame goes out the smoke descends, which is a thing I never observed before, and by that he do know the instant when to bid last, which is very pretty.*

Samuel Pepys, diary entry, Wednesday 3 September 1662

The popularity of selling by the candle seems to have waned by the early 1700s, although the tradition is retained in some places. In Hubberholme, North Yorkshire, a candle auction is held on the first Monday of January. The local vicar is in charge, and the winning bidder gets the use of a 16-acre field, known locally as 'the Poor Pasture', for one year (under certain terms and conditions, of course).

## MODERN CHANDLERY

While most candles are now mass-produced, individual craftspeople still make candles in the traditional ways (although most avoid tallow). Candle making is also a popular pastime, with equipment such as plaited cotton wick, waxes, moulds and dyes readily available from craft suppliers.

# Chimney Sweeping

## SWEEPING CHIMNEYS

When wood or coal is burned in a fireplace, it causes a build-up of soot in the chimney above. Without regular cleaning the chimney becomes partially blocked, and the chances of a chimney fire are greatly increased. Chimney sweeping has a chequered past. It was once a job that was carried out by cottagers, using a bundle of holly and a rope, but in the Victorian era it was one of the least pleasant jobs to have, and many small children died sweeping chimneys.

## SWEEPING WITHOUT A SWEEP

An early method of sweeping a wide chimney over a wood fire, without employing a chimney-sweep, involved a rope, a bundle of holly twigs and two people (one of whom needed a head for heights). One person would take the rope and climb onto the roof of the house. They would then drop the rope down the chimney, and the person at the bottom would tie a bundle of holly twigs half way along the rope – the bundle would need to be big enough to scrape the sides of the chimney and to clean the soot away, but not so big that it got stuck. With the rope held tightly at both ends (one end on the roof, the other on the hearth) the holly was pulled up and down to clean the chimney, before eventually the person at the top let go, and the rope, holly bundle and a great deal of soot were pulled down into the fireplace.

## TERRIBLE TRADE

Chimney sweeping in the early 19th century has a deservedly bad reputation. Master sweeps sent small boys up the tall, narrow chimneys of the growing industrial towns, with a brush and a scraper for cleaning off soot. These boys were often orphans, or were sold into the trade by their desperately poor families. Many children died – some while they worked, through becoming stuck and suffocating or from falling, while others died later, as years of exposure to carcinogens in the soot led to testicular cancer. The plight of these 'climbing boys' was raised as early as the 1760s, but the initial legislation was not stringent enough to be truly helpful. In 1788 an Act decreed merely that they should attend church on a Sunday, and it was not until the mid-19th century that an effective ban on the use of children for chimney sweeping came into force. Their use was replaced by the familiar screw-together rods and brush, carried on their backs by soot-faced adult sweeps.

## A SEEMINGLY UNLUCKY PROFESSION
## APPARENTLY BRINGS LUCK

Chimney-sweeps have given rise to a number of superstitions. One belief is that to meet a chimney-sweep in the street is lucky, and that when you do meet one you must greet him courteously, perhaps even bowing. Sweeps are also said to be particularly lucky at weddings, perhaps guaranteeing fertility in the marriage, and in the second half of the 20th century it was maintained that sweeps could make more money from their paid attendance at weddings than from cleaning chimneys.

Folklorists have found no evidence of sweep-related superstitions before the Victorian period, although some claim links to ancient customs. One suggested reason for greeting a sweep for luck is found in a story relating to the monarchy: a King George (perhaps George II) is said to have been rescued by a sweep when his carriage horses bolted, and to have been in the habit of saluting any chimney-sweeps he saw from that time on. Exactly why a sweep should be an omen of fertility is not known.

## NOT SWEPT AWAY

While it was no longer such a dirty and dangerous craft (industrial vacuum cleaners made the job much cleaner), the number of chimney-sweeps declined dramatically with the switch from coal fires to other forms of domestic heating in the 1960s and 1970s. But chimney-sweeps are still needed, and not just for guest appearances at weddings. The National Association of Chimney Sweeps (www.nacs.org.uk) is a modern professional body for sweeps, and a National Vocational Qualification in chimney engineering and cleaning can be completed at their Chimney Training Centre, while the Guild of Master Sweeps (www.guild-of-master-sweeps.co.uk) oversees the City & Guilds qualification in sweeping.

# Making Besom Brooms

## BESOM BROOMS

A besom broom is made from a bundle of twigs – traditionally birch, or less commonly heather – attached to a long handle.

*Making besom brooms from hazel, Penmach, Caernarvonshire, 1940s*
© *Mary Evans Picture Library*

## BROOM SQUIRES AND BROOM HORSES

For making a birch besom, the birch brushwood was cut from coppiced birch trees during winter, made into bundles called faggots, and stored so the wood became seasoned. Seasoning was essential to avoid brittleness, which would have led to a broom that shed more than it swept up. Besom broom makers were often known as broom squires, and they worked astride a broom horse. Also known as a besomer's horse, this was a wooden frame with a specially designed clamp at one end for holding broom handles steady so they could be worked and smoothed.

Once the birch twigs were ready, the broom squire would arrange a bundle of them into a head, rolling them backwards and forwards on his leather apron. The twigs were around 90 centimetres (3 feet) long, and two sizes of head were made: the smaller with a diameter of 25 centimetres (10 inches) and the larger with a diameter of 30 centimetres (12 inches). Once they were in a satisfactory bundle, the twigs were tied, traditionally with small rods of willow or hazel, and more recently with wire. Then the butt end of the head was trimmed with a billhook or axe around 2.5 centimetres (1 inch) above the top bond.

Straight poles of either hazel, birch or lime were popularly used as besom handles, although other woods could be used. They were also cut from coppiced trees, poles of around 1 metre (3 feet 4 inches) being selected for the purpose. With the pole held in the clamp of the broom horse, the broom-maker would remove the bark and roughly shape the handle with a 'draw knife' – a blade with a handle on each end, which was operated with two hands. It was then finished and smoothed, and an axe was used to sharpen one end to a point. The two parts of the besom were then ready to be put together. The sharpened end of the handle was rammed into the butt end of the head. An auger or hand drill was then used to bore a hole through the head and handle so that a wooden peg could be driven in to fasten the two together.

## BROOM LORE

Brooms have had various superstitions attached to them over the years. In Yorkshire it used to be said that 'if a girl strides over a besom-handle she will be a mother before she is a wife'. This belief caused some anxiety among mothers no doubt, and led boys to leave brooms on doorsteps to see if any unmarried women would step over them without thinking. In the 19th and 20th centuries there seems to have been a widespread belief that it was unlucky to buy a broom in the month of May, or to use one that had been bought in that month. In Scotland, there are some references to it being lucky to throw a besom after someone (or something, such as a new fishing net), and there was also a popular belief that a besom laid across a doorway would keep a witch away. This last superstition is perhaps linked to the now common association between witches (and more recently wizards) and the besom. While folk tradition had witches flying in or on all manner of items, including pitchforks and pig-troughs, in modern fiction and art the witch is inevitably seated on a besom.

## TODAY'S BROOM SQUIRES

Besom brooms are still made in the traditional way today, although not in the same numbers as they were in the past. If you would like to make your own besom, but do not have access to birch twigs, you might try making one with a head of heather. Cut bushy stems of heather in February or March, ensuring that the stems are supple, not brittle, or they will snap when the broom is used. They should be stored somewhere dry and airy, just as cut birch twigs should be, until you are ready to make your broom.

# Patchwork and Quilting

## PATCHWORK AND QUILTING

Patchwork and quilting are distinct crafts, although the two skills are so often used in combination that their separate nature can be forgotten. Patchwork is specifically the sewing together of small patches of different fabrics to create a multicoloured design. Quilting is the sandwiching of a piece of wadding between two pieces of fabric, the three layers then being held together with often decorative stitching. Patchwork, while often quilted, is not necessarily so, and can also be 'flat'.

## PATCHWORK

Patchwork was initially associated with thrift as it involved reusing fabric, the patches being cut from worn-out garments and bed linen. Few examples of early English patchwork are still in existence, possibly for the very reason that the patches were nearly worn through by the time they were sewn into their new form, and what's more these were practical, not necessarily decorative, pieces. One of the earliest examples of English patchwork to survive is thought to date from 1708 (and is on display at Levens Hall in Cumbria), but it is a sophisticated piece and by no means the first patchwork item to have been sewn, combining as it does practical function with artistry.

To create the heirloom pieces we associate with patchwork, identical patches were cut using templates. These could be diamond-, hexagonal- or square-shaped pieces of wood or card, although – for those who could afford them – templates were also made from more expensive materials, including pewter and brass. The template was used to create a paper pattern for every piece of the patchwork, the paper shapes being tacked to the material being used before the patches were cut out. The edges of the patches were then sewn together in tile-like patterns, the paper backing often left in place on the inside of the quilt.

Patchwork thrived as those from the working classes sewed it for themselves and for sale to the higher classes. In time the middle classes adopted patchwork as a craft – in 1811 Jane Austen, along with her mother and her sister, made a quilt with diamond-shaped patches – and it became a hobby practised by those who had no need to reuse old fabric.

While British patchwork had become increasingly decorative, it was in America, with the early colonists, that patchwork truly developed into an art form. It also became a social occasion: women sewed patchwork during the winter, then met in groups in the spring for 'quilting bees', in which they quilted it. Quilts were made for women who were to be married, and friendship quilts were made to be given on special occasions, often with different women providing different blocks of the quilt, which were then sewn together at a bee. It is said many traditional North American quilts contain a deliberate mistake in the sewing, to show that only God is perfect, but these were nevertheless beautifully crafted pieces of work.

*Quilt by Harriet Bradbury, New Hampshire, USA, c.1876*
© *Visual Arts Library (London) / Alamy*

## QUILTING AND QUILTED PATCHWORK

The practical application of quilting is to provide additional warmth, particularly to bedcovers, and it is thought that clothes and bed linen have been quilted since at least the 14th century. The best quilting is done on quilting frames – made from strips of wood, these hold the layers of fabric (with wadding in the centre) taut and together, making the work easier and the sewn pattern more prominent when the quilt is released from the frame. Quilted bedcovers were either made of one plain fabric with a sewn pattern, or from different fabrics with a pattern added using appliqué (sewing pieces of fabric onto the top layer of the quilt to form patterns), or by using patchwork as the top layer of fabric. In American quilting bees, groups of women met and worked around a quilting frame to complete a single piece.

## HEYDAY OF NEEDLEWORK

In both Britain and America, the 'golden age' of patchwork and quilting came between the late 18th and late 19th centuries. After this, industrialization began to take its toll, and by the mid-20th century ready-made clothes and bed linen were the norm. However, a revival did begin in the late 20th century, when, in America in particular, quilts and patchwork began to be recognized as important artefacts of women's history. Early quilts have been collected as museum pieces, and quilting and patchwork again taken up as hobbies, although not on the same scale as they were practised previously. Groups such as the Quilters' Guild of the British Isles (www.quiltersguild.org.uk) continue to promote the tradition, both as art and craft, and many books are available – both manuals describing the techniques employed and accounts of the history of patchwork and quilting, particularly in North America.

# Making Rag Rugs

## RAG RUGS

Rag rugs are made from small strips of fabric (rags), pushed or pulled through a backing material such as hessian. The exact history of rag-rug making is not known, although it has been suggested that Viking settlers brought the craft to Britain. Traditionally made from old clothes and other recycled material, rag rugs had their heyday in the 19th century, when they were made by poorer families, often providing the only floor covering in the house. Few early rag rugs exist, as these were utilitarian pieces of work, never considered as heirlooms. New rugs were often made in the winter, and old ones were moved around the house, the best rug being kept in front of the fire and older ones placed in less prominent positions, until the oldest and most worn rug was thrown out, often onto the compost heap. By the mid-1900s, the association of rag rugs with poverty meant that they dropped out of favour – people did not want to be considered so poor that could only have rag rugs on their floors. However, a revival of interest in traditional crafts at the end of the 20th century included rag-rug making, and they are now made by hobbyists and craftspeople.

## PROGGY, PRODDY, HOOKY, PEGGY, STOBBY AND BODGY RUGS

Rag rugs, or rag mats, have been known by many different names in various parts of Britain, including those given above. No matter what they were called though, the materials used to make them were, in the past, free: the rags were old clothes and scraps of material cut into strips; the backing was a hessian sack, obtained at no cost from a farmer or merchant who had no further use for it; and the key tool for rag-rug making, a prodder, was often home-made, perhaps whittled from a peg. The fabric was prepared by cutting it into strips around 1.25 centimetres (½ inch) wide and 5–7.5 centimetres (2–3 inches) long, depending on the length of pile required or the amount of material available. The backing was sometimes attached to a wooden frame to tauten it and make working easier.

The prodder was used to create two holes next to each other in the hessian by separating the weave. One corner of a rag strip was held over one hole, and the prodder was used to push the fabric through this and then through the second hole, thus creating the pile, with the two ends of the fabric sticking up from the backing. As the weave of the sacking became full of rags, it tightened, so the fabric strips were held in place with no need for knotting (although some rag-ruggers do now knot the rags). By selecting which fabrics to use for each part of the rug, any pattern could be created, either by eye or by marking the design on the hessian before the rags were added, although by the late 18th century, those who could afford it could buy hessian with a pattern already marked on it. They could also buy a specially designed tool to replace the simple prodder. This was pushed into the backing, making the two holes, and held in place there. Spring-loaded jaws could then be opened, which grabbed the fabric, and by pulling the tool out of the backing, then opening the jaws, the fabric was woven through it.

## FROM RAGS TO RUGS

Rag rugs are essentially made in the same way today as they have always been, although hessian must generally be bought, as jute sacks have become somewhat rarer than they once were. Rag-rug tools are available from craft suppliers, although you might like to whittle your own prodder for authenticity. Beamish Museum (www.beamish.org.uk) in County Durham has a collection of some 250 rag rugs if you need some inspiration, and a number of books on rag rugging are available, as well as workshops and courses (including some accredited by City & Guilds). Other rag-rug techniques are also taught, including the plaited, rather than prodded, version: strips of fabric are sewn together into long lengths, the long lengths plaited together in threes, and the plaits then sewn together in a coil, from the centre outwards.

*Spinning*

## SPINNING

Spinning is the process of creating yarn or thread by twisting fibres of wool, cotton or hair together in order to make them usable for sewing, knitting and weaving. It is an ancient craft – the basic method of spinning by hand involves the use of a 'drop spindle', a shaft with a round weight at the bottom, and spindle weights have been discovered that date back to Neolithic times. A brief overview of the traditional spinning of wool is given here.

## SORTING AND CARDING

Sheep were shorn in the early summer, providing the fleeces, or raw wool, needed by the spinner. Wool quality varies not only between breeds of sheep, but also within a single fleece (the best quality fleece being that from the shoulders), so fleece was sorted before spinning. Very dirty fleeces were washed, but as the natural oils in wool actually aid the spinning process, washing was usually left until afterwards.

After sorting, the next task was to prepare the wool for spinning by gently pulling the fibres apart by hand, separating them and removing any foreign matter. For fine thread, the fleece was then carded between a pair of boards with handles ('cards'). The inside of the cards was traditionally covered with teasel heads, but these were later replaced by fine wire hooks. A small amount of wool was placed on one of the cards, and the other card was drawn across it. This was repeated a number of times, with the wool being periodically transferred between the cards. Eventually, with the wool evenly spread across one of the cards, the back of the other card was used to roll the wool fibres off, and into a light, fluffy roll known as a rolag.

## SPINDLES AND DISTAFFS

A spindle consists of a central wooden shaft, often with a notch near the top, and a circular weight, or 'whorl', near the bottom. The top of the shaft

was attached to a rolag held in the hand, the whorl was turned with the other hand, and as the weight gave the spindle momentum, it would turn and drop towards the floor, twisting the wool fibres into a length of yarn. The yarn was then wound around the central shaft, and the process repeated. This simple but skilled form of spinning was sometimes aided by the use of a distaff. This was a wooden stick on which the raw wool fibres (or flax fibres, if spinning thread for linen) could be held. The distaff was usually held under the left arm, while the right hand fed fibres from it to the spindle. That spinning was considered women's work is shown in the use of 'the distaff side', and earlier 'the spindle side', to refer to the female line of a family.

*Carding and spinning
wool, Scotland, 1909*
© *Hulton Getty*

## SPINNING-WHEELS

The spinning-wheel superseded the drop spindle in Europe in the 15th century. In a spinning-wheel, the spindle is held horizontally, and turned not by the fingers but by a wheel-driven belt. Most spinning-wheels are operated by a crank connected to a foot treadle, leaving the hands free to feed raw wool onto the spindle.

# MECHANIZATION: JENNIES, FRAMES AND MULES

Spinning was mechanized during the late 18th century. James Hargreaves invented the 'spinning jenny' in around 1764; Richard Arkwright patented his 'spinning frame' in 1770; and in 1779 Samuel Crompton produced his 'spinning mule', so called because it was a cross between Hargreaves's jenny and Arkwright's frame. These were the first machines that allowed spinning on more than one spindle at a time, and took spinning from the cottage to the factory or mill.

## MAKING YOUR OWN WOOLLEN YARN

If you live in a sheep-farming area, it is possible to collect enough wool from fences and hedges to try spinning your own yarn. When you have collected a good amount, use your fingers to tease the fibres apart (or if you know someone with cards, borrow these for the job). An improvised drop spindle can be made by inserting a skewer through a small potato. To make

*Hargreaves's spinning jenny*
© *Classic Image / Alamy*

something a little more elegant, carve a small round section of wood, make a hole in the centre and push a piece of wooden dowelling through this so that it sticks out around 2.5 centimetres (1 inch) at the bottom. Then cut a small upward-facing notch near the top of the dowelling.

To get started you'll need a bit of ready-made yarn. Tie this just above the wooden disc (or potato), then wind it under it, round the bottom of the dowel, and back up to the notch. Make a loop (or half-hitch knot) here to keep the yarn in place. Next, take a handful of your teased wool, fold the end of it over the end of the starter yarn at the notch and, pinching the join together with one hand, twist the spindle in a clockwise direction with your free hand. The starter yarn and the wool should twist together. Holding the spindle against you to prevent it from untwisting, tease out some more of the wool, move your hand to the untwisted part, and turn the spindle again. Keep working in this way until you have created a length of yarn. Unhook it from the notch at the top of the spindle, and wind it round the dowelling or central part of your spindle. Reattach your yarn at the notch, as you did with the starter yarn, and keep working, swapping to a new handful of wool as needed. To begin with, your yarn will inevitably be a bit lumpy, and you might find that it breaks rather often, but this will improve with practice.

## MORE YARN

Many books are available which include instructions on spinning, and courses are also available, including residential workshops (a search online should find one near you).

# WEAVING

Weaving is essentially the criss-crossing together of yarns in at least two directions to produce a textile. Weaving is an ancient craft, and the oldest known woven cloth dates from around 7000 BC. It is thought early weaving may have been carried out with strands of yarn stretched between pegs driven into the ground, or on a simple frame on which a set of strands of yarn, called 'weft', could be passed over and under a set of lengthwise threads called 'warp'. Over time, the simple frames developed into hand-looms of both vertical and horizontal types, with hand- or treadle-operated devices which lifted alternate warp strands, creating an opening through which the weft strand could be passed. From the Middle Ages onwards, weaving was a major source of employment in Britain, and the craft was carried out by individual cottagers and urban guild members. Weaving did not become mechanized until the 1820s and 1830s (somewhat later than spinning), and in Britain hand-looms were in common use until the Victorian period.

## HAND-LOOMS

While many different styles and designs of hand-looms were developed, most of them work to the same basic principles. The warp is held taut between two beams so that the weft can be interwoven between them to create the woven textile. The warp threads are separated alternately by lifting 'heddles', either by hand or by means of a foot treadle. A heddle is a rod placed across the warp, to which every other warp thread is attached.

By lifting a heddle, half the warp threads are lifted, creating an opening called a 'shed', through which the weft thread (attached to a shuttle) can be passed without the need to weave in and out of the individual strands. This heddle can then be dropped and the other heddle lifted, creating another opening, the 'countershed', through which the weft can be returned. A comb-like implement is then used to close any gaps in the weave. Rollers at each end of the loom allow pieces larger than the loom frame itself to be woven, and patterns are created by using threads of different colours.

## TABLET WEAVING AND INKLE WEAVING

*Inkle weaving at a medieval fair*
© *Ian Townsley / Alamy*

Tablet weaving and inkle weaving are both traditional, and ancient, methods of producing decorative bands. Unlike the weaving discussed above, which produces a plain weave (where both the warp and weft threads are visible in the finished textile), tablet weaving and inkle weaving produce what is known as a bound weave, and specifically a warp-faced bound weave, where only the warp threads are visible.

Tablet weaving uses small square tablets (or cards) with a hole in each corner to hold the warp threads. In the past these were made from wood, ivory or bone, but many modern tablet-weavers cut them from cardboard, trim down playing-cards, or simply use beer-mats. Separate lengths of yarn are threaded through each of the holes in each of the tablets. The tablets are then placed together side by side, and one set of yarn ends is tied to a fixed object, while the other is tucked into the weaver's belt. Leaning back slightly to keep the warp threads taut, the weaver passes a weft thread through the space (again known as the shed) between the top and bottom warp threads, then turns all of the tablets through a quarter-turn. The shed is found again, the weft thread passed back through, and the tablets turned through another quarter-turn. The weaving is kept tight, and not gappy, by 'beating' or pushing the shed. The pattern created varies depending on the way in which the warp threads are threaded, and by changing the direction of the quarter-turn.

*Weaving*

Inkle weaving is done on a small, specialized inkle loom – the narrow bands it produces are known as inkles:

*'As thick as Inkle-Weavers' is a very familiar expression, used by persons who mean to imply that 'close fellowship' exists between particular parties to whom they might refer. Now inkle is an old provincial name for tape, which was, nearly a century ago, manufactured to a great extent at Newbury, in Berks. The tape-looms, on which the threads were prepared, were so narrow, and so closely connected in position, that the weavers sat in close proximity to each other. Hence the expression, 'as thick as inkle-weavers.'*

John Timbs, *Things Not Generally Known, Familiarly Explained* (1859)

## WEAVING ON A SIMPLE FRAME

A very simple hand-loom is easy to make. It is possible to start small, on a frame that can be used to make woven squares (these can be sewn together like patchwork to produce a larger piece) before working up to bigger looms. Join four pieces of wood, each 13 centimetres (5 inches) long, in a square frame shape, and tap in small-headed nails along its sides, leaving them proud so that you can wrap the yarn around them. When that's done, string the warp threads by winding your yarn lengthwise, up and down between the nails from left to right. Next, use a large needle to weave the 'weft' through the warp, going over one warp thread, under the next, and so on. When you reach the end of the warp threads, work in the opposite direction, this time going over the warp threads you went under before, and under those you went over. On a small frame like this, you can use your fingers to push the weft threads down tight against the previous worked row to keep your weaving neat.

## TANGLED WEB

If you are drawn into the tangled web of hand-weaving, there are many books and courses available to help you learn more. You can start weaving on any scale, and soon create both practical and decorative textiles, but it is also a skill, and many say that to progress to a hand-loom it is best to learn in the presence of an expert. The London Guild of Weavers, Spinners and Dyers (www.londonguildofweavers.org.uk) and the Association of Guilds of Weavers, Spinners and Dyers (www.wsd.org.uk) are two of the organizations that work to preserve and promote the craft.

## Brewer's Clog
Pattern No. 45

Made from Extra Strong Leather.
Strong Beech Soles. Ironed and Tipped.
Double Watertight Tongue.
Copper Bound Toes.

**All Boot Sizes**     per pair

## Blucher Clog With Flap
Pattern No. 46

Used largely by Mineral Water Manufacturers
and Laundries. Well made to resist water.
Ironed and Tipped. Toe Plates.

**Boot Sizes 2 to 5**     per pair
    „    6 to 10     per pair
**Derby Tongue 5d. per pair extra**
**Can be had in Rubber. Patt. No. 46a**
2 to 5     per pair.     6 to 10     per pair

## One Bar Clog
Pattern No. 47

A General Purpose Clog for Light Work.
Ironed and Tipped.     Toe Plate if desired.

**Boot Sizes 2 to 6**     per pair

## Felt Lined Garden Clog
Pattern No. 40

Made from Good pliable Leather and Lined
with Finest Quality Felt.
A boon for the gardener.

| Boot Sizes 2 to 5 | per pair | Extra for Irons |
|---|---|---|
| „   6 to 10 | „ | 4d. pair. |

## Wellington Clog
Pattern No. 52

Strong Waterproof
Leather Uppers.
Beech Soles.
Iron and Tipped.
Copper Toe Plate

12" high     per pair
14" high     per pair

**All Boot Sizes.**

## Carriage Wash Clog
Pattern No. 53

Fits Over Boot.
Used Mainly By
Garages.
Strongly Made.
Soles Ironed
and Tipped.

**Extra Stout Leather**
20" high     per pair
22" „     per pair
**Stout Leather**
20" high     per pair
22" „     per pair

## Moulder's Clog
Pattern No. 48

Well-made with Beech Soles. Ironed and
Tipped. Toe Plate. Open Front. Used largely
in Iron and Steel Works.

**Boot Sizes**     per pair

**Can be had with Watertight Tongue, which renders
it suitable for any Trade 6d. pair extra.**

## Moulder's Spa
Pattern No. 49

Height 11"
**Price per pair**
LEATHER
RUBBER
Carriage paid on 6 pairs

Well-made from Stout Waxed Le
Can be had in Rubber (Re-inforce
Mineral Water Manufacturers, e
Can be had any height. Prices on app

# *Making Clogs*

## CLOGS

Unlike Dutch clogs, which are made entirely of wood, traditional British clogs consist of a carved wooden sole and a leather upper. The origins of clog making are somewhat obscure, but clogs have been worn since the early Middle Ages. They are most commonly associated with the northern industrial towns of Lancashire and Yorkshire, and particularly with textile mill workers.

## CLOG MAKING

*At other times you will find the woodmen cutting down the alder trees in the swamps, for the chair-makers and clog-makers. All up in Lancashire and a great part of Yorkshire the common people wear huge thick wooden clogs, which are almost always made of alder-wood. Patten-makers and ladies' clog-makers are great consumers of alder-wood. In the manufacturing districts a vast quantity is used in spoles, bobbins, and various other things in the spinning mills. So the woodmen cut it and square it ... and cut out the clog-wood into little logs of the requisite size. Rich and red the chips and the hewn parts of this wood look; and the whole process makes an agreeable variety in wood scenery.*

William Howitt, *The Boy's Country-Book* (1863)

Alder was one of the most popular woods for making clogs, although sycamore, willow, beech and birch were also used. The first task in clog making was cutting blocks of wood to be made into soles. Sole-block cutting was either carried out by clog-makers (or 'cloggers') themselves or, particularly when clogs were in greatest demand, was a separate trade. The work was done in the woods during spring and early summer. Trees were felled and the wood trimmed into blocks of four different sizes: men's; women's; middles or boys'; and children's. Once this had been done, a stock knife – a long, slightly curved blade, attached at one end to a wooden bench – was used to roughly shape the blocks into soles. The wooden block was held in one hand, and downward cutting strokes were made into it by the knife held in the other hand. The blocks were then stacked in heaps according to size, with gaps left to allow air to circulate freely. Once seasoned, they were ready to be made into clogs.

A clog-maker did the final shaping of the wooden sole with three further knives. The first was similar to a stock knife, but smaller, and was used to shape the outline and underside of the sole. The next was a hollower, which was used to shape the top of the sole, where the foot sits. The third was the grip or gripper. This had a narrow V-shaped blade, which was used to cut a groove around the top edge of the sole, into which the leather upper would fit. Once the sole had been smoothed and finished, clog 'irons' were nailed to the base. These were essentially horseshoes for clogs, and were originally hand-forged by the local blacksmith. The soles completed, the upper was then made, generally from either one or two pieces of leather, although sometimes three were used. The leather was marked using a paper pattern, and the pieces were cut with a razor-sharp knife, a process known as 'clicking'. To increase the comfort of the final shoe, the inside of the leather that would form the heel and tongue was 'skived' – that is, scraped with a knife to make it thinner. The pieces were then stitched on a curved block, before being shaped on a wooden last. After shaping, the upper was removed from the last, and the edge of the leather inserted into the groove cut in the sole. The upper was then tacked into place, before being finally nailed with short flat-headed nails.

*On-the-spot clog making*
© The Scotsman Publications Ltd Licensor www.scran.ac.uk

A narrow strip of leather was placed over the junction of upper and sole, and tacked into place. Fancier clogs had a brass toe-plate fitted as a final touch.

## CLOGS TODAY

Clogs were once the working footwear of choice. They were said to be warm in winter and cool in summer, and if the irons were replaced from time to time, the soles would last for many years. But clogs declined in popularity from the 1940s onwards, when fashions changed and many saw clog wearing as a sign of poverty. However, clog making as a craft has never entirely disappeared, and a revival in clog dancing in the latter part of the 20th century has led to a continued demand for clogs. Most soles are now machined rather than made by hand, but traditional clog-making methods – a combination of skilled carpentry and leatherwork – are still favoured by a few craftspeople.

# Kitchen Gardening

## GROW YOUR OWN

In its widest sense, kitchen gardening can describe anything from the window box or patio pot full of culinary herbs to the vast, formal potagers of the châteaux and country houses of France. Distinct from the commercial enterprise of market gardens, kitchen gardens are a means of providing food for the household – however grand that may be. They reached their peak with the walled gardens of the Victorian era, where a year-round supply of fruit and vegetables was grown, including many exotic varieties, rivalling the range of choice now only achieved by supermarkets through the use of global sourcing and transportation.

## A GROWTH INDUSTRY

The grand kitchen gardens of the Victorian era had their roots in the kitchen gardens of the Renaissance, which, in turn, grew out of the medieval monastic tradition. The abbey gardens of the Middle Ages served a number of purposes – medicinal, decorative, spiritual and, above all, culinary. This style of gardening lives on in possibly the most famous example of a French formal potager (kitchen garden) at Villandry on the Loire. However, on a less grand scale, growing your own food – in the cottage garden, strip field, allotment or elsewhere – was, until the modern era, an essential part of survival. Even in more recent times, temporary revivals of 'growing your own' have helped to sustain populations in the industrialized world during times of crisis.

The archetypal image of the small-scale kitchen garden is that of the English cottage garden, in which vegetables, herbs, ornamental plants and even livestock (such as chickens) jostle for space. This romantic image has driven many attempts at a revival of kitchen gardening and self-sufficiency over recent decades. However, in reality, such gardening has always been the privilege of the few rather than the true experience of the many. The Industrial Revolution took the majority of people directly from a subsistence-farming style of vegetable growing to an urban life with no growing space or, at best, only a tiny area in which to produce a few bits and pieces to supplement their diet. Later on, with the provision of better housing and the creation of allotments in many communities, it became possible again for those in the working class to grow their own vegetables. However, during the 20th century the rise in the value of urban land and the declining interest in vegetable gardening led many councils to sell off their allotments. At the same time, there has been a tendency for gardens to become decorative extensions of the house, or areas for parking cars – a trend that has recently started to be reversed with a growing awareness of the value of eating fresh fruit and vegetables and, more particularly, an interest in organic means of production.

*Kitchen garden,*
*Villandry, France*
© *Bildarchiv Monheim*
*GmbH / Alamy*

Meanwhile, in the upper echelons of society, as the masses moved towards the industrial centres, those who made enough money were able to employ staff to work their gardens. Vast areas were enclosed within walls to grow food to feed the family, staff and guests at the big house. The original purpose of the walls is a matter of debate, although they are often thought of as a means of providing a controlled climate, which they may well have done in very small settings. However, most country house walled gardens were huge (Queen Victoria's walled garden at Windsor covered an area of 32 acres), rendering the windbreak effect of the walls negligible. It is equally possible that the purpose of the walls was security, protecting the food crop from theft.

At the top of the staff pyramid was the head gardener, who had overall responsibility for supplying the house with produce. It would take many years, working up through the ranks from garden boy, to gain the knowledge necessary to be able to provide (and store) fresh fruit and vegetables, including an ever-widening range of exotic varieties, all year round. In a world of highly toxic pesticides and no health and safety regulations, even surviving long enough to reach such a lofty position was no mean feat.

In addition to manpower and know-how, the head gardener had a (sometimes bizarre) range of tools, structures and equipment available to him. The tools used were often custom-made, each with its own specific purpose, and most have now fallen out of use. Larger gardens would have had their own tool sheds, in which the equipment could be stored, maintained and repaired.

## PUTTING IT ALL TO BED

The layout of walled kitchen gardens usually involved geometric arrangements of large square or rectangular beds, with the vegetables arranged in rows. Between the beds would be central walkways.

*Whatever shape be adopted, borders should always be introduced on each side of the main walks. Nothing tends more to relieve the heavy appearance of large masses of vegetables than such borders. They are separated from the main vegetable compartments by small walks, from 18 inches to two feet wide. These walks can be edged with pebbles, and have a sprinkling of gravel, or simply cut off as alleys, and left solid earth. If formed of some hard substance, all the wheeling can be performed on them instead of on the main walks.*

Samuel Orchart Beeton, *All About Gardening* (1871)

In addition to this, arrangements of fences, sticks, hurdles and banks would be used to train climbers, provide windbreaks and create microclimates for specific plants. By positioning sloping beds and banks so that they faced south, the heat of the sun could be used to maximum advantage. Likewise, the shade provided would protect other crops from full sun, preventing them from wilting or 'bolting' (going to seed). This all helped to extend the season over which they could be harvested.

Soil preparation involved backbreaking manual labour – digging, turning, raking, weeding and the regular addition of huge amounts of organic matter in the form of home-made composts and animal manure.

## SUNTRAPS, HOTBEDS AND GLASSHOUSES

For whatever reason the walls were originally built, they became one of the most important tools available to the Victorian kitchen gardener. The walls were often three metres (ten feet) or more in height, and their construction was an art in itself. Red brick was used, on the inner face at least, because of its heat-retaining properties, and south- and west-facing walls were often built taller to take full advantage of the available sun. A south-facing wall could be used for growing peaches, nectarines, plums and tomatoes, while the cooler north-facing walls were reserved for cool-loving blackberries, gooseberries and currants. The west-facing wall might be used for pears and figs.

The walls could also be used to provide support for structures such as sheds. More importantly, following the abolition of the taxes on glass and windows and the invention of plate glass in the 1840s, there was a boom in the construction of glasshouses, which were often built in the form of a lean-to against the south-facing wall. This vastly increased the possibilities for growing exotic varieties and, combined with the installation of coal boilers and central heating systems, extended the growing season right through the winter. The wealthy Victorian landowner could now show off home-grown grapes, citrus fruits and melons among other things, and put fresh fruit on the table even in the middle of winter.

The height of such showing off was, perhaps, the pineapple pit. This was a type of hotbed – a bed under glass, kept at a high temperature using the heat produced by rotting horse manure. The construction used a double-skinned wall, with the manure placed in the space in between. Heat was allowed to circulate through the growing space via carefully positioned holes. Several tonnes of manure might be used, and it all had to be changed every few weeks to maintain the necessary temperature.

Even after the crops had been harvested, the job of the gardeners was not complete. The larger gardens would have had several dry rooms (often on the second floor) for the storage of harvested fruit. By controlling the light, temperature and humidity, the period of storage could be extended, or ripening could be timed for a particular moment to meet with the requirements of the family of the house.

## NEW GROWTH

In the early 20th century, changes in economic and social conditions brought about a decline in kitchen gardens, and their number dwindled rapidly after World War I. A lack of manpower, a reduction in wealth and the easier availability of transported goods were all contributing factors. Many walled gardens have been lost, although recent efforts at restoration on the part of the National Trust and other bodies have led to interesting rediscoveries of some craft skills that might otherwise have been lost for ever.

There are a number of organizations dedicated to the restoration and preservation of walled kitchen gardens, and some rely on the help of enthusiastic volunteers. The National Trust (www.nationaltrust.org.uk), the Garden History Society (www.gardenhistorysociety.org) and English Heritage (www.english-heritage.org.uk) are all possible starting points for those who would like to dig deeper.

For those who want to have a go on a smaller scale at home, the Royal Horticultural Society (www.rhs.org.uk) and Garden Organic (www.gardenorganic.org.uk) can offer advice on growing your own fruit and vegetables.

# Using
## Herbal Remedies

## HERBAL REMEDIES

We can only assume that wild plants and herbs have always been collected and used medicinally. A number of Anglo-Saxon manuscripts describe the medicinal use of herbs, and in medieval times herb gardens were a feature of monasteries and country houses. Some herb lore was collected in books such as *The Herball* (1597) by John Gerrard and *The Physical Directory* (1649) and *The English Physitian* (1652) by Nicholas Culpeper, but much traditional knowledge of herbal remedies has been lost, as it existed in oral tradition alone, in recipes passed on between family members. However, interest in herbal remedies has never disappeared. Modern medical herbalists continue an ancient tradition, although what was once a rural craft, known by many, is now a specialist profession. Herbal medicine has its own professional body in the UK, the National Institute of Medical Herbalists, and to be a qualified practitioner a herbalist must complete an approved degree in herbal medicine, or phytotherapy.

*Dandelions and nettles*
© *Peter Titmuss / Alamy*

## 'AN EASY AND NATURAL METHOD OF CURING MOST DISEASES'

John Wesley, best known as the founder of Methodism, published widely on a number of subjects, and his *Primitive Physic, or an Easy and Natural Method of Curing Most Diseases* (1747) was reprinted throughout the 19th century. A few of his remedies are included here, for interest rather than as recommendations.

## Coughs

In an edition of his book published in 1780, Wesley included remedies for eight different types of cough.

### 56. A COUGH

*Every cough is a dry cough at first. As long as it continues so, it may be cured by chewing immediately after you cough, the quantity of a pepper corn of Peruvian bark. Swallow your spittle as long as it is bitter, and spit out the wood. If you cough again, do this again. It very seldom fails to cure any dry cough. I earnestly desire every one, who has any regard for his health, to try this within twenty-four hours after he perceives a cough.*

*Or, drink a pint of cold water lying down in bed.—Tried.*

*Or, make a hole through a lemon and fill it with honey. Roast it and catch the juice. Take a tea-spoonful of this frequently.—Tried.*

## 'A venomous sting'

### 213. A VENOMOUS STING

*Apply the juice of honey-suckle leaves.*

*Or, a poultice of bruised plantain and honey.*

*Or, take inwardly, one drachm of black currant leaves powdered. It is an excellent counter-poison.*

## Baldness

As there is still no known cure for baldness, it seems unlikely that any of Wesley's three suggestions work, although his note in the text suggests that he tried at least one of them.

### 11. To cure BALDNESS

*Rub the part morning and evening, with onions, till it is red, and rub it afterwards with honey.*

*Or, wash it with a decoction of boxwood.—Tried.*

*Or, electrify it daily.*

## HERBAL TEA

The most widely used herbal remedies today are herbal teas. While these are available to buy in dried form, either in tea bags or as loose leaves, many prefer to prepare their own from freshly picked leaves and flowers. Always ensure that you know which plants you are picking, and take care where you pick them from (see some of the recommendations in the section on wild food, p99). Wash your collected leaves or flowers in cold water before making your tea. This is done by placing the herbs in a teapot, pouring on water that has just boiled and putting on the lid (covering is said to stop the beneficial essential oils from disappearing in the steam). After five to ten minutes strain into a cup. Don't add milk, but if you like you can sweeten herb tea with honey. Herbs can have quite strong effects, and it is sometimes recommended that no more than three cups of herb tea should be drunk in a day. Also, if you want to treat a specific medical condition, it is always best to consult a doctor and see a qualified medical herbalist.

### Dandelion tea

Dandelion tea is a diuretic, and is said to be good for cleaning the liver and expelling toxins from the body. Use a small bunch of leaves to make a pot of tea.

### Nettle tea

Nettle tea is thought to be a good general tonic and system cleanser. Again a small bunch of fresh leaves will make a pot of tea.

### Peppermint tea

Peppermint has long been used to aid digestion and ease nausea. Buy a small mint plant, and simply pinch out a few fresh leaves each time you want some tea.

### Elderflower tea

Tea made from elderflowers is most commonly used to ease the symptoms of colds and flu, and some believe it is also good for hay fever.

### Lemon balm

Tea made with lemon balm leaves is a mood-lifter, said to help with mild depression. It is also said to relieve stomach upsets.

## LEARNING MORE

There are many books and websites on herbal remedies, should you wish to know something more about this huge craft. An excellent introduction to the medicinal uses of herbs can be had from visiting the Chelsea Physic Garden (www.chelseaphysicgarden.co.uk). The garden was founded in 1673 by the Worshipful Society of Apothecaries, and still works to conserve and research the properties of over 5,000 species.

# *Creating Topiary*

## TOPIARY

Topiary is the art of clipping trees and shrubs into ornamental shapes. Extremely popular in 17th-century France, topiary is an older craft than many people think, and has been in and out of fashion since ancient times.

## ANCIENT CLIPPING

The ancient Romans were fond of formal gardens with clipped hedging, maintained by a slave called a *topiarius*. In one of his letters, Pliny the Younger (c.62–c.113 AD) described the garden of his Tuscan villa, which contained fantastic topiary forms:

*You descend, from the terrace, by an easy slope adorned with the figures of animals in box, facing each other, to a lawn overspread with the soft, I had almost said the liquid, Acanthus: this is surrounded by a walk enclosed with evergreens, shaped into a variety of forms. Beyond it is the gestatio, laid out in the form of a circus running round the multiform box-hedge and the dwarf-trees, which are cut quite close ... In one place you have a little meadow, in another the box is cut in a thousand different forms, sometimes into letters, expressing the master's name, sometimes the artificer's, whilst here and there rise little obelisks with fruit-trees alternatively intermixed.*

This was fashionable gardening for the wealthy. With the decline of the Roman Empire, the next people to take up topiary were the medieval monks, who used it somewhat less extravagantly – in herb beds divided by low clipped hedges. Topiary then declined somewhat, but was made fashionable again in the large formal gardens of Renaissance Italy, where shrubs and trees were trained and clipped into every conceivable shape, the design for one 15th-century garden including topiary donkeys, oxen, vases, urns, warriors and apes.

In 16th-century England, knot gardens – intricate patterns of dwarf hedging – were popular, and in 17th-century France, tightly clipped box hedges were planted in increasingly complex patterns to create formal beds called parterres. The golden age of topiary came perhaps in the late 17th century, and the garden at Levens Hall in Cumbria was planted at that time, containing bizarre and intricate topiary which is still maintained today.

Yew topiary, Crathes
Castle, Aberdeenshire
© The National Trust for
Scotland Licensor
www.scran.ac.uk

## FAMOUS CRITICS

In Britain at least, the early 18th century brought a backlash against topiary. Joseph Addison preferred to see a tree of a natural shape:

*Our British gardeners ... instead of humouring Nature, love to deviate from it as much as possible. Our trees rise in cones, globes and pyramids. We see the mark of the scissors on every plant and bush. I do not know whether I am singular in my opinion, but for my own part, I would rather look upon a tree in all its abundance and diffusions of boughs and branches, than when it is cut and trimmed into a mathematical figure; and cannot but fancy that an orchard in flower looks infinitely more delightful than all the little labyrinths of the most finished parterre.*

Joseph Addison, in *The Spectator* (1712)

And Alexander Pope was another critic of topiary:

*We seem to make it our study to recede from nature, not only in various tonsure of greens into the most regular and formal shapes but even in monstrous attempts beyond the reach of the art itself. We run into sculpture and are yet better pleased to have our trees in the awkward figures of men and animals than in the most regular of their own.*

Alexander Pope, 'Verdant Sculpture' (1713)

But the popularity of topiary revived again in the early 19th century, and while topiary is now generally used for a few specimen shrubs rather than an entire garden, it remains popular.

## TOPIARY FOR BEGINNERS

Topiary essentially requires patience and judicious clipping. While topiary developed in the grand gardens of the wealthy and influential, it is possible to create topiary on a smaller scale in any garden. Some of the key plants used in topiary are box (*Buxus*); yew (*Taxus baccata*); Portugal laurel (*Prunus lusitanica*); and Leyland cypress (*Cupressocyparis leylandii*). To create a simple cone, buy a suitable plant, make a cone-shaped frame of canes, trim the plant to within the canes (waiting for the plant to grow first if necessary), then remove them. Frames are available in a wide range of shapes for more intricate designs, and cutting guides can be made with wire. For inspiration, visit one of the many topiary gardens that are open to the public, such as Levens Hall (www.levenshall.co.uk). To find out more about topiary, get in touch with the European Boxwood and Topiary Society (www.boxwoodandtopiary.org).

# Maze Laying

## HEDGE MAZES

Modern hedge mazes are puzzles – hedges are planted in such a way that when you enter the maze, the way to the middle is not obvious but involves lots of twists and turns (and dead ends). Puzzle mazes developed in the 17th century. Prior to this, hedge mazes (which have probably been planted since the medieval period) were based on single-path labyrinths, which had quite different intentions behind them.

## EARLIER LABYRINTHS

Early mazes, or labyrinths, were not puzzles but single-track coiling patterns. You don't get lost in this type of maze, as you can always see where you are going. In Britain, labyrinths were cut in the turf, and were apparently used for fun – the object being to run along the path to the centre and back again without stumbling or falling (quite tricky and slightly dizzying when running around the sharp curves of the coil). A number of these turf labyrinths survive, including one at Wing in Rutland and another at Winchester in Hampshire, although it is known that many more have been lost – either destroyed or simply neglected. One such 'lost' maze was the 'Shoemaker's Race' in Shrewsbury. This was maintained by the Shrewsbury shoemakers' guild in the 17th century, and used in their Whitsun festivities. In France and Italy, labyrinths had a more obviously spiritual function, representing penance, and were laid in the floors of churches and cathedrals – the path to be followed at a walk, not a run. These were sometimes called 'Roads to Jerusalem', and it has been suggested that walking the labyrinth, or going round it on your knees while praying, was a substitute for pilgrimage. Whether or not this was the original intention, the labyrinth at Chartres Cathedral is still used in this way. Some believe that the English turf labyrinths were also created for spiritual reasons, but records reveal only their non-religious use, although it may be that only later were they adapted or created for fun.

## PUZZLE MAZES

Puzzle mazes developed from low-hedge mazes, which mimicked the earlier labyrinths. During the 16th and 17th centuries, full-height hedges were gradually introduced, and more complex designs were used. Britain's most famous puzzle maze, and possibly the most famous hedge maze in the world, was planted at Hampton Court as part of the gardens laid out there between 1689 and 1695. Early 18th-century hedge mazes still survive in Denmark, France and Italy, and mazes were often part of the public parks and leisure gardens of the 19th century, designed to provide entertainment and exercise. But

*Maze, Hampton Court Palace, Surrey*
© *Cephas Picture Library / Alamy*

not all hedge mazes are historic. The hedge maze at Longleat House in Wiltshire was laid out in 1975. It is made up of more than 16,000 yews and covers around 1.48 acres (0.6 hectares), and the total length of the path is around 1.69 miles (2.72 kilometres).

## MAIZE MAZES

In recent years maize mazes have become popular (and are inevitably dubbed 'amaizing'). Unlike a hedge maze, which can last for centuries, maize mazes are only usable for two months before the maize is harvested. A maize field is planted in spring, paths are cut through it in June, the maize is tall enough in July or thereabouts to make the maze fun, and in September the field is harvested and the maze is gone.

## MAKE YOUR OWN HEDGE MAZE

Making a hedge maze is quite an undertaking. You need the space, the plants (any good hedging plants will do; commonly evergreen conifers are used – fast-growing ones if you are impatient) and a plan. A puzzle maze should be planned out on graph paper before you mark it out on the ground. Remember to leave enough room for the plants to grow (this means very wide paths to begin with, unless you want the maze to be particularly claustrophobic). The plants will need to be cared for in the usual way, both when you plant them and afterwards. An earlier-style maze, without the puzzle, can be laid out with the plants of your choice.

*Engraving of mazes,*
*1900*
© *The Bridgeman Art Library*

# Practical Crafts

# Stonemasonry

## STONEMASONRY

Skills ranging from cutting, splitting and dressing blocks of stone for building through to the intricate carving of decorations and sculptures all form part of the historical stonemason's craft. Although modern quarrying methods, saws and other cutting equipment have simplified the initial stages, stone carving still requires the expert, artistic eye of an experienced craftsman.

## A CHIP OFF THE OLD BLOCK

Stone has been worked and dressed since prehistoric times – the megalithic monuments at Carnac in Brittany and Stonehenge in Wiltshire bear witness to the skills in cutting and working stone that were available thousands of years ago in Europe, while the huge carved statues of Easter Island tell a more fantastic story still. In Britain, stone has been used in the construction of dwellings since at least the Iron Age, while craftsmen were already famously carving stone to produce columns, decorative façades and sculptures in ancient Greece.

Within Europe, a great tradition of stonemasonry grew up with the construction of churches, cathedrals and castles from the early medieval period onwards – expanding with the spread of Christianity and the power and influence of the new Christian kingdoms. The highly skilled masons of Norman France brought their knowledge and techniques with them to Britain following the conquest of 1066, giving rise to a great boom in the construction of Norman and then Gothic churches and cathedrals there.

The larger cathedrals would have required hundreds of skilled masons in addition to the labourers and other craftsmen involved. At the head of each project was a master mason – a wealthy professional. The master mason often effectively worked as the architect, using his knowledge of geometry and a few basic tools (including the set of compasses that later became one of the symbols of freemasonry) to make the drawings on floors covered in soft plaster from which the templates for the construction were made.

Stonemasons travelled many hundreds of miles around Europe, taking their skills from project to project, and formed themselves into

organizations within which they shared their secrets – the lodges that are cited as the precursors of modern freemasonry. Each mason also had his own mark, or 'sigil', which he carved into finished pieces to ensure that his work could be identified and paid for.

As the work on new cathedrals gradually lessened in the later Middle Ages, so the requirement for highly

*Tools for stonemasonry*
© 67photo / Alamy

skilled masonry diminished. 'Rough' masonry, used in the construction of stone houses, cottages and farm buildings, became more common. Skilled stone carving underwent something of a resurgence in the 18th and 19th centuries with the construction of grand town and country houses for the new wealthy class, and with the growth in the requirement for monumental masonry for the ornate memorials to the dead that became popular, particularly in the urban cemeteries of the larger towns and cities. However, by the 20th century the art of stone carving had gone into a serious decline, and it is only in very recent decades that the drive to restore and conserve important buildings has reversed this.

## CARVING OUT A NICHE

Where smooth, dressed surfaces and decoration were required, 'freestone' was used – so called because its fine grain allows it to be cut and worked freely (limestone and sandstone are both examples of this type). Historically, there were two types of mason. Once the stone had been quarried, 'banker' masons cut the stone to the shape of a template and carved any patterns and decorations into it. First, the stone was split using larger chisels and wedges to form the basic shapes. Further stone was then removed in stages, using gouges, chisels and mallets, with finer tools being employed at each stage. The banker mason passed the finished stone on to the 'fixer' mason, who set the stone precisely in place.

## FINDING OUT MORE

Stonemasonry is a highly skilled craft that doesn't lend itself to having a go at home. A good starting point for those wishing to find out more is the Stone Federation Great Britain (www.stone-federationgb.org.uk), the trade organization that has taken over from the older Masons Company (www.masonslivery.co.uk), a medieval guild which is one of the Livery Companies of the City of London.

# Building with Wattle and Daub

## WATTLE AND DAUB

Wattle and daub, or wattle and dab, is a truly ancient building technique, found worldwide in the construction of dwellings. Primitive buildings were constructed by placing poles vertically in the ground, creating walls by weaving thin branches between the poles (wattle), and coating these with a mud-based filling (daub). Wattle and daub was later used to fill in the gaps of timber-framed buildings.

## LONG USE

*As for 'wattle and daub' I could wish that it had never been invented. The more it saves in time and gains in space, the greater and more general is the disaster that it may cause; for it is made to catch fire, like torches. It seems better, therefore, to spend on walls of burnt brick, and be at expense, than to save with 'wattle and daub', and be in danger ... But since some are obliged to use it either to save time or money, or for partitions on an unsupported span, the proper method of construction is as follows. Give it a high foundation so that it may nowhere come in contact with the broken stone-work composing the floor; for if it is sunk into this, it rots in course of time, then settles and sags forward, and so breaks through the stucco covering.*

Vitruvius, *The Ten Books on Architecture* (1st century AD)

While the Roman architect Vitruvius was no fan of wattle and daub, it was in constant use in Britain until the 19th century, although by that time the craft was less widespread than in earlier centuries, and was associated with lower-status housing. From the mid-12th century, timber framing, with wattle-and-daub panels filling the spaces between the timbers, was the dominant form of building in much of Britain:

*The greatest part of our building in the cities and good towns of England consisteth only of timber, for as yet few of the houses of the commonalty ... are made of stone ... Certes this rude kind of building made the Spaniards in Queen Mary's day to wonder, but chiefly when they saw what large diet was used in many of these so homely cottages; insomuch that one of no small reputation amongst them said after this manner, 'These English,' quoth he, 'have their houses made of sticks and dirt, but they fare commonly so well as the king.'*

William Harrison, *The Description of England* (1587)

While early wattle-and-daub buildings were self-built by peasants, this method of construction later became a skilled craft, and 'daubers' – also known as 'daubatores', 'mud-plasterers' or 'torchers' ('torching' is used synonymously with daubing in medieval documents) – worked alongside the somewhat better-paid carpenters and stonemasons in building houses for the wealthy. The demise in daub came with the increased use of brick nogging to fill in the spaces between timbers and with the move away from timber framing to stone and brick construction.

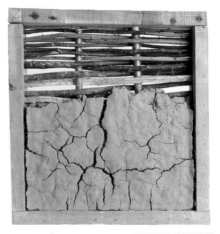

*Wattle-and-daub wall construction*
*Tim Ridley © Dorling Kindersley, Courtesy of Avoncroft Museum of Historic Buildings*

## HOW IT WAS DONE

The wattle matrix was woven in the same manner used in making hurdles – withies, or thin wands of wood, often from coppiced woodland, were closely woven around a number of uprights. The wood used for weaving was that which was locally available, although hazel was typical, and willow and ash were also common. The vertical staves of the structure were often oak or elm. Daub was also composed of locally sourced ingredients, and typically consisted of subsoil, cow dung, chopped straw and water. Crushed chalk, crushed stone or sand was often added. This mixture of ingredients was used to create a daub that had body, held together well and didn't shrink or crack too much once it had dried. The daub was mixed by treading, either with human feet or by penned animals (which no doubt added dung to the mix as they worked, leading some to suggest that the dung was less a deliberate addition than an incidental one, coming direct from the treading animals or in reused straw). The daub was applied to both sides of the wattle at once to ensure that it would stick together. It took some weeks to dry, and once it was hardened a limewash or lime plaster was applied. Walls created in this way, and repaired as necessary, provided good insulation, and lasted for centuries.

## MODERN DAUBERS

While most craftspeople skilled at working with wattle and daub use the technique to repair surviving timber-framed buildings, modern versions are also being experimented with (in combination with modern technology) in order to build homes with minimal environmental impact. Courses are available for the interested amateur, including from the Weald and Downland Open Air Museum (www.wealddown.co.uk).

# *Cob Walling*

## COB

Cob consists of subsoil mixed with water and straw, and from the 13th to the 19th centuries was the traditional building material of those parts of the West Country which lacked good building stone. The county of Devon has the highest density of cob buildings – it has been estimated that there are 20,000 houses there built partly or wholly of cob.

The eventual decline in cob building came with the widespread availability of cheap bricks, increasing labour costs, and changing building regulations. For a time, building with cob almost completely disappeared, although it has undergone something of a revival since the end of the 20th century.

## CONSTRUCTING COB WALLS

*Before we enter into cob in the abstract, we must dispose of it in the concrete. In putting our readers in possession of the most approved method of constructing cob, we take as our basis the workmanlike account of that careful compiler Mr. Loudon, who derived his information from a Devonshire clergyman, one born in a cob parsonage, and himself a grand compounder thereof. The cob walls of the West of England are composed of earth and straw mixed up with water, like mortar, and well beaten and trodden together; the earth nearest at hand is generally used ... These mud walls are made two feet thick, and are raised on a foundation of stone-work ... After a mud wall is raised to a certain height, it is allowed some weeks to settle ... The first layer or rise (Devonicé raise) is from three to five feet high, while every successive raise is diminished in height as the*

*work advances. The solidity of cob walls depends much on their not being hurried*
*in the process of making; for if hurried, they will surely be crippled, and swerve*
*from the perpendicular.*

*Quarterly Review* (Volume LVIII, 1837)

Good cob relies on good subsoil, and one of the reasons for the proliferation of cob buildings in Devon is the level of clay in this soil which, along with sand and fine gravel, improves the strength of the mix.

Traditionally, the soil was dug very close to the site of the house, and mixed with chopped straw (to bind the cob together) and water by treading, either with human feet or with help from cattle (in the same way

that daub was mixed for wattle-and-daub constructions). Once it had reached the correct consistency, the cob was used to build upwards from a prepared stone plinth. Clods of cob were lifted onto the plinth, where they were compacted by stamping from above and beating and shaping from both sides – as the wall grew in size, some workers stayed at the bottom, lifting fresh cob up to those who stood on the top. The wall was built in 'raises', or layers, and once a raise was complete, it was allowed to dry completely (a process that could take months in poor weather) before the next raise was added (the height of the raise being often dependent on the quality of the cob). The walls were anything between 60 and 120 centimetres (2–4 feet) thick at the bottom, and tapered to the eaves, while corners were rounded, both for ease of construction and because rounded corners were less prone to erosion.

*Learning cob-walling*
*techniques, Weald &*
*Downland Open Air*
*Museum*
© *Weald & Downland Open*
*Air Museum, Singleton, Nr*
*Chichester*
*www.wealddown.co.uk*

## A GOOD HAT AND STOUT BOOTS

It has long been said that the key to building with cob is to provide the house with 'a good hat and stout boots' – traditionally, a good thatched roof and raised stone foundations. With these, and any necessary repairs along the way, cob buildings can last for centuries, as shown in many of the villages of Devon. Without these, and with the ingress of water that this would cause, cob walls return to mud and collapse. Any moisture which does get into the walls of a cob building must also be allowed to escape again, and for this reason they are traditionally coated with lime-based render followed by limewash, which are porous and allow for this essential evaporation.

## OTHER EARTH BUILDINGS

Other areas of Britain, again where good building stone was not readily available, had their own traditions, and names for constructing buildings from earth. Parts of East Anglia had 'clay lump', also known as 'cob lump' or 'clay bat'; Cumberland had 'clay daubins' or 'dabbins'; and Hampshire had 'dob'. And while the richer nations largely abandoned building with earth, elsewhere it remained an important technique of construction. However, earth building is undergoing a minor renaissance in a number of countries where the craft seemed lost, its practitioners being increasingly called on to create new, environmentally responsible homes, as well as to repair houses from earlier times. A number of courses on cob building are available if you would like to learn more, including some run by the Weald and Downland Open Air Museum (www.wealddown.co.uk), which also runs courses in other traditional building methods, or the Devon Rural Skills Trust (www.devonruralskillstrust.co.uk). The Devon Earth Buildings Association is one of a number of regional groups working to promote earth building (www.devonearthbuilding.com).

*Pargeting*

## PARGETING

Pargeting is decorative external plasterwork, the decoration ranging from relatively simple geometric designs to extravagant sculptural reliefs. In Britain, it is particularly associated with the counties of Suffolk and Essex, where not only grand homes but also humbler dwellings were often decorated by the pargeter. The term (said with a soft 'g') is thought to derive from the Old French *parjeter*, meaning 'to throw all over'.

## HISTORY OF THE CRAFT

*It is a miserable shift to try to hide the offices of a house, which, if well arranged and brought into view, give character to the dwelling and insure the better conduct of the domestics. Where old walls require external plastering, let it be the old-fashioned pargetting instead of rough cast, or modern-scored stucco. The recovery of old parget patterns and the invention of new, is a field of architectural study hitherto most undeservedly neglected.*

*The Quarterly Review* (Volume XCVI, March 1855)

The original purpose of plasterwork was functional – to provide some protection to the wall behind – but the possibility of decorating it was soon exploited. Early pargeting was used to decorate the external plaster panels of timber-framed buildings of the Tudor period. The plaster was made from lime, sand, water and hair (which bound it together), although many other ingredients, including dung, urine and tallow, were added in an attempt to produce plaster of a workable consistency.

Early designs were fairly simple: herringbone patterns or freehand swirls were marked in fresh plaster with a pointed implement. During the 16th century, plasterwork in England became increasingly sophisticated. It is often said that Henry VIII did much to popularize elaborate pargeting when he hired Italian plasterers to add external decoration to Nonsuch Palace in Surrey.

For the next 100 years or more, pargeting was extremely fashionable, but by the late 17th century it had gone into decline. Much of the pargeting created in its heyday has been lost, with many of the remaining examples found in Suffolk and Essex. Perhaps more truly lost than many other crafts, pargeting is kept alive by a small number of pargeters, who work mostly in the conversation of existing plasterwork, although they are sometimes commissioned to create new designs.

## TOOLS AND TECHNIQUES

The very simplest pargeting is created by drawing a sharp stick across wet plaster. Comb-like tools were also used to mark lines in the plaster, or fingers to make dimples. Moulds and presses were employed to stamp repeating designs such as leaves, flowers, scallops or chevrons. In freehand sculpted work (perhaps the most skilled technique), the drying plaster is shaped by hand in situ, either into abstract designs or into representations of birds, animals or people.

*Pargeting, Saffron Walden, Essex*
© *Brian Harris / Alamy*

*Thatching*

## THATCHING

Thatching is a traditional style of roofing that has been used, at different times, in many parts of the world. In Britain, thatching is thought to date back to the Iron Age. The materials used would have varied, depending on what was available close by, and over the centuries bracken, broom, heather and sedge were all used by thatchers, although eventually the three styles of thatching still in use today came to dominate – long-straw, combed-wheat and water-reed.

Although associated with poorer rural housing (and with traditional building techniques such as cob, where the walls could not support a heavier roof), thatch once covered the roofs of castles and churches as well as poor farm cottages and animal sheds. Thatch was also common in towns, and as early as 1212 regulations were issued in London which attempted to limit the use of thatch, or at least thatch that was not covered by a layer of plaster to limit its fire-spreading properties (although it is unlikely that the regulations were rigorously enforced, as thatched buildings were still common at the time of the Great Fire of 1666).

Although the use of thatch dwindled in towns, it remained popular in the countryside until improved transportation (and railways in particular) led to the more widespread use of Welsh slate in the early 19th century. Certainly, by the late 19th century thatch was thought of as a poor man's roofing material, and as such quite undesirable, a situation entirely different from today – thatch is now an expensive roof covering, associated with high-status rural properties.

## LONG-STRAW THATCH

Long-straw thatching was once the most widespread of the three main forms of the craft. It was practised in the Midlands and the south-east of England. Long straw was a by-product of the grain harvest, and consisted of the broken or bruised stems left after the crop had been threshed. The straw was shaken, thoroughly wetted with water, then gathered up (or 'drawn') into bundles most commonly known as yealms, the straw being gathered any way up, with butt ends and ear ends of the straw appearing at both ends of the bundle. A carrier made from a Y-shaped stick, sometimes known as a yoke, was then used to transport the yealm to the roof.

If the roof was being rethatched, only the top layer of existing thatch was removed, and the new material was fastened on to an earlier layer. The long-straw thatcher works in narrow courses upwards from the eaves to the roof, the thatch being traditionally fixed with 'sways' (lengths of round hazel or willow), which were held down with 'spars' (also known as spics and broaches, these are essentially staples of sharpened split hazel or willow rods, twisted into shape). The eaves and gables were also held with external 'liggers' (tapering lengths of split hazel or willow), which again were fixed with spars.

*The stages in the creation of a thatched roof*
*Dave King / Paul Lewis – modelmaker © Dorling Kindersley*

While thatchers who work with long straw use a tool called a side rake to neaten the completed thatch and remove loose material, this form of thatching still has the shaggiest appearance, which – along with the often decorative pattern of liggers – make it quite distinctive.

## COMBED-WHEAT THATCH

Combed-wheat thatch (also known as Devon-reed, combed-straw or wheat-reed thatch) evolved in the West Country. Unlike long-straw thatch, the straw is carefully combed to remove any short straws and unwanted material (originally a task done by hand), and when it is formed into bundles (known as nitches) all the butt ends of the straw are at one end,

which is made even by 'bumping' or 'butting' (essentially dropping the end of the bundle onto a board to neaten it). This treatment leads to a much neater finished roof, and a material that can be used in a very similar way to water reed (see below). As with long-straw thatch, a new layer of straw is added on top of the old, but in regular horizontal layers, often extending to the full length of the roof, rather than upwards in narrow courses. The butts of the straw lie downwards, and are knocked neatly into place with a tool called a leggett (a flat piece of wood with a grooved face, fitted with a handle), which leads to a very even, bristly finish to the thatch.

## WATER-REED THATCH

*Tusser's 'Five Hundred Points of Husbandry' were reprinted in Numbers, with Notes, about a century ago, by the title of Tusser Redivivus. I happen to have a single number of the work, that for May, in which are the following lines, and the subjoined note upon them:*

> *Where houses be reeded (as houses have need)*
> *Now pare off the mosse, and go beat in the reed:*
> *The juster ye drive it, the smoother and plaine,*
> *More handsome ye make it, to shut off the raine.*

*'Reeding is no-where so well done as in* Norfolk *and* Suffolk, *and is certainly, of all covering, the neatest, lightest and warmest; neither will it (like straw) harbour any vermine, and besides comes very reasonable and cheap. If it be now and then cleansed from moss, which stops the water and rots it, and smooth beaten, to be sure it will last the longer; but it is not very apt to gather moss, and will bear a better slope than any other thatch.'*

*The Gentleman's Magazine* (August 1814)

Water-reed thatch is principally associated with East Anglia, although its use later became more widespread. When rethatching with water reed, all of the existing thatch is removed, rather than simply the top, or damaged, layer. As with combed-wheat thatch, a leggett is used to produce an even finish, but the face of a water-reed leggett is studded with nails rather than being grooved. Reed is not pliable enough to be bent over the ridge of the roof (while straw is), and sedge or rye is traditionally used to form the ridge of a water-reed roof.

## AGRICULTURAL THATCH

Historically, thatch has not only been used on buildings – thatched ricks were once a common way of protecting a grain harvest (see the section on harvesting, p35). This work was generally done with long straw, and was carried out either by a farm worker who was competent at the task or by a thatcher.

## THE THATCHER'S SIGNATURE

*Leggett for reed thatching*
*© Paul Felix Photography / Alamy*

*A thatcher of Thatchwood went to Thatchet a thatching,*
*Did a thatcher of Thatchwood go to Thatchet a thatching?*
*If a thatcher of Thatchwood went to Thatchet a thatching,*
*Where's the thatching the thatcher of Thatchwood has thatch'd?*

James Halliwell Phillipps, *The Book of Nursery Rhymes Complete* (1846)

Many thatchers add a straw ornament to a completed thatched roof (often in the shape of a bird, such as a pheasant, or other animal) which acts as their signature to the work. These perhaps developed from the straw ornaments added to thatched ricks, which superstition said would protect the farmer's crop from birds and witches. Some rick ornaments took the shape of something that represented the owner of the rick, while others represented the person who thatched it – in either case it was commonly said in the past that they were only made by those who had more time than sense, as the thatch added to a rick was only a temporary covering, unlike the thatch on a building, which lasts for many years.

## THE MODERN THATCHER

It is thought that there are around 1,000 thatchers working in Britain today, and in many ways the traditional techniques of thatching remain unchanged. However, there has been a significant change in the sourcing of thatching materials. From the mid-20th century onwards, mechanization in farming (particularly the use of the combine harvester), the increased use of artificial fertilizers, and newer, shorter wheat varieties have all led to a decline in material for straw thatching, and particularly for long-straw thatching. Whereas in the past thatching straw was a by-product of grain cultivation, by the late 20th century it was a specially grown crop. Thus water-reed thatching has become more widespread, and today it relies heavily on imported supplies as well as British-grown reeds.

*Tiling*

## ROOF TILES

Thatch is not the only traditional roofing material – over the centuries various materials have been used to tile roofs. These were traditionally sourced locally, leading to regional variations in roof style. Shingles are wooden tiles, traditionally made from cleft oak; plain tiles and pantiles are both forms of clay roof tiles; while slate tiles are the form of roofing we are most familiar with today.

## SHINGLES

*SHINGLE: a wooden tile, used for covering roofs, spires, &c., made of cleft oak. Shingles were formerly very extensively used in some districts, but their use has, for the most part, been superseded by more durable kinds of covering; they are however still to be found on some church roofs, and on many timber spires, especially in the counties of Kent, Sussex, Surrey, and Essex.*

John Henry Parker, *A Glossary of Terms used in Grecian, Roman, Italian and Gothic Architecture* (1845)

Wooden tiles, known as shingles, were in use as a roofing material from Roman times to the Middle Ages, when they were gradually replaced by tiles made from clay. In Britain, they were traditionally made from oak, which weathers over time to a silver-grey colour. Shingles were split from oak logs, and dressed and finished with an axe and a drawknife. They were thicker at one end, and were attached to a roof with this thicker end downwards, in overlapping rows. An oak shingle roof can last for up to 100 years. At one time, shingles were found only on church spires (Sussex has the greatest number of these), but there has been a revival of interest in roofing with shingles, and in recent years a number of buildings have been constructed with roofs made from hand-split sweet chestnut or oak shingles, and a number of courses are available which teach this craft. For more information on how cleaving creates durable, waterproof items, see the section on green woodworking, p279.

*Right. Wooden shingles on spire of St Peter's church, Newenden, Kent*
© *Michael Grant / Alamy*

*Far Right. Slate roof, Cotswolds*
© *Nick Turner / Alamy*

## CLAY ROOF TILES

Although the Romans made and used fired clay tiles in Britain, the practice then ceased for many centuries, and clay tiles did not become widespread until the 13th century. Early plain tiles resembled shingles in shape and size, and were made wherever suitable clay deposits were available. Pantiles were curved, often S-shaped clay tiles, which were introduced to eastern Britain from the Netherlands in the 17th century. Clay tiles became a serious competitor to thatch in the 17th century, when improvements in the manufacturing process made them cheaper and more reliable. In turn clay tiles had to compete with slate, when Welsh slate became more widespread.

## SLATE

*In like sort, as every country house is thus apparelled on the outside, so it is inwardly divided into sundry rooms above and beneath; and where plenty of wood is, they*

*cover them with tiles [shingles], otherwise with straw, sedge, or reed, except some*
*quarry slate be near-hand, from whence they have for their money so much as may*
*suffice them.*

William Harrison, *The Description of England* (1587)

Welsh slate has been used in various parts of England since medieval
times, but it was not until the early 19th century, when rail transport
made Welsh slate accessible to all, that it became the dominant form of
roofing in Britain, and roofs throughout the country began to look the
same. Before this time, regional slate had also been used: for example, the
grey-green Cornish slate, known as Delabole, and the blue-grey slate of
the Lake District. These are true slates – the tiles originally split by hand,
into thin layers, from metamorphic rocks. Stone slates were also used in
some areas: 'Horsham slate' or 'Horsham slab' is a type of sandstone once
used on roofs in parts of Sussex, Surrey and Kent; and Purbeck limestone
roofs occur in Dorset. Stone slates were heavy roofing materials, and
were generally restricted to larger buildings or roofs with a very low
pitch. Today, while there has been some interest in reviving local roofing
traditions, many slates are imported from Brazil.

## WEATHER VANES AND WEATHERCOCKS

A weather vane is essentially a revolving pointer that indicates the direction of the wind (that is, the direction the wind is coming from rather then where it is going to). A weathercock is specifically a vane in the shape of a cock, historically one of the most popular designs used in weather-vane making. Weather vanes are thought to be one of the oldest instruments of weather prediction.

## BLOWING IN THE WIND

*WEATHERCOCK. It is related that Andronicus Cyrrhestes built an octagonal tower at Athens, having at each side a statue of the God, to whom the wind blowing from that quarter was dedicated, and in the middle of the tower was a small spire, having a copper Triton, which being put in motion by the wind, pointed to the deity from whom it proceeded. The custom of placing vanes on the top of church steeples, is at least as old as the middle of the ninth century, and as these vanes were frequently made to resemble a cock, the emblem of clerical vigilance, they received the appellation of weathercocks.*

Francis Sellon White, *A History of Inventions and Discoveries: Alphabetically Arranged* (1827)

The elaborate weather vane erected by Andronicus in the first century BC is generally regarded as the earliest recorded example of this type of device, although no doubt simpler methods, and simpler vanes (such as fabric pennants), had long been used to ascertain changes in wind direction, and were used on ships as well as on buildings. In the 9th century, the Pope reportedly decreed by papal enactment that a weathercock should be placed on every church steeple to remind all those who passed to be on their guard against sin (the shape of the cock refers to the story of St Peter, who denied Christ three times before the cock crowed), and presumably to show them which way the wind was blowing too.

Heraldic weather vanes were popular in Tudor times, and consisted of the insignia of a nobleman's coat of arms on a metalwork banner attached to an upright rod.

The Victorians returned the weathercock to favour, as well as many other elaborate metalwork designs created by blacksmiths.

## NOTABLE VANES

The weathercock on the church in Ottery St Mary, Devon, is often cited as the oldest in Britain. It is thought to date to around 1340, and its design includes a number of tubes which once whistled when the wind blew, imitating a cock's crow. Unfortunately, the cock is now silent, as its whistling tubes have been blocked. The weather vane at the Royal Exchange in London is in the shape of a grasshopper, the creature which appears on the crest of Sir Thomas Gresham, who founded that institution in 1565. According to Gresham family legend, the founder of the family was abandoned as a baby, and left in some long grass. He was found by a woman whose attention was directed to the right place by the chirruping of a grasshopper – a pleasant but unlikely story. A more recent famous weather vane was that presented to Lord's Cricket Ground in the 1920s, in the shape of 'Father Time'.

*Weathercock*
*© Caro / Alamy*

## TAKE ONE COATHANGER

A very simple weather vane can be made from a wire coathanger, a sheet of paper and some sticky tape. The end product will be neither elegant nor durable enough to grace a church steeple, but it will work on the same principle as its more decorative counterparts, and show you the direction of the wind. To make your vane, place one end of the hanger on the paper, and draw around it (from the 'neck', round the end and half way along the bottom). Join the open ends with a straight line, and cut out the shape. Stick this to one end of the hanger with the sticky tape, ensuring there are no gaps where the paper meets the wire. Hang the coathanger (now a weather vane) from a piece of string, and check that it is evenly balanced (if not, add paperclips to the end which is higher). Then hang the weather vane somewhere where it can turn freely in the wind. The movement of air will push the paper-covered end downwind, and the end that isn't covered will point to the direction from which the wind is blowing. Rather more substantial, and artistic, weather vanes are still made, often by blacksmiths working with wrought iron, or by coppersmiths.

*Making Rope*

## MAKING ROPE

Once carried out on a vast scale in the coastal towns of Britain to supply the demand for sailing-ship rigging, rope making by hand is a long-established craft. The basic principle involves twisting together suitable fibres, first in one direction to form thin strands, then twisting the strands together in the other direction, creating tension which holds the fibres together through the action of friction to form a strong, continuous length. Rope can be made from a range of materials, both natural and man-made, including hemp, coir, flax, sisal and 'bast' (taken from the inner bark of certain trees).

## THE ROPE-MAKING LINE

Rope has a history stretching back many thousands of years. The earliest, prehistoric ropes and cords were made by braiding or twisting plant fibres, reeds or strips of animal hide by hand. However, there is evidence to indicate that the Egyptians, and other sailing peoples of the ancient world, used ropes made of strands that were twisted by simple mechanical means.

During the Middle Ages, rope was made throughout Europe using the 'rope-walk' method, which required the lengths that were to be twined to be drawn out in a straight line to beyond their final length. The main benefit of this approach (and the reason for its development) is that much longer ropes can be made, removing the need for splicing together shorter lengths – particularly important where ropes were required for rigging taller sailing ships. Rope manufacture became vitally important to the maritime power (naval and trading) of seafaring nations. In Britain, rope-yards grew up all around the coastline to feed the demand for miles and miles of rope in a variety of thicknesses and types. Many streets still bear names such as 'Rope Walk' or 'Roper Lane' as testament to their one-time use. Bridport in Dorset (a county with farmland particularly suited to growing hemp and flax) still exhibits evidence of rope-walks in the width of the pavements in some streets – originally built to allow room for the walks.

To make longer lengths of rope, rope-walks had to stretch for some distance – often several hundreds of metres. The standard rope length used by the Royal Navy was 120 fathoms (720 feet, or approximately 220 metres). The walks were often constructed outside, with rows of trees providing the only protection from inclement weather. Later, covered walks were built, and in some places advantage was taken of natural features such as caves. A good example of this is the Peak Cavern near Castleton in Derbyshire, where rope was still made by hand, on a small scale, until well into the 20th century.

In the earlier years of rope making, a simple 'jack' was used. This piece of equipment would put one twist into the cord for each turn of the jack. During the Middle Ages, jacks were developed which could be turned with a handle, and which geared up the number of turns produced in the rope for each turn of the handle – firstly using pulleys, and later using cogs. This sped up the process greatly, although it was still extremely time-consuming when compared with the powered industrial machinery used now.

## FROM HECKLING TO SPLICING THE MAINBRACE

The hemp from which the majority of rope was once made was known colloquially as 'neckweed' or 'gallows grass' – a darkly humorous allusion to one of the end uses of the rope it produced. The first stage of the rope-making process is the extraction of the strong fibres of the outer casing of the hemp stalk. When this was carried out by hand, the harvested hemp was first dried in bundles, then threshed to remove the seeds. Once this had been done, it was soaked in water or left at the mercy of the elements for a few days to allow the softer tissue to rot away – a process known as retting.

To clean, straighten and align the fibres, they were 'heckled' – a similar technique to the carding carried out before spinning wool. Handfuls of hemp fibres were softened with oil (often whale oil) and drawn repeatedly through the pins of a heckle board. The 'streak' that was formed would then be spun on the rope-walk. One end was attached to a rotating hook on a large spinning wheel (turned by a helper), and the remainder was wrapped around the waist of the spinner, who walked steadily backwards, feeding out the fibres to produce a yarn.

Many rope-makers bought in the yarn, and it is likely that it is from this point that the modern small-scale rope-maker would start the process. First the yarns must be 'warped'. The yarn is payed out along the rope-walk, laid over T-shaped supports to keep it off the ground, to form the warp. The number of times it is payed backwards and forwards depends on the required finished thickness of the rope or cable being made. For a three-stranded rope, three separate sets of yarn will be laid out.

Each set is then attached at one end to a hook on the rope jack (which has three or four separate hooks that can be rotated together at the same speed by turning the handle at the rear), and the other ends are all attached to a single hook on the 'traveller' or 'sledge' at the other end. The hook on the traveller is initially fixed in place, while the handle of the jack is turned to twist each

*Ropewalk, 1890*
*© Royal Photographic Society*

of the sets of yarn into a separate strand. Once the required amount of twist has been put into each strand, the 'top' (a conical piece of wood, grooved to receive each strand) is inserted to separate the strands, thin end towards the traveller, at the traveller end. A helper continues to turn the jack handle as the rope-maker moves forward, sliding the top steadily towards the jack. As the top moves forward, the right-hand twist in the separate strands causes them to form up to make a single, left-hand twisted rope behind it. The rope-maker uses his experience to judge the speed of movement to adjust the lay, and so the hardness, of the finished rope. As this process is carried out, the traveller will move towards the jack as the twisting reduces the overall length of the warp by about a quarter.

The final step involves splicing or knotting the end of the finished rope to prevent it unravelling. Heavier ropes might involve the use of a significant amount of manpower, huge tops and even horses to hold the tension at the traveller end. Ropes could also be twisted together in turn to form heavy cables. The mainbrace, which supported the mainmast, of the largest sailing ships was so thick that splicing the end to secure it was a huge task, earning the issue of a special rum ration on completion.

There are a number of different types of cordage, each with its own name depending on thickness, material, purpose and length. However, the basic techniques employed in their manufacture are similar. Lighter-weight rope is known as line, and thinner cord as twine. Historically, a number of rope products were made to exact lengths and in particular styles – including animal ties, which often incorporated horsehair to help them slip more easily, making them easier to tie and untie, even when wet. Another particular type of cordage can be made from lime bast – bast being the fibrous material of the inner bark of trees. Lime trees provided the best bast of the trees available in Europe, and it has been made into rope for many thousands of years. The resulting rope is of low weight, and is less absorbent and of lower elasticity than hemp rope. However, it is also less strong and requires considerable initial input to make the narrow strips of bast from which the first cord is twisted.

## LET'S TWIST AGAIN

To make rope (or, more realistically, thinner cord) at home on your own or with a helper, some form of jack will be required as an absolute minimum. Patterns for home-made jacks are available on the internet, or you may be lucky enough to come across a ready-made mechanical jack for sale. However, if you have a number of friends to help you, the basic principles can be used to twist together strands of bought twine to form a thicker rope. One person operates as the traveller, holding three or more strands together at one end. The others each take a single strand, hold it steadily in tension and turn it (as evenly as possible with the other helpers) to tighten the twist that is already in place. Then, continuing to hold the tension, the three strands are brought together and twisted (in the opposite direction to their own twist) to form a rope. The lay might not be even, but it will be yours.

*Tanning*

## TANNING HIDES

When an animal skin has been removed and dried it becomes hard, and is of little use. Very early on, either through accident or experiment, mankind developed the craft of tanning in order to turn skins into leather. It is essentially a chemical process – the skin is soaked in a solution which contains tannin (in Britain this was most commonly obtained from the bark of oak trees). This preserves the animal skin, making it pliant, resistant to decay and insoluble in water.

## THE PROCESS OF TANNING

Tanning was originally carried out by individuals, who preserved the skins of their own animals after they had been slaughtered for food. It later became a cottage industry, then a larger-scale manufacturing operation.

The first process was the washing of the skin to remove the blood, which would discolour the leather. This was often done in a stream so that the impurities were simply washed away, and as the skin would undergo several washes on its way to becoming leather, early tanneries were generally located next to streams. At this stage the skin would still have a coating of hair on one side and a layer of flesh on the other. Both had to be removed before tanning took place. At first, this work would have been done with a stone scraper after keeping the hide somewhere warm until the hair and flesh had just started to rot; later, the skins were immersed in lime pits or soaked in a solution of lime in order to loosen the hair and flesh, before the 'beamsmen' of the professional tanneries, who worked with the skin laid over a beam, used a blunt knife to remove the hair and a sharp knife to scrape away the flesh. Little was wasted: the hair was sold to upholsterers, while the flesh was used in glue. The de-haired and de-fleshed skins would still be full of lime, and while some could be thoroughly washed and squeezed to remove it, others (such as kid hides) were too delicate for this, and one of the most unpleasant parts of the process ensued:

*The absorption of lime in the afore-mentioned process makes the skins hard and thick; to render them supple, and prepare them for receiving the tan liquor, they are*

*thrown into a pit called the poke, or mastering-pit, which contains a quantity of putrescent dung diffused in water: the dung of dogs, pigeons, or sea-fowl, is preferred for this purpose, that from cows and horses not being sufficiently powerful ... When the skins have become perfectly soft, they are taken out of the putrescent pit, and cleansed on the beam, when they are ready for tanning.*

Luke Hebert, *The Engineer's and Mechanic's Encyclopaedia* (1836)

The tanner, colour plate, 1849
© Science Museum Library

Next, the hides were cut up, as some parts of them needed to be soaked for longer than others. Then came the actual tanning – in some respects a simple process compared to the complexities of preparing the hide. Ground oak bark would be left in water for various lengths of time (up to several weeks) to produce different strengths of tannin solution. The solution was held in a series of pits, from the weakest to the strongest. The hides were placed in the weakest solution first, before progressing to the stronger ones, and then were piled up together along with powdered oak bark and the used tannin solution. This final part of the chemical process would take a long time, perhaps nine months. After that, the hide was ready to be washed, rubbed to remove any bloom, and oiled to prevent it from drying out too quickly.

## FROM THE TANNER TO THE CURRIER

*The business of the currier is to prepare hides which have been under the hands of the tanner, for the use of shoe-makers, coach-makers, saddlers, bookbinders, &c.*
John Souter, *The Book of English Trades* (1818)

Once the tanner had finished his work, the leather was sent to the currier, whose skill lay in cleaning, stretching and softening the leather, preparing it for its final use. One of his skills was 'skiving' – paring away at the flesh side of the leather with an exceptionally sharp knife to reduce the leather's overall thickness, without piercing through the leather and spoiling it. Various other currying processes followed, including oiling and polishing, perhaps adding a further three months to the preparation time.

## SPECIALIZED CRAFT

The crafts of the tanner and the skinner were eroded by the development of factory methods. Mineral treatments became available that were quicker-acting and more adaptable than the tannin from oak bark, and artificial solutions replaced the putrescence of the mastering-pit. In 1809, a splitting machine was introduced. This sliced one piece of thick leather into two pieces of thin leather, removing the need for the currier's skiving. Some oak tanners do remain, continuing a highly specialized craft, although the process has been much modernized. Hobbyists also continue the tradition.

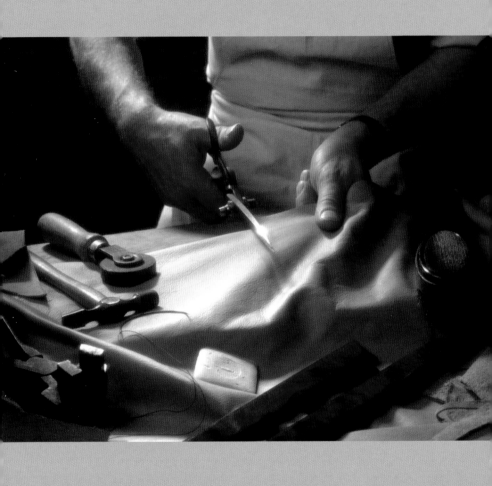

*Working with Leather*

## LEATHER

Once an animal hide has been tanned, and then finished by a currier (processes described in the section on tanning, p255), the resulting leather can be fashioned into any number of both practical and decorative items. Leather working has long been closely associated with saddlery (also described in a separate section, p262), but over the centuries many other items have been fashioned from leather. These include (most obviously) boots and shoes as well as other items of clothing such as gloves, and leather has also been used in bookbinding, furniture making, vessel making (leather jugs and tankards are a particularly English tradition), and to make items of luggage. The various leather trades were at their height in Britain in the latter part of the 19th century, when leather goods fashioned there were exported all over the world.

*Leather working*
© Ian Fraser / Alamy

## VICTORIAN SWEAT SHOPS

While some became prosperous through the export of British leather goods to the countries of the British Empire, the conditions of the craftspeople who worked in the leather industry were not good. Many worked in small backyard workshops, although a number of large leather-working factories also existed. The Sweated Trades Commission of 1889 reported that conditions were poor, and that these highly skilled workers worked long hours for very little pay, with women earning even less than their male counterparts (men were paid by the hour, while women were paid for completed items). Even in the large factories, considered to be modern facilities, earnings were further reduced by deductions made for heating and lighting. Saddlery and harness making, which had long been the mainstay of the leather industry, went into decline in the early part of the 20th century. Light leather goods, such as hat boxes, travelling bags and wallets, were made in place of horse-related items. Today, more leather goods are imported than exported, but leather working continues with the production of luxury, hand-crafted goods, and with individual leather-workers continuing the craft.

## CUTTING AND STITCHING LEATHER

While different skills must be learned for many of the specific leather trades, such as shoe and boot making, the cutting and stitching of leather is a skill that can be used in everything from saddlery and wallet making to dog collars. The tools used are relatively simple, and fulfil the three tasks of cutting, punching and stitching the leather. Cuts are made with very sharp knives or, for long straight lines or the parallel cuts needed to make strips of leather, a tool called a 'plough gauge' is used. The plough gauge has an adjustable width gauge, so can cut accurately to the width required. It is pushed along the leather with one hand, a vertical blade making the cut, while the other hand pulls aside the piece being cut.

Holes are punched in leather to allow for the addition of rivets (a method of joining and decorating leather), or to make holes for buckles or lacing. Sharp punches are used, in combination with a hammer, to cut such holes. Holes can also be made for stitching (a necessary requirement in heavier or thicker leathers). The stitch holes can first be marked with a rotary pricking wheel (to give even spacing to the holes), and then created with an awl. Alternatively, a pricking iron is used. This is a punch with a series of evenly spaced sharp points. The sewing line is often marked with a creasing iron, or 'creaser'. This has a blunt metal point which is heated over a flame, and then drawn along the leather to create a permanent indentation.

A variety of strong needles, both curved and straight, are used for stitching leather. The pieces of leather to be sewn are held between the knees or in a wooden clamp. Strong waxed thread is used, and in the past linen thread was preferred, the leather-workers twisting together strands of linen to create thread of the desired thickness, and drawing it through a lump of beeswax before use. A number of stitches are used, similar to those used in stitching clothes, but the strongest stitches are made by using two needles at once, one at each end of the thread. Known as saddle stitch, opposing stitch, or double-handed sewing, one needle is pushed through the first hole, and the thread pulled half way through. After this, both needles are pushed through each hole in opposite directions (one from the front of the work and one from the back) and the thread pulled tight.

# *Saddlery*

## THE SADDLER'S TRADE

The principle behind all saddles is to provide protection for the horse's back, and security and comfort for the rider's seat. The first horseback riders rode bareback, a situation which continued for many years (the Macedonian cavalry of Alexander the Great rode and fought bareback, without a saddle or stirrups). The exact history of the saddle is somewhat uncertain. Basic padding was probably used by some very early riders, but precisely when the first 'tree' (a piece of wood that spreads the rider's weight in such a way as to be comfortable for the horse) was used is disputed. It was certainly in use by nomadic tribes in Asia in around 200 BC, and by the 3rd century AD the Sarmatians had added stirrups. The tree formed a core part of the leather saddles that became widespread in medieval Europe and that evolved into the saddles still made today.

## CONSTRUCTING A SADDLE

*The frame of a saddle is called a* tree: *it is not made by the saddlers, but by persons who confine their attention to this branch of business ... In making a common saddle, the workman proceeds thus: He first extends two strips of* straining web *from the pommel to the hinder part of the tree, and fastens them with tacks: the tree is then covered on the upper side with two thicknesses of linen cloth, between which a quantity of wool is afterwards interposed: a covering of thin leather, usually made of hog's-skin, is next tacked on, and the flaps added: under the whole are placed the pads and saddle-cloth; the former of which is made of thin cotton or linen cloth, and thin leather, stuffed with hair. The addition of four straps, two girths, two stirrup-leathers, and as many stirrups, completes the whole operation. Saddles are often covered with buckskin.*

Edward Haze, *The Panorama of Professions* (1836)

Saddlery has always been a skilled craft, at its height when horses were in common use in transport and agriculture. The finest quality leather is used for the best saddles, and while saddles are now available which use synthetic materials, bespoke leather saddlery remains a relatively small but thriving trade.

## THE WALSALL CONNECTION

While many people know that Walsall Football Club's nickname is the Saddlers, few know of this West Midland town's connection with the craft and trade of saddlery. Walsall firms provided saddles and harnesses for the British Army during the Crimean War, and supplied equipment for both sides during the Franco-Prussian War. At the craft's peak in 1901, as many as 6,830 saddlers and harness-makers were employed in the town – the centre of Britain's saddle industry. While such numbers have now dwindled dramatically, there are still over 70 saddle manufacturers in Walsall, which is probably the highest concentration of saddlers in the world.

## A QUALIFIED CRAFT

The Society of Master Saddlers (www.mastersaddlers.co.uk) was formed in 1966. It oversees the training of its member (saddlers, harness-makers, and saddle-fitters). Saddlers and harness-makers work hard to become qualified – a master saddler will have gained three City & Guilds qualifications in saddlery or have completed a four-year apprenticeship, as well as having worked in the trade for at least seven years. The earliest records of a guild of saddlers in London date back to the 12th century, although the guild itself could be even older. The Worshipful Company of Saddlers still exists (www.saddlersco.co.uk), one of a select group of surviving medieval craft guilds.

# Blacksmithing and Farriery

## THE BLACKSMITH AND THE FARRIER

The craft of the blacksmith is old and varied. Prior to the Industrial Revolution, the blacksmith was a vital part of the rural community. There would have been at least one blacksmith in every village, working in his smithy to forge items out of metal, and making and repairing agricultural and domestic ironwork. While farriery is a separate trade, involving the shoeing of horses, in the past many village blacksmiths were the local farriers as well, and people would bring their horses to the local smithy for shoeing. Some blacksmiths would have taken the examination of the Worshipful Company of Farriers (a guild established in 1356) to become Registered Shoeing Smiths. This tested not only the manual skill of shoeing, but also knowledge of a horse's anatomy and diseases (and treatments) of a horse's foot, considered key parts of the farrier's work.

Both blacksmithing and farriery are highly skilled crafts, and while both suffered a decline post-industrialization, both trades continue – the blacksmith now often producing decorative or artistic pieces, and the farrier commonly buying in horseshoes to keep horses well shod.

## IRONWORK

Iron has been extracted from the ground and shaped into tools and weapons for thousands of years. The earliest blacksmiths were itinerant. They travelled from manor to manor with their equipment: simple bellows, an anvil, hammer and tongs. Their forge was a fire built in a hole in the ground, but even with this simple equipment they would smelt their own iron, melting it to separate it from its ore. Later, blacksmiths set up permanent workshops, often at a crossroads or the centre of a village, and bought their iron ready-smelted.

## THE VILLAGE SMITHY

*Under a spreading chestnut tree*
*The village smithy stands;*
*The smith, a mighty man is he,*
*With large and sinewy hands;*
*And the muscles of his brawny arms*
*Are strong as iron bands.*

*His hair is crisp, and black, and long,*
*His face is like the tan;*
*His brow is wet with honest sweat,*
*He earns whate'er he can,*
*And looks the whole world in the face,*
*For he owes not any man.*

*Week in, week out, from morn till night,*
*You can hear his bellows blow;*
*You can hear him swing his heavy sledge,*
*With measured beat and slow,*
*Like a sexton ringing the village bell,*
*When the evening sun is low.*

Henry Wadsworth Longfellow, 'The Village Blacksmith' (1841)

The forge was the centrepiece of every smithy, where a glowing fire of coke and coal was originally brought to heat by a pair of leather hand-bellows. Most blacksmithing is done with hot metal, heated to the precise level of softness that makes it easy to fashion, a skill learnt with experience. The different levels of heating are known by nicknames rather than temperatures, based on the colour and appearance of the metal. For example, 'snowball heat' makes iron white-hot, but is too hot for steel. Go above snowball and metal will burn. Below this are various welding heats, including 'slippery heat', then lesser heats such as 'dull red' for flattening, shaping and finishing work.

Once heated, hot metal is taken to the anvil for working. Anvils are said to have been perfected by the time of the Middle Ages. Most work is done on the 'face', the flat section on the top of the anvil. A step down from this is the 'table', softer than the face, and sometimes used for cutting. Next comes the 'beak', a long pointed part used for anything that requires a curved section, including horseshoes. The underside of the beak is known as the 'throat'. At the back of the face is the square 'heel', near which are two holes – a square 'hardie hole' used in shaping work, and a round hole used when punching holes in metal (such as the nail holes in horseshoes). The anvil was raised to working height by being attached to a huge block of wood (often a section of the trunk of an elm tree). The block would be set into the floor of the smithy to make sure it didn't move, and was said to give 'life' to the anvil – if the anvil was well set on its wooden block, it would give spring to the hammer, and take some of the effort out of lifting it after each blow.

## FARRIERY

While farriery is an old craft, it is not so old as that of the blacksmith. The Romans shod their horses with leather and metal shoes called 'hipposandals', which were tied on with straps. The nailed-on horseshoe was a later invention, probably dating from the 6th or 7th century, and not widespread in Europe until the 11th century. When

*Smithy, Walls, Shetland*
© Shetland Museum
Photographic Archive
Photographer J Peterson

shoeing a horse, the farrier examines the hooves, then removes the old shoes. Once this is done, the hooves are trimmed and smoothed. New shoes are then checked for fit, with any necessary adjustments being made to their shape. When the farrier worked from the smithy, much of the shoeing he did was done 'hot'; that is, the horseshoe was heated before it was applied to the horse's hoof. Latterly, with farriers travelling to the horse rather than the horse being taken to the farrier, cold-shoeing is more common. In either case, the shoe is nailed to the hoof, a job that is painless for the horse so long as it is done properly.

## HORSESHOES FOR LUCK

Horseshoes are one of the most widely recognized symbols of luck. Actual horseshoes are still often nailed to doors to bring good fortune, although the earliest recorded superstitions relating to horseshoes suggest that it was the finding of a horseshoe that was considered lucky. Nailing them up came later, in the 16th century, as a method of keeping witches away:

*To show how to prevent and cure all mischiefs wrought by these charms and witchcrafts ... One principal way is to nail a horse shoe at the inside of the outmost threshold of your house, and so you shall be sure no witch will have power to enter thereinto. And if you mark it, you shall find that rule observed in many country houses.*
Reginald Scot, The Discoverie of
Witchcraft (1584)

There are two distinct camps when it comes to deciding which way up to hang your lucky horseshoe. Those who hang them with the open end up claim that if you hang them with the open end down, the luck will fall out. Those who hang them with the open end down sometimes counter this by saying that with the prongs up the Devil can sit in the shoe.

## MODERN TRADES

*Shoeing a horse*
*© Peter Titmuss / Alamy*

The National Association of Farriers, Blacksmiths and Agricultural Engineers (www.nafbae.org) works to ensure the future of these crafts. BABA, the British Artist Blacksmiths Association (www.baba.org.uk), is a blacksmithing organization which, among other things, holds master-classes and publishes a magazine and newsletter. Their website includes a list of training courses – smithing can be learned in a number of ways, including both private and college courses – as does the website of the Worshipful Company of Blacksmiths (www.blacksmithscompany.org.uk). You must now be a member of the Farriers Registration Council before you can legally practise farriery (whether on your own horse or someone else's), and those wishing to train for farriery must complete a four-year apprenticeship, including National Vocational Qualification Level 3 in Farriery and the Diploma of the Worshipful Company of Farriers (www.wcf.org.uk).

_Wheelwrighting_

## WHEELWRIGHTING

The invention of the wheel is often cited as a pivotal point in history. The manufacture and repair of wooden wheels for carts or wagons was once an essential craft – vital for the movement of goods, livestock and people on land. As most communities had their own wheelwright, and as potential customers were limited in number, his skills often also extended to those of carpenter and wainwright (manufacturer and repairer of cart and wagon bodies).

## REINVENTING THE WHEEL

Wooden wheels began to be used about 6,000 years ago, and until the 20th century very little had changed in the basic principles of the craft since the solid wheel began to be replaced by the spoked wheel approximately 2,000 years ago.

## THE WHEELS OF INDUSTRY

In Britain, the heyday of the craft coincided with the boom in agricultural production from the mid-18th century onwards. In rural communities at this time, the work of the wheelwright was mainly confined to repairs to existing wheels, as farm vehicles were built to last, and farmers would try to ensure that they did. Much of this work was carried out when farm vehicles were overhauled in the spring and early summer. Within towns, a much wider potential clientele existed – tradesmen, shopkeepers, merchants and haulage firms all needed carts, wagons and wheels to keep their businesses turning over.

*It will appear by a very superficial examination, that such a business is of very great consideration, inasmuch as it contributes largely to the facilitating of our first necessities, by supplying the means of ready transit for articles of all descriptions, as well as in offering a similar comfort of quick communication for ourselves; and it is pleasing to reflect, that amidst all the various improvements in arts and manufactures, that this of wheel carriages has been by no means neglected. Our artisans in this line stand pre-eminent, our carriages are manufactured on better principles, as well as more neat in their execution, than are to be found in any other country.*

Thomas Martin, *The Circle of Mechanical Arts* (1813)

## THE END OF THE ROAD

Despite the undoubted skill of its practitioners, the craft of the wheelwright suffered a dramatic and almost total demise with the arrival of motor vehicles and the pneumatic tyre at the end of the 19th century. This was exacerbated when the armed forces disposed of vast quantities of horse-drawn vehicles immediately after World War I, simultaneously ending its status as a major customer of the wheelwright and flooding the market with cheap carts and wagons.

## TURNING A HAND TO THE CRAFT

As with any woodworking craft, wheel-building begins with the selection, cutting and seasoning of suitable wood. Traditionally, the wheelwright would select his own timber: elm was the preferred sort for the hub (known as the stock or nave); oak for the spokes; and ash for the 'felloes' (pronounced 'fellies') that formed the rim. The wood was cut in winter, when the trees were dormant, and then left to season – usually for several years.

A wheel is essentially made up from three separate components – the hub, the spokes and the rim. When viewed from the side, the wheel must be perfectly circular so that it runs true. When viewed from the front, a cartwheel is slightly 'dished' – the spokes are tilted outwards from the hub. This feature, combined with the fitting of the wheels and axles so that the top of the wheel tilts outwards (often significantly), results in greater strength and resistance to the sideways forces produced by the motion of the drawing horse.

There are a range of tools specific to the craft of the wheelwright, each with its own specialized purpose. Among these are the spokeshave, tyre dog, jarvis, samson, bruzz, spoke set gauge, spoke lever, boxing engine and traveller.

Firstly, the stock (hub) is hewn from the solid heart of an elm round, drilled and turned on a lathe to form a barrel or cylindrical shape wide enough for the nave bonds (iron hoops) to be placed around each end. An even number of spoke holes are then carefully marked out, bored with

an auger and finished with the bruzz (a three-cornered chisel). The correct angle for the dish is set using a gauge stick.

The spokes are cut and roughly shaped with a drawknife, 'feet' are added at each end (to fit the holes in the stock and rim) and then they are finished with an axe, spokeshave and jarvis (a specialized type of plane). Once the spokes have been

Tyring the wheel
© Paul Felix Photography / Alamy

driven home into the stock, and checked to ensure they are at the correct angle, the business of adding the rim can begin. The rim consists of a number of separate curved sections, known as felloes. Each is cut, shaped and drilled to take the ends of two spokes. To make sure the ends of the spokes meet with the holes, they must initially be forced together using a spoke dog, before the felloe is hammered home and the spokes move apart slightly into their final position.

When all of the felloes are in place, the metal tyre can be added. The circumference of the wheel is measured using the traveller and an iron hoop is then made. The hoop is made to a slightly smaller circumference so that when heated, fitted and then cooled, it binds the wheel together tightly and stays in place. Carrying the red-hot tyre to the wheel (fixed in place on a tyring bed) and hammering it into place must be done very quickly, and usually requires at least three people. At this point, if the calculations are wrong, the wheel will buckle or break – a real moment of truth. Finally, a tubular metal bearing (or 'box') is fitted to the centre of the stock and held in place by driving in oak wedges, before the wheel is mounted on the axle, where it is prevented from falling off by the insertion of a linchpin.

## THE WHEELS KEEP ON TURNING

The Worshipful Company of Wheelwrights (www.wheelwrights.org), one of the Livery Companies of the City of London (born out of the much older guild, and incorporated in 1670), is still very active in the support and development of the craft. They hold a list of practising wheelwrights in England, Wales and Northern Ireland. Training in wheelwrighting, to NVQ level, can be undertaken at Herefordshire College of Technology (www.hct.ac.uk).

## COOPERING

Coopering is the name given to the craft of wooden-barrel making or, more correctly, wooden-cask making. Such wooden casks traditionally came in a wide variety of sizes, from the diminutive 4.5-gallon (20-litre) 'pin', through the 36-gallon (164-litre) 'barrel', to the huge 108-gallon (491-litre) 'butt'. The craft of their manufacture was once common and widespread throughout Europe, where they were the standard form of packaging for wet and dry goods for many centuries.

## ROLL OUT THE BARREL

Although it is now a rare and specialized skill, practised more for the purposes of repair than manufacture, there was a time when most villages would have had at least one cooper. It is known that casks were used in ancient Egypt, and it is believed that the craft of manufacturing wooden casks has changed little since the time of the Romans, whose word for vat or cask, *cupa*, gave the trade its name. Now more often seen as items of garden furniture, even as late as the first half of the 20th century wooden casks would have been a common feature of commercial and industrial life, stacked high in the docks and warehouses of the world.

It is not only the brewing, wine-making and distilling trades that have historically relied on the skills of the cooper. Until the advent of modern metal, cardboard and plastic packaging, almost all goods carried by sea were transported in wooden casks – including sugar, spices, salted fish, oils and gunpowder. Even as late as the 19th century, coopers formed part of the crew of cargo ships. As the ships sailed out of European ports, they would carry with them the materials for the coopers to manufacture the casks for the return cargo. In more recent times the craft became confined to dry land, with individual coopers and small workshops being replaced by larger manufacturing enterprises attached to breweries and warehouses. In Britain, as metal replaced wood as the material of choice for the storage of beer, even these concerns died out – despite the efforts of campaigning groups such as the Society for the Preservation of Beers from the Wood, formed in the 1960s, which argued that storage in wooden casks contributed a vital element to the complex flavour of traditional ales. However, the recent increase in demand for malt whisky, which derives its colour and much of its flavour from maturation in breathable, tannin-rich wooden casks, has ensured that, at least for the time being, there is still some commercial demand for the skills of the cooper.

## A BARREL OF LAUGHS

As such a venerable and long-established trade, coopering naturally has its own set of customs – the best known being the ceremony of 'trussing the cooper' or 'trussing-in'. The trussing rite was usually associated with the celebration of the end of an apprenticeship, with the unfortunate victim being built into a cask (in later years usually symbolically), covered in something unpleasant and rolled around. In one example, caught on film at Buckley's Brewery in Wales in 1934, an apprentice was initiated into the craft by being covered in flour, treacle and sawdust before taking his tour of the factory floor.

## FLAGGING, JIGGING, SHAVING AND BILGE

The cooper's craft is physically demanding, highly skilled and considered to be one of the most difficult in which to achieve any degree of proficiency – a substandard cask is of no use to anyone. Those who wished to practise the trade served a long apprenticeship, at the end of which they would manufacture casks without resorting to precise plans or written measurements, relying only on their experience and judgement of shape and form to produce containers to a specific capacity that were tight against leaks. In practice, the nature of this 'by eye' manufacturing method and the behaviour of wood as a material meant that some allowance was always made for variation in the volume contained. The volume of a wooden cask also decreases slightly in use as the metal hoops are hammered down to keep the wooden staves firmly pressed together.

There are two main categories of cooper – wet and dry. The former are the more specialized as their products have to be suitable for holding liquids; the latter often make their casks from inferior wood, which are then lined with sacks to stop the dry goods escaping. A third category, the white cooper, is also recognized. These craftsmen use coopering techniques to make other vessels and utensils for agricultural, domestic and decorative purposes. The basic process is similar for each.

The first stage is the selection of suitable wood. Oak is considered to be the best. Staves are cut (or preferably 'cleaved' – that is, split) from trees that are ideally over 100 years old, with particular attention being paid to the direction of the grain, before they are air-dried for anything from 18 months to 3 years.

After that, the staves are dressed using a curved drawknife, known as a backing knife, before the inside is shaped using a hollowing knife. The dressed staves taper towards each end to allow for their curving later on to form the distinctive barrel shape – growing in girth from the narrower 'croze hoop' at each 'head' to the wider bulge or 'bilge' in the middle. The edges are then bevelled by being worked against the 'jointer', a huge, stationary, upside-down plane.

Once all the staves are ready, the barrel

is 'raised' by fitting all of the staves into a raising hoop at the top end, before the first truss hoop is hammered down. Now the staves can be bent into shape, using heat (in the form of boiling water or steam, or by assembling the cask around a fire contained in a metal pot at its centre). Pressure is usually applied at this point by hammering on progressively smaller truss hoops, although there are variations on this method.

The last stages of the manufacturing process, before the final shaping and finishing, involve the levelling of the ends with an adze and topping plane, the bevelling of the top inside edge to form the 'chime' (rim), before a wide, shallow channel is made with a 'chive', and a 'croze' is used to make the deeper channel into which the head (lid) will fit. Finally, the ends of the staves are released so that the heads can be hammered into place, before permanent iron hoops replace those used during construction.

The whole process requires a range of specialized tools peculiar to the trade, including the dowelling stock, side-axe, bick iron, round stave, bung-hole borer, chive, topping plane, flagging iron, driver, adze, diagonals, croze, inside shave, swift, downright, buzz, heading knife, jigger and hollowing knife.

## THE END OF THE BARREL

The Worshipful Company of Coopers (www.coopers-hall.co.uk) is the oldest surviving coopering organization in the UK. One of the Livery Companies of the City of London, gaining its royal charter in 1501, it was born out of a much older medieval craft guild, although it is now a corporate body, dedicated mainly to charitable work. There are very few working cooperages left in Britain, although cask making can still be seen at the Speyside Cooperage (www.speysidecooperage.co.uk) in the heart of the primary malt whisky producing region of Scotland.

*Green Woodworking and Woodturning*

## GREEN WOODWORK

The term 'green' is used to refer to wood which is freshly cut – as opposed to seasoned wood, which has been stored (sometimes for a number of years) to condition it before use. Traditionally practised (at least in the early stages of production) in the woods, where the raw material is first cut, green woodworking is intimately linked with coppicing (an ancient form of woodland management described in a separate section, p12) and is sometimes thought of as the poor country cousin of woodworking trades such as joinery, cabinet making, carpentry, coopering and wheelwrighting. But for the practitioners of the craft, green wood offers the major benefit that it is easier to cleave (split), carve and turn than seasoned timber. Over the centuries, products made with green wood have included hurdles, tools, furniture, simple structures, baskets, wattle walls, kitchenware and, in recent years, garden sculptures (some of these items are dealt with more specifically elsewhere in this book, in the sections on wattle hurdles, p9, and wattle-and-daub, p230). Green woodworking has also given us the 'bodger', whose craft is the subject of the separate section on chair making, p284.

## MEN OF THE WILDWOOD

The practice of the craft of green woodworking reached its peak in the Middle Ages, when woodsmen spent their working lives in intensively managed coppiced woodland, making a range of products season after season. Rather than transporting wood (and labour) to a workshop, they carried out much of the manufacturing on site in temporary shelters built for the purpose. The craftsmen usually led a solitary existence, although in later years larger teams were hired to work estates or were employed by small commercial enterprises. There were two distinct seasons, both requiring intensive labour and long hours of hard work; during the winter the wood was harvested (while the trees were dormant) to provide the timber for the summer season, when it was worked. The woodsman's craft went into decline from the 18th century, but more recently there has been a renewed interest in the sustainable nature of green woodworking practised hand in hand with coppicing and woodland management. In these modern times, the range of items produced has, inevitably, widened to include more luxury and decorative items, such as plant supports, sculptures, 'rustic' garden structures and high-quality household items, recognized as much for their aesthetic and tactile qualities as their practical value.

## WOODSMANSHIP

*There is not a more noble and worthy husbandry than in this ...*
John Evelyn, *Sylva, or a discourse on forest trees* (1664)

Devotees of green woodworking argue that its primary benefit, when practised in conjunction with coppicing, is that it involves working in harmony with the wood (and woodland). By paying close attention to the wood at every stage, working with the grain, employing tried and tested techniques and selecting the right piece of wood for the right task, items can be produced with strength, durability and a quality of finish that cannot be matched by cutting and machine-working dry timber.

### Horses and beetles

Many of the tools and items of equipment used by the green woodworker can be made in situ. A simple sawhorse can be made by hammering three pairs of crossed poles into the ground and bracing them with horizontal poles at the points of intersection. A shaving-brake, used for peeling the bark from newly cut poles, can be made in a similar way. The shaving-horse (or draw-horse) is more likely to be made as a portable item. This consists of a thicker shaped horizontal seat on three legs, which is straddled by the user. A pivoting vice mechanism is attached to the front, to which pressure can be applied using the feet, bringing down a wooden bar to hold the piece of work in place so that both hands are free to shape it using drawknives and other shaving tools. The green woodworker uses a number of specialized cutting, peeling, shaving and splitting tools, including wooden wedges and mallets known as 'beetles', 'mauls' or 'froe clubs'.

## Cleaving

The most important technique practised by the green woodworker is 'cleaving' or 'riving'. This involves splitting wood down its grain. Unlike sawing, this avoids the destruction of the cellular structure which gives the wood its natural strength, preserves its resistance to water and also exposes any knots or other weaknesses. Timber of any thickness can be 'cleft' or 'riven' and, once the skill has been mastered, the process is far quicker than sawing. Ash, hazel, chestnut and willow are the preferred species for this approach.

Cleaving green wood
© Paul Felix Photography /
Alamy

Poles of small to medium diameter are cleft from the end. Using a sharp tool, such as a billhook, a diametric split is made from the thinner end going through the central point of the concentric rings – the resulting clefts will be stronger and less likely to warp where the growth has been even and the ring structure is broadly symmetrical. Where possible, the cleft should be made so that it travels between, rather than through, any knots. Once the split has been made, the two halves can be separated by careful bending, paying attention to the direction of the split and adjusting the direction of the pull by turning the pole over if the split begins to go off to one side. For thinner poles, leverage can be applied if necessary by bracing them against your thigh. For thicker poles, a 'cleaving brake' (two horizontal poles attached to uprights hammered into the ground) can be used to apply greater leverage. One of the tools traditionally used for this process is the froe (a metal blade set at right angles to a wooden handle), which can be used to start the split and worked along the split to help lever it open.

Short logs can be cleft by placing them upright on a hard surface and hammering a splitting wedge or hatchet into the upper end. Longer logs are split by hammering wedges in from the side while they are lying (braced horizontally) on a hard surface. The wedges are hammered in lightly every 30 centimetres (12 inches) or so, then hammered home in sequence from one end. Where possible, cleaving should be carried out by halving and halving again, so that the two sections are even each time.

*Pole lathe, Dorset*
*© Edward Parker / Alamy*

## Peeling

If the final product requires wood without the bark attached, the bark should be peeled from the logs or poles as soon as possible after they are cut – the drier the wood, the more difficult it is to peel. Larger poles and logs are peeled from the centre, working towards the ends using a peeler shaped like a sharpened spade. Smaller poles can be peeled using a drawknife while they are held at a comfortable working height on a shaving-brake.

## Turning

For making turned items, the green woodworker employs the pole lathe – a simple lathe made from green wood. A wooden frame is constructed (in the past, it would have been constructed on site and fixed firmly to the ground or tree stumps), to which two wooden 'poppets' are attached to hold the pivots that grip the ends of the wood to be worked. A tool rest is placed to one side to allow tools to be held firmly in position. The mechanism that turns the wood is made by lashing the thicker end of a long pole to a stake driven into the ground. The pole is rested on a support made from forked poles so that the thin end is above the lathe. A cord is attached to the thin end, then wrapped around the wood to be turned, and attached to a treadle below the lathe.

Once the piece of wood to be turned has been roughly shaped by shaving, it is placed between the two fixed points, which are adjusted to hold the ends tightly in place. The operator pushes down the treadle to produce the cutting stroke; the upstroke is provided by the return pull of the bent pole. The cutting tool is applied only on the cutting stroke, and the expert user builds up a steady rhythm so that the turning is carried out smoothly and quickly. The main benefit of turning in this way is that it requires no electricity supply. It is also considerably safer than using a powered lathe, and turning green wood on a pole lathe produces no splinters or dust.

## CONTACTS

Green woodworking has grown in popularity over recent years. A number of organizations offer courses and advice on getting started. Points of contact for those interested in giving it a go include: the British Trust for Conservation Volunteers (www2.btcv.org.uk), the Small Woods Association (www.smallwoods.org.uk) and the Green Wood Centre (www.greenwoodcentre.org.uk).

# Making Chairs

## WOODEN CHAIRS

The manufacture of wooden chairs of the style known as 'Windsor' chairs (where the legs are fitted into the underside of the wooden seat, and are entirely separate from the back) is the craft that gave us the 'bodger'. Contrary to the connotations that the word has gained in modern times, the bodger was a highly skilled green woodworker, responsible for buying standing wood, then cutting, splitting, shaping and turning it, usually on site in the woods, in order to manufacture the legs and stretchers upon which the chair was built. The production of the remainder of the chair involved a number of other craftsmen in workshops, sometimes many miles away.

## BODGING

Bodging is one of the many branches of the green-woodworking craft and has a history stretching back at least 500 years. Beech is the best wood for the manufacture of chair legs because of its straight, close grain – consequently, the craft of chair making has historically been associated with the Chilterns in Buckinghamshire (particularly the town of High Wycombe), where beech woodland was once widespread. However, the craft was also practised in a number of other areas, and other types of tree, such as ash, yew and apple, were also used.

Often working in pairs, the bodgers selected timber from coppiced woodland and usually carried out all of the stages of their part of the chair-manufacturing process right there – bodgers were often itinerant and not only worked, but also lived in the woods. Once cut, the wood was cleft (split) to form 'billets' for the various turned sections of the chair – the legs, stretchers (struts to brace the legs) and back rails. The billets would then be shaped, firstly using a side-axe to trim them to a rough six-sided section, then by shaving them using a drawknife while they were braced on a shaving-horse. All the while, the bodger's aim was to leave as little waste as possible.

The final turning was carried out on a pole lathe. The legs and other parts were then stacked and left to season, after which they were ready to be transported to town to sell to the chair factories, where they were completed by the framers and master chair-makers. The legs were usually sold by the gross and the purchasers, knowing they had the upper hand in the transaction, often paid rock-bottom prices, thus forcing many bodgers to work long hours for a pittance. However, bodged legs were considered superior to those made using machinery in factories and a few bodgers resisted the inevitable takeover by mechanization until the middle of the 20th century.

## BENDERS, BOTTOMERS AND BENCHMEN

The rest of the process of chair making was carried out production-line style by a number of different craftsmen, traditionally divided into two categories – benchmen, who prepared the seats and other parts not made by the bodger, and framers, who assembled and finished the final chairs (there being a number of different roles within each category).

The chair seats were first cut to shape, using saws, from planks (usually of elm) by the benchman. They were then carved, shaped and hollowed to give the classic saddle shape by a benchman known as a 'bottomer', using an adze. If the design required it, the 'bender' would shape the split stakes used for the bowed back of the chair and bend this into shape using boiling water or steam to make it pliable. Finally, the framers and finishers would drill the necessary holes, slot the chair together (including the stage known as 'legging'), add arms if required, and carry out any further finishing that was necessary. Some Windsor chairs also had a 'splat' (a central, flat, decorative strut) added to the back.

Rocking chairs were made in a similar way, except for the addition of rockers, made from shaped, steam-bent split stakes, to the bottom of the legs.

*Making Chairs*

## BODGE IT YOURSELF

The craft of making Windsor chairs effectively combines two distinct sets of skills. If you would like to have a go at bodging, good starting points include the Association of Polelathe Turners and Greenwood Workers (www.bodgers.org.uk) and the Working Woodlands Trust (www.workingwoodlands.info). Further information on the techniques involved are included in the green-woodworking section of this book on p279. There are also a growing number of craftspeople now making complete Windsor chairs, both in Britain and the United States, several of whom offer courses teaching all of the necessary steps.

287

# Making Walking Sticks and Shepherds' Crooks

## WALKING STICKS AND SHEPHERDS' CROOKS

Sticks and staffs of some description have always been made and used. Since early days, those travelling by foot equipped themselves with a stout stick, pulled from a tree or hedgerow, and used it as a support as they walked, and as a useful weapon if they were set upon along the way. Shepherds also used sticks, again for support as they walked with their flocks. The distinctive shepherd's crook perhaps developed when a stick with a branch at the end (useful for catching a sheep by placing it around their neck) was replaced with a stick attached to a roughly shaped ram's horn. In Britain at least, these early sticks and staffs were useful rather than decorative and only roughly shaped, but by perhaps the 14th century professionally made sticks, carefully shaped and finished, had appeared, and the level of stick dressing, or decoration, increased.

> Shepherds' crooks
> © Andrew Davis / Alamy

## MAKING A WALKING STICK

In Britain, hazel, ash, blackthorn and holly are among the most popular woods used in stick making, although any wood that will make a strong straight shaft can be used. The sticks are best cut in winter, when they contain less sap, as they won't shrink so much when they are left to season, and less shrinkage leads to a lower likelihood of splitting. Reasonably straight sticks can be cut from most hedgerows or woodlands, while professional stick-makers often managed their own coppiced 'stick plantation' in order to grow suitable material. The sticks must be seasoned (ie left to dry) for at least a year before they can be used, and can be wrapped in bundles to help keep them straight. Some are chosen because they have natural handles, while others will have separate handles added to them, or a handle can be shaped by applying steam to the stick and bending it (a process also used to remove unwanted kinks in the shaft). A simple 'thumb stick' has no handle, the wood being chosen for a naturally occurring Y-shaped fork.

When the seasoned sticks are ready, they can be worked and shaped by sawing, rasping and filing, the skill of the craftsman coming to the fore in knowing how to make the best of the grain and of any knots in the wood. The bark can be left on, or removed if a highly polished finish is desired; while the handle can be simple, or ornately carved – representations of the heads of birds and animals being among the most popular designs. Whatever type of stick is made, be it ornate or fairly rustic, the final stage is to add a ferrule, or tip, to the bottom of the shaft, to protect the end of the stick from excessive wear.

## TRADITIONAL SHEPHERD'S CROOK

The shank of a shepherd's crook is longer than that of a walking stick, but is made in the same way. While some shepherds' crooks are made entirely from wood, with a crook head carved from a block of wood, there is a long tradition of making the head of the crook from an old ram's horn (horns from younger sheep or from ewes are often not solid enough to work well). Shepherds used to make their own crooks on winter evenings, a tradition which survived into the 20th century.

First, the end of the horn is cut off, then the horn is heated so that it can be flattened or twisted to remove the natural curl (although some sticks are now made which incorporate this curl). Heating can be done by holding the curved part of the horn over a flame, and gradually twisting the curl out between repeated heatings, or by placing the horn in boiling water until it becomes malleable, and pressing the horn flat under a weight. The final shape of the horn is set by heating the horn again, placing it in a vice or similar, and forcing it into shape. It is then left, clamped or tied in place, so that the new shape will hold.

Next, the horn is filed (first the inside curve, then the outside curve to follow this), then it is smoothed and finished. The horn is usually attached to the staff by shaping a peg at the top of the shank, and drilling a hole in the horn into which this will fit. A collar of horn or metal is then fitted over the joint. The shepherds of the past created very beautiful, as well as functional, pieces.

## STICKS WITH A HIDDEN AGENDA

*It is recorded by Holinshed in his* Chronicles of England, *that in the hollow of a pilgrim's staff, the first head of saffron was secretly brought from Greece, at a period when it was a capital crime to take the living plant out of the country ... [and] the silkworm was also introduced into Europe in the hollow of a pilgrim's staff ... That ancient contrivance of making a repository in the hollow of a walking-stick is not yet obsolete; in the Great Exhibition of 1851, Dr Gray of Perth displayed a medical walking-stick which contained an assortment of instruments and medicines; and the same principle has been employed for the portable conveyance of telescopes, instantaneous-light apparatus, and many other important articles. There were also exhibited in the Exhibition of 1851 several varieties of sticks enclosing in them swords, dirks, and spring-spears, the principle of their construction being, that they required a heavy blow to be given with the armed end before the strong spring could be overcome which held back the spear end.*

William and Robert Chambers, *Chambers's
Journal* (Volume XIX, 1863)

Hollowed-out sticks have certainly been used in the past for the purposes of smuggling or secreting small objects, and sticks containing gadgets were once also popular. Henry VIII was a great popularizer of the walking stick or cane (the name given to elegant sticks made from exotic woods), and a manuscript of his time describes a stick that had perfume, tweezers, a knife, a file and a golden footrule among its many contents.

## STICK AND CROOK MAKING TODAY

The craft of stick and crook making is popular today, although most stick-makers are hobbyists rather than commercial manufacturers. The British Stickmakers Guild (www.your-adviser.com/bsg), founded in 1984, counts both professional and amateur stick-makers and collectors among its members, and many regional stick-making groups also exist. Stick-making competitions are held at a number of country shows.

*Making*

*Sussex Trugs*

## SUSSEX TRUGS

A Sussex trug is a shallow oblong basket, made from strips of willow, with a hooped handle attached halfway along the long sides. Trugs are used chiefly in the garden, for carrying vegetables, fruit or flowers. The invention of the Sussex trug (still made today and known as such) is attributed to Thomas Smith of Herstmonceux in East Sussex, who started making trugs in the 1820s. Smith sent one of his trugs to the Great Exhibition of 1851, where it apparently met with favour from Queen Victoria, who is said to have ordered several of them, leading to their increasing popularity among discerning gardeners. However, it is likely that trug-like baskets have a somewhat longer history than this – some suggest that they have been made since the 16th century.

The precise origin of their unusual name is not known. 'Trug' could simply be a variant of 'trough', while it has also been suggested that it derives from the Anglo-Saxon *trog*, meaning boat, and refers to its boat-like shape and overlapping 'clinker-built' construction. The word 'trug' was also used as the name for an old local measure for wheat, and early trug baskets were used for measuring grain.

## MAKING A SUSSEX TRUG

The first stage in trug making is shaping the rim, and then the handle (a hoop which completely encircles the trug to give it strength). The rim and handle are traditionally made from coppiced sweet chestnut or hazel: rods of around 2.5 centimetres (1 inch) in diameter are split in half and the inner surface is smoothed, while the bark is left intact on the outer surface. The lengths are then steamed to make them pliable, and bent around a jig or former to form a rectangular rim with rounded corners (the ends being secured with flat-headed copper nails) which is left to cool and set. The hooped handle is made in the same way, and the framework for the trug is created by attaching the handle to the rim at right angles, halfway along the long sides.

The boards which form the body of the trug are cut from willow, traditionally cleft with an axe-like tool called a froe, but now often machine-cut. The boards are thin, only a few millimetres thick, and are shaved smooth with a drawknife while held on a shaving-horse. They are then finished to suit their position in the completed trug – the central board is longest and has almost straight ends, while the boards on either side of it are shorter and have increasingly tapered ends. The boards are then either steamed or soaked in water, again to make them pliable, and bent inside the rim. The central board is the first to be inserted into the frame created by the rim and the handle. It is secured to the rim and handle by being nailed to them from the inside. The rest of the boards are then added, each one overlapping the last, to complete the body of the basket. Finally, small blocks of wood are often fitted to act as 'feet'.

## CONTINUING POPULARITY

Sussex trugs are still popular, and while cheaper imported (and even plastic) versions are widely available, a number of traditional trug-makers continue to make them by hand in Sussex. While more expensive to buy, for the time being handcrafted traditional trugs still have an important place in many gardens, enjoyed for their usefulness, durability and pleasing design.

# Making Baskets

## BASKET MAKING

Basket making is the craft of making containers by interlacing pliable strips of wood or other vegetable fibres using a technique similar to weaving. It is one of the oldest crafts, and examples of it have been found in Iraq that are thought to date to 5000 BC.

## HISTORY

An ancient craft, basket making reached its peak in Britain in the 19th century with the increased demand for baskets for the storage and carriage of goods. In the census of 1891, there were 14,000 basket-makers in England, working in both towns and rural areas. However, the craft soon went into decline, partly because of the importation of baskets and partly because of a transition from basketwork containers to cardboard boxes and paper sacks, and later, from the 1960s onwards, plastic containers. Historically, baskets were practical items, designed for their usefulness rather than their aesthetic qualities, and hundreds of different types of basket were made, all of which were light in weight but strong and durable. Baskets were used to store and move produce, to carry peat and logs, or to catch fish. Basketwork techniques were also used in hurdle making and in wattle-and-daub buildings (on which there are separate sections elsewhere in this book, on p9 and p230 respectively). Traditional basket-makers still work today, and while their products are often bought more for their decorative nature than for their practical applications, the recent trend for sustainable rather than plastic packaging has resulted in an increase in their commercial use.

## THE RAW MATERIAL

*Baskets are made either of rushes, splinters or willow, which last are, according to their growth, called osiers or sallows. They thrive best in moist places; and the proprietors of such marsh lands generally let out what they call the willow-beds to persons who cut them at certain seasons, and prepare them for basket-makers. To form an osier-bed, the land should be divided into plots of six, eight or ten feet broad, by narrow ditches, and if there is a power of keeping water in these cuts, at pleasure, by means of a sluice, it is highly advantageous in many seasons ... When the osiers are cut down, those that are intended for white-work, such as baskets used in washing, are to be stripped of their bark or rinds while green. This is done by means of a sharp instrument fixed into a firm block: the osiers are passed over this, and stripped of their covering with great velocity. They are then dried and put in bundles for sale.*

John Souter, *The Book of English Trades* (1818)

*Traditional willow basket making, Willows and Wetlands Visitor Centre, 2007*
© *Neil McAllister / Alamy*

In Britain, willow is the traditional material used in basket making. The willow, known as osier or basket willow, was once grown in plantations throughout Britain, on any suitable land (it grows best in a rich soil with a high water table), but most osier cultivation is now limited to Somerset. The osiers are cut as annual coppice shoots, which grow up each year from permanent 'stools'. Most of the harvesting takes place in winter, the rods traditionally being cut by hand with a reaping hook, with a second crop taken in spring.

Basket-makers use three types of rod: white, buff and brown. White rods have their bark removed – a job traditionally done manually by individually drawing each stem through a hand-brake, a simple tool consisting of two pieces of metal set close together to form a V-shape. Peeling is best done when the sap is rising, so spring-cut osiers are the easiest to peel, while winter-cut rods are kept alive by standing them in ditches until they are stripped in spring. Buff rods are also peeled, but first they are boiled in water. As they are boiled, the tannin in the bark stains the rods to their 'buff' colour. Brown rods have the bark left on. Before they are stored, the osiers are dried, to prevent mildew.

Large quantities of willow are now imported, but some basket-makers continue to grow or harvest their own rods.

## MAKING A BASKET

*So far as it is practicable to describe the manipulations without a series of illustrative figures ... A common English mode is, to begin by laying three stout ozier-rods on the floor, parallel and in contact, and three others above them at right angles, all six being cut to a length a little exceeding the diameter of the basket. The basket-maker now puts his foot on the centre of intersection of the six rods, and interweaves smaller rods around and among them in a spiral form, opening the six rods from time to time, so that ultimately they stand equidistant, like the spokes of a wheel. The weaving being carried on to the full diameter of the bottom, the latter is now turned upside down, and, the points of the radiating ribs being cut off, a willow rod is inserted on each side of each rib, and turned upwards. These upright rods become a warp, into which smaller rods can be woven to form the side of the basket. The upper ends of the rods are finally brought down and plaited into a sort of rim or edge, and a handle is added if necessary.*

*The Penny Magazine* (November 1842)

The description above refers to one of the common methods of making a basket. Three types of rod are needed: stout rods for the 'slath', or base, also called bottom sticks; strong but pliable rods for the side stakes; and rods known as weavers, which do the weaving. Once the rods are sorted, they are soaked in water to make them pliable, then the slath is started. Rather than placing a foot on the intersection of the first six rods, it is common to cut slits in three of them and poke the others through these slits to form a cross.

The most common weave for working the base is called 'pairing'. One method of achieving this is to insert the sharpened ends of two weavers into the split in your base cross. For the first two or three 'rounds', the weavers bind the cross together without separating the bottom sticks, then they are woven in between them, creating the spokes of a wheel as described above. When the base is complete, the side stakes are added

– the simplest method of adding side stakes is to use a bodkin to insert a side stake in either end of each of the bottom sticks. Once inserted, the side stakes are temporarily held in place with a hooped rod.

The basket is then ready for the 'upsett', the name given to the next stage, which is critical in determining the final shape of the basket. For this a weave called 'waling' is used. Fairly strong weavers are used, almost as thick as the side stakes, and these are added by 'slyping' the ends (slicing the end of the weaver to create a point) and pushing them into the weave. After a few rounds of waling, a choice of weaves can be used to complete the sides of the basket – two of the commonest forms are known as 'slewing' and 'randing' – until the top of the basket is reached, and a border completes the work. The simplest border is a 'track' border, where the top of each side stake is bent over, and woven through the third or fourth stake to its right.

*Right. Randing*
*Middle right. Slewing*
*Far right. Waling*
© *The Willows and Wetlands*
*Visitor Centre*

The basket-maker uses few tools, and these have changed little over the centuries. Among those most used are: a bodkin for separating the weave to add a new rod; secateurs or sharp shears for cutting; a sharp knife for cutting and trimming; and a beater or rapping iron to tap down each row of weave and keep it tight.

## LEARNING MORE

The Basketmakers' Association (www.basketassoc.org), formed in 1975, works to promote knowledge of basket making, and its website includes a list of some of the many short courses available on the craft. A number of books and manuals are available which show the different weaving techniques and the variety of items that can be made. The Willows and Wetlands Visitor Centre (www.englishwillowbaskets.co.uk) near Taunton in Somerset combines a willow and basket museum with the commercial production of everything from dolls' cradles to willow coffins.

# CHARCOAL BURNING

Charcoal burning is an ancient woodland craft. Charcoal is made by the controlled burning of wood, using insufficient air for rapid or complete combustion. The charcoal thus produced was used primarily as fuel, particularly in medieval and early modern iron furnaces, as it burns with intense heat and no smoke.

## THE WOOD COLLIER'S CRAFT

*The wood is charred in the following manner. It is piled first into heaps of a spherical form, and covered with leaves and dirt. The fire is applied to the wood, at the top, and when it has been sufficiently ignited, the pit is covered in; but to support combustion, several air holes are left near the ground. The colliers are obliged to watch the pit night and day, lest, by the caving in of the dirt, too much air be admitted, and the wood thereby be consumed to ashes. When the wood has been reduced to charcoal, the fire is partially extinguished by closing the air-holes. The coals are drawn from the pit with an iron-toothed rake, and while this is being performed, the dust mingles with them, and smothers the fire which may remain.*

Edward Hazen, *The Panorama of Professions and Trades* (1836)

The craft of charcoal burner, or wood collier, changed little over many centuries. A sense of mystery often surrounded the colliers themselves, as they were often solitary, living where they worked in temporary huts in the wood, the huts being constructed from poles and turf sods. The essence of charcoal burning is to burn wood in a very controlled way, with very little air, in order to produce as much carbon as possible with the minimum amount of ash. To do this, the collier first constructed a chimney, formed around a tripod of wood. Then lengths of wood were placed around this, forming a widening circle on the ground, and further lengths were placed in tiers on the top of this stack, giving it a dome-like profile.

When the construction was complete – after it had reached around 7 metres (23 feet) in circumference – most of the air was excluded by covering it with turf or soil. To start the burning, red-hot charcoal was dropped down the chimney. The top of the stack was then sealed. The burning process took several days, with the burner checking the stack every couple of hours, as any cracks or gaps in the covering of turf or soil needed to be repaired immediately, or all the wood would simply burn to ash.

*Charcoal burning, New Forest, c.1910s*
*© 2005 Credit:Topfoto TopFoto.co.uk*

When burning was completed, the stack was opened, with buckets of water on hand in case the fire flared up and the charcoal re-ignited. The charcoal could then be sorted and bagged for sale, primarily for smelting and glassmaking, while charcoal from alder wood was used in the manufacture of gunpowder.

## SMALL-SCALE CHARCOAL BURNING

There are a number of methods for the production of charcoal on a very small scale. One involves digging a trench: once the trench is complete, it is filled with wood, which is then set alight. When the fire has definitely caught, a sheet of corrugated iron is placed over the top of it, and earth is quickly shovelled on top of that. Care must be taken that the fire doesn't spread outside the pit. Several days later, when everything is cool, the trench is opened up, and it is hoped that charcoal will be found inside.

Another method, which again needs minimal supervision, employs a steel drum. One end of the drum is removed, while several holes are made in the other end. The drum is then used as an improvised kiln: the end with the holes is placed on top of some bricks, a fire is started inside the drum, and logs are piled onto this fire. To control the burn and create charcoal, a lid is placed on the open end, and soil is laid on this and piled up around the base of the drum.

## NOT QUITE UP IN SMOKE

In the 17th century charcoal was the major product of many coppiced woodlands, but the craft dwindled, particularly from the 18th century onwards, when a process for smelting iron with coke (produced from coal) was introduced. Some traditional charcoal burners were still working in the first half of the 20th century, but their numbers were small, and the craft all but died. However, there has been a revival in charcoal burning in recent years, as part of sustainable woodland management and to cater for the growing demand for environmentally sensitive barbecue charcoal – a welcome alternative to imported charcoal, which is often produced from endangered tropical forests. A number of associations, including local wildlife trusts and the Forestry Commission, have supported charcoal-burning projects, and traditional charcoal-burning demonstrations are offered at a number of sites (the details of many of these can be found by searching online).

# Making Clay and Briar Pipes

## PIPES

Pipes consist of a narrow tube with a bowl at one end – tobacco is burned in the bowl, and smoke is drawn along the tube and into the mouth. The tobacco plant is native to South America, but by 1500 BC it was being smoked in pipes in North America. It did not reach Britain until the Elizabethan period, and then it was initially smoked in small silver pipes, as befitted its status as a luxury good available only to the wealthy. Soon the tobacco plant was cultivated in Europe too, making it more abundant and therefore less expensive. Cheaper pipes were needed to match this, and clay-pipe making began.

Early attempts were made to curb tobacco smoking: James I wrote a pamphlet, 'A Counterblaste to Tobacco' (1604) – describing it as 'a custom loathsome to the eye', 'hateful to the nose', 'harmful to the brain' and 'dangerous to the lungs' – and also imposed a tobacco tax, but this did little to limit the growing popularity of pipe smoking.

## ELIZABETHAN BAD HABITS

*Smoking-pipes are of a great variety of kinds. The simplest, and one of the most esteemed, is the clay-pipe. These are formed in moulds, the hollow in the tube being made by running up a wire; the pipes are then dried and baked in a furnace moderately heated.*

*The Popular Encyclopedia* (1837)

Clay pipes were first made in potteries which also made other items, but demand was such that clay-pipe making eventually became a separate craft, well established by the mid-17th century. By the late 1600s, almost every town in England had its own pipe-maker, as did many large villages, and millions of pipes were produced. Early pipes are notable for their small bowls, but over time these gradually increased in size. They were also relatively plain, although decorated pipes – made by the larger manufacturers and with elaborate patterns adorning the outside of the bowls – were popular by the mid-1800s.

Clay pipes were fragile, and pipe-makers were kept busy as the pipes they made soon cracked, were thrown away and a replacement was sought. Clay pipes with a very long curving stem, known as 'yards of clay' or 'churchwardens', were popular with the upper classes (the length of the stem allowed the smoker to lean the bowl, in his hand, on the arm of his chair, while a small nub of clay on the bottom of the bowl prevented the chair arm from burning), while the poorer classes smoked pipes with a shorter stem. Fragile clay pipes were progressively replaced by wooden pipes, the briar pipe being the wooden pipe of choice, and competition from these, and from cigars and cigarettes, sent the craft of clay-pipe making into a sharp decline at the end of the 19th century.

## BRIAR PIPES

*In the dim light of the lamp I saw him sitting there, an old briar pipe between his lips, his eyes fixed vacantly upon the corner of the ceiling, the blue smoke curling up from him, silent, motionless, with the light shining upon his strong-set aquiline features.*

Arthur Conan Doyle, 'The Man with the Twisted Lip' (1891)

Sherlock Holmes is one of the most famous of pipe-smokers (fictional or otherwise). He did not limit himself to his 'old briar pipe' (in 'A Case of Identity' he smoked an 'old and oily clay pipe'), but by the late 19th century many other pipe-smokers did. Briar-pipe making is generally said to have begun in France in around 1840. The pipes (bowl and stem in one piece, with the mouthpiece added later) are, somewhat confusingly, carved from the seasoned root of the tree heath (*Erica arborea*) and not from the briar. Their name comes from the word 'bruyère', the French name for this shrub. The tree heath only matures sufficiently for pipe making in the

Mediterranean, and its roots were imported to Britain when this method of pipe making became popular. Traditionally hand-turned, but increasingly machine-made, briar pipes are still made today for a dwindling number of pipe-smokers – as, on a very small scale, are clay pipes, their use primarily limited to historical re-enactments.

*Making Bobbins*

## BOBBINS

Bobbins are vital in the craft of making bobbin lace, also known as bone lace or pillow lace (a craft described on p334). They are essentially thin pencils of bone or wood, around which the lace-making thread is wound. They fulfil several purposes: storing the thread; acting as handles to move the thread around; and acting as weights to keep the thread in tension. Many early bobbins were made from turned bone (some think that this led to the term 'bone lace', but the derivation is uncertain), while hardwood is the other traditional material used in bobbin making. Metals such as brass and pewter were also used, although rarely. Bobbin-lace making requires the use of dozens of bobbins. It became popular at the end of the 16th century, and from that time onwards specialist bobbin-makers, working by hand with a lathe and often adorning their bobbins with intricate decoration, began to supply the lace-makers' needs.

## BOBBINS AND SPANGLES

Many bobbins, both bone and wood, are fitted with a 'spangle', a ring of coloured beads or other ornaments that gives the bobbin extra weight, and helps it to remain steady against the pillow on which bobbin lace is worked. Honiton bobbins are one exception – the 'lace sticks' used for working Honiton lace being pointed and light and without a spangle. 'Mother and babe' is the name given to bobbins which have a hollowed-out shank, in which either a miniature bobbin or glass or wooden beads are visible.

In the past, bone bobbins (which were more expensive than wood, but lasted longer) often carried inscriptions, created by drilling small dots to form the letters, the dots then being filled with coloured pigment. Some inscriptions were of a religious nature, or celebrated births or anniversaries or love. Somewhat darker inscriptions were put on bone bobbins now known as 'hanging bobbins'. Commemorating executions by hanging, these were inscribed with the name of the unfortunate criminal, the word 'hung' and the year, and at one time seem to have been popular souvenirs in Bedfordshire. One surviving example of a hanging bobbin is that relating to Joseph Castle, hanged in public in 1860 for the murder of his wife. Legend has it that his wife's friends held a ball or party after his death, and presented each guest with a bobbin as a memento.

## BOBBINS TODAY

A decline in traditional bobbin making matched the decline in the craft these tools were specially made for, but while machine-turned and plastic bobbins are now commonly used by lace-makers, a number of specialist bobbin-turners still make traditional bobbins, in wood and bone, and hand-painted bobbins are also available. Because of the variety and artistry exhibited, bobbins are also popular with collectors, who may or may not be lace-makers themselves.

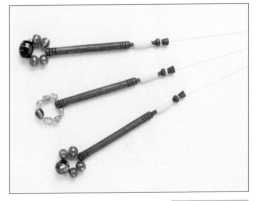

*Bobbins with spangles*
© *Dorling Kindersley*

*Making Paper*

## MAKING PAPER

The word 'paper' is ultimately derived from 'papyrus', the plant used by the ancient Egyptians to make writing media. In simple terms, making paper involves pulping suitable fibres in water, and then draining the liquid from the resulting mixture while it lies flat.

## RAGS TO RICHES

The papyrus used by the Egyptians was not, in fact, true paper in the modern sense – it was made by weaving together layers of slices from the pithy stem of the papyrus plant, before pressing, drying and finishing. However, as a portable writing surface, lighter and easier to write on than clay tablets, it represented a step on the road to the production of what could be argued to be the most important product in recent human history. Chinese tradition has it that true paper was invented by a court official at the beginning of the second century AD – although there are indications that paper was being used in China long before then. The fibres for this early paper came from a variety of sources, including the paper mulberry, rags and hemp. Elsewhere in the world, other writing media were being made from tree bark, woven bamboo and leaves.

By the 8th century, the skills required to manufacture paper had spread from China to the Middle East. The first true paper used in Europe was imported from the Middle East, and for some centuries the city of Damascus was an important supplier. Eventually the techniques of paper manufacture were brought to Europe via North Africa and Spain by the

Moors. Prior to this, monastic manuscripts and earlier Hebrew scrolls were written on parchment, made by separating and stretching layers of animal hide, or the more expensive and thicker vellum, made from whole skins.

When paper began to be made by hand in Europe, the main source of fibre was rags – from linen or hemp fabric, often from old clothes. Parchment and vellum remained the materials of choice for monastic handwritten texts but, with the growth of printing, demand for rag paper grew rapidly. Rags were collected and sold to paper-makers, and bones were also needed to make 'size' for finishing the paper surface to prepare it to receive ink – the beginnings of the rag-and-bone trade.

The earliest surviving reference to a paper mill in Britain, that belonging to John Tate in Hertford, appeared in a book printed by Wynken de Worde in around 1495:

> *And also of your charyte call to remembraunce*
> *The soule of William Caxton first printer of this boke*
> *In laten tonge at Coleyn himself to auance*
> *That euery well disposyd man may thereon loke*
> *And John Tate the yonger joye mote he broke*
> *Whiche late hathe in Englond doo make this paper thynne*
> *That now in our Englyssh this boke is printed inne.*

From the 'Prohemium' of John Trevisa's translation of
*Bartholomeus de Proprietatibus Rerum* (c.1495)

Once the rags had been collected, they were mashed with water, by foot, in stamping mills. The resulting slurry of water and fibres was then lifted out on a 'deckle', a mesh screen with a wooden frame. The deckle was carefully shaken and tilted to evenly distribute the fibre, and the water then drained through the mesh, leaving a rough, damp sheet of paper. This sheet was then pressed in a stack with others, interleaved with felt. Finally, the sheet would be dried and possibly pressed further, before sizing – coating with a solution of gelatine or similar to prepare the surface to receive ink.

The Industrial Revolution brought with it the steady mechanization of the paper mills. The rag-engine was introduced at the end of the 17th century for pulping rags, and the methods for weaving the wire mesh of the deckle were improved, removing the 'laid lines' that its wires had previously left in the finished paper. However, the major change in paper manufacture was driven by the lack of suitable white rags to fuel increasing demand at the turn of the 19th century. This led to improvements in bleaching and, most significantly, the development of methods for extracting fibres from wood pulp – first by mechanical, and later by chemical, means.

The whole process is, of course, now entirely mechanized. During the 19th century deckles, producing one sheet at a time, were replaced by mesh conveyors on which huge rolls of paper could be produced, rolled flat and then artificially dried before cutting. However, a small demand for high-quality, hand-made paper has remained and, in recent decades, there has been a growth in the small-scale craft production of paper using a variety of sources for pulp – including recycled paper, hemp and sheep droppings (the idea being that the sheep's digestive system separates and breaks down the grass fibres naturally).

*Using a deckle*
© *Napier University,*
*Department of PMPC*
*Licensor www.scran.ac.uk*

## HOME-MADE PAPER

If you would like to make paper at home, you can now buy kits which include all the necessary equipment. However, if you are of a more adventurous nature, paper can be made using a selection of readily available household items. This description outlines the basics, so don't expect anything other than a very rustic outcome to start with. Some experimentation and adaptation of the equipment and ingredients will be required to produce something of a realistically usable quality.

The first stage involves making your pulp, or fibre soup, from your chosen source. It is probably best to carry out initial experiments using old scrap paper – printed newspaper works well, but the ink will result in a very grey finished product. If you are using plant fibres, keep your cut plants damp and store them until they begin to rot before you go on to the next stage. Add your material to a large pan of water and boil it for several hours to break it down further. If necessary, the resulting pulp should then be ground down using a pestle and mortar, or mallet and slab (chop up any longer fibres with scissors or shears). The more work you put into the pulp, the finer the resulting paper.

The deckle can be made by attaching a sheet of perforated zinc to a wooden frame, or by stretching mesh fabric (such as net curtaining) over it. Dissolve your pulp in warm water in a suitably large container (you need to be able to lay the deckle flat in it) – the exact consistency will require experimentation. Dip the deckle into your mixture, slosh it around gently and lift it out, continuing to move it to distribute the pulp evenly as the water drains through the mesh. Once the water has stopped dripping through, turn out your sheet onto an old flat blanket, or preferably a sheet of felt. Several sheets can be stacked, interleaved with blankets or felt, and then pressed using boards and a heavy weight. Finally, the sheets should be hung up separately to dry.

## FIND OUT MORE

If you would like to find out more about the history of paper making, or learn the subtleties of the craft, the British Association of Paper Historians (www.baph.org.uk) is a good starting point. Specialist equipment for paper making can be obtained from a number of craft shops and suppliers.

*Making Quill Pens*

## QUILL PENS

Before the advent of mass-produced fountain pens and the modern biro, writing with ink required the use of an implement that could be repeatedly dipped into a reservoir of this liquid before applying it to the writing surface. The process of writing was laborious – only a few marks could be made after each dip. Writing implements can be made from a range of items, but for many centuries they were most commonly made from reeds or from quills (the stems of bird feathers). The technique for cutting a quill to make a pen was once taught in schools.

## HISTORICAL WRITINGS

Mark making, drawing, painting and, later, writing using liquid 'ink' have been carried out for millennia. At its most basic, a finger or stick could be dipped into the writing medium. Later, chewed-stick or animal-hair brushes were made. As writing developed, at first in the ancient civilizations of the Middle East, the method of mark making employed was linked to the availability and choice of writing surface. The earliest surviving examples of writing are scratched into the surface of clay tablets. By the first millennium BC, fine brushes were being used for writing in China and the Egyptians were writing on papyrus 'paper' using reed pens.

When the European monks of the early Middle Ages began to produce and copy their handwritten illuminated manuscripts, they continued to use the established techniques for cutting nibs in reed pens. However, following the fall of the Roman Empire, reeds from Egypt were not always available, so the hollow stems of feathers began to be used as an alternative. The method of cutting and making a pen was similar for both.

Quills eventually became the writing implement of choice, and remained so for many centuries. Geese were farmed throughout Europe, providing a steady supply of feathers – although feathers from a number of different birds could be used, including crows, whose feathers were apparently particularly suitable for making fine lines. Quill pens required

*Stripping the barbs for a quill pen*
© *Dorling Kindersley*

regular trimming to maintain the nib and had a useful lifetime of only a few days' writing. At its peak, demand for quills went into tens, or even hundreds, of millions every year in Britain alone.

The steel-tipped pen didn't become widely available until the 19th century, although there is evidence to suggest that metal pen-nibs were being used by some long before this. A bronze-nibbed pen has been found in the ruins of Pompeii. The quality of metal nibs improved during the Victorian era, bringing about a decline in the use of quills, and making quill pens was no longer widely taught in schools. By the beginning of the 20th century practical, mass-produced fountain pens (which removed the need to keep dipping into the inkwell) gained rapidly in popularity and the quill pen disappeared from use.

## DIP INTO THE CRAFT

Despite the impracticalities involved in using quill pens, the flexibility and adaptability of the hand-cut nib allow for subtleties of style and changes in line thickness by adjusting pressure that cannot be replicated using modern pens.

To make a quill pen, you will first need to obtain a suitable feather. Historically, the five outer wing feathers of a goose (or swan if you were very privileged) were used. Those from the left wing curve most comfortably for a right-handed writer, and vice versa. The quills were dried and hardened before use – a range of methods were used, including burying them in hot sand. In the absence of a large supply of goose feathers, the techniques can be practised using a plastic drinking straw.

The cuts can be made using a sharp penknife (the purpose for which such a tool was originally intended), taking care at every stage to keep your fingers away from the blade and always to cut away from your body. The quill is less likely to break during cutting if the end is first softened by dipping it into boiling water.

Before cutting the nib, shorten the feather to a comfortable length and strip away the barbs that would otherwise rest uncomfortably against your hand as you write. You may also wish to trim the plume further, or even remove it completely. Although writers are often depicted holding a magnificent plume, in practice the novelty of being tickled while writing probably soon wore off. Cut away the end of the quill (now the barrel of your pen) at a shallow acute angle to the line of its length. Then remove any material from the inside. Make a slit, about 1 centimetre (0.4 inch) in length, in the top of the barrel (the opposite side to the point formed by the first cut), by placing the point of the knife inside the barrel and gently levering it upwards until a split forms. Then turn the barrel over and cut a scoop from what will become its underside, starting approximately three times the length of the slit in from the outer end of the slit, removing about half of the diameter of the tube, and continuing out to the tip. Finally, shape the nib from each side in turn, trimming it to make the desired width at the point.

Before writing with the pen, you may need to lightly scrape the underside to make it flat, rather than concave. The nib can be further improved by thinning the end – carefully scrape the top (the outside), working towards the tip. The nib will need to be regularly scraped and trimmed during its short life to preserve the quality of writing.

## PUTTING PEN TO PAPER

Making your pen is only the beginning. A good starting point for ideas on how to use it to best effect might be the Calligraphy and Lettering Arts Society (www.clas.co.uk).

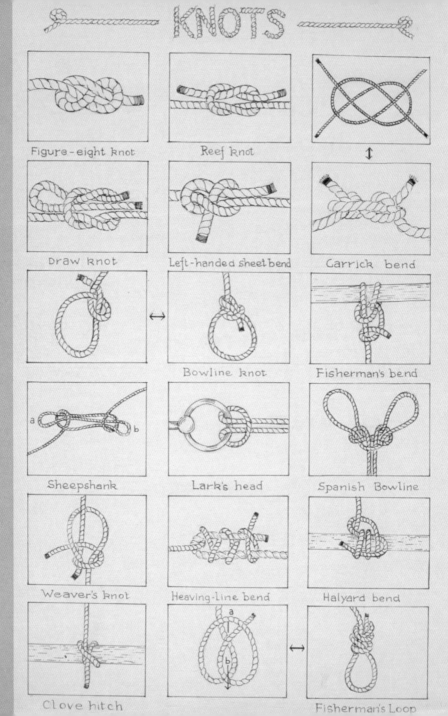

# KNOTS

Figure-eight knot

Reef knot

↕

Draw knot

Left-handed sheet bend

Carrick bend

↔

Bowline knot

Fisherman's bend

a Sheepshank b

Lark's head

Spanish Bowline

Weaver's knot

Heaving-line bend

Halyard bend

Clove hitch

a b ↔

Fisherman's Loop

*Tying Knots*

## KNOTS

Knots are formed by interlacing a cord or cords, twisting the ends around
each other to form loops, then pulling the loops tight. Humans have
tied knots since prehistoric times, and while they are predominantly a
practical invention, they have also been used for decoration in jewellery
designs and in art.

## A KNOTTY PROBLEM

*The uses of knots are infinite; in the commonest occasions of life, one or two simple
knots are indispensable; in building, mining and almost every land occupation, knots
of curious form are employed; while on shipboard, knots may be almost numbered by
the dozen, and each is appropriated to a specific duty.*

Chambers's Encyclopaedia (1863)

While specific hobbies and interests have to some extent kept the craft
of knot tying alive (sailing enthusiasts, for example, will know many
sailing knots, and rock climbers will know the knots they need to tie),
many people no longer know how to tie more than one or two knots. The
problem for the beginner is that there are thousands of knots, and the
true art of knot tying involves not only knowing the knot, but knowing
the appropriate use for it.

## KNOT LORE

Since at least medieval times, the true-love's knot (or true-lover's knot) has been a symbol of true love – the interlaced cords in the knot representing the interwoven affection of two people. It is a complicated and ornamental knot, often made of two intertwined loops or a bow with two loops, although it exists in several forms.

*The Endless Knot of Love, engraving, c.1790*
*© Mary Evans Picture Library / Alamy*

*Together fast I tie the garters twain,*
*And while I knit the knot repeat this strain:*
*Three times a true-love's knot I tie secure,*
*Firm be the knot, firm may his love endure!*
John Gay, 'The Pastoral' (1714)

Knots were also once used for love divination. A young woman would tie knots in her garter (all the while speaking an incantation) and place it under her pillow or around the bedpost before going to sleep. It was said that she would then dream of her future husband. The tying and untying of knots also formed part of other magical ceremonies. It was said that sorcerers could control the wind with three knots tied in a rope, and that the action of a spell recited while a knot was tied would come about when the knot was undone.

## ESSENTIAL KNOTS

There is no definitive list of essential knots, and different knot experts will recommend different knots as the best to learn. The knots described below are just some of the most useful. All you need in order to learn how to tie these knots is a couple of lengths of rope, string or cord (plus a handy pole for the clove hitch), and some patience.

## Bowline

The bowline is a very useful knot. It makes a single fixed loop which is reasonably secure. It is also fairly easy to tie and untie, so is a good place to start. It has uses in yachting, and a variant, the double bowline, is commonly employed by climbers (alternatively, climbers use a bowline followed by a 'stopper' knot to make a truly secure loop).

The tying of this knot is often described in terms of rabbits and trees, and those with a scouting or guiding past will probably remember learning it that way ('the rabbit comes out of the hole, round the tree ...'). These instructions should get you there too:

1 *Make a small loop near one end of the rope, with the longer end crossing over the shorter end*
2 *Bring the long end of the rope up through the loop, around the back of the short end, and back down through the original small loop*
3 *Pull the knot tight*

## Sheepshank

The sheepshank is used to shorten a rope temporarily (without resorting to cutting it). It can also be used to take up the slack in a rope that is already attached at both ends, or to help to protect a damaged section of rope. There are two methods of making a sheepshank.

First Method:

1 *Arrange the middle section of a rope into the shape of the letter Z*
2 *Close up the Z so that the rope is lying in three parallel lines, with outward-facing U-shaped bends at each end*
3 *Twist the bottom rope to create a simple loop (or 'crossing turn') below the topmost U-shaped bend, with the free end of the rope passing behind the horizontal part, then turn the loop 90° to the U-shaped bend so the righthand side of the loop turns toward the back, and push that U-shaped bend through it*
4 *Pull the rope to make sure the knot is tight*
5 *Repeat at the other end with the top rope*

Alternatively:

1   *Make three simple loops in the middle section of a rope, ensuring that in each case the leading end of the rope (the left) is on top of the trailing end (the right)*
2   *Turn each of the two outer loops 90° so the righthand side of the loop turns towards the back, then put your hands through the two outer loops from the outside*
3   *Hold on to either side of the middle loop, and pull gently while keeping some tension on the rest of the rope*
4   *The middle loop should now be pulled through the two outer loops. To tighten the sheepshank, pull on the free ends of the rope*

## Clove hitch

This is a quick-to-make, temporary knot (as used by cowboys in a hurry to tether their horses). Because it will slip, it cannot be used as a permanent fastening without the addition of further knots.

1   *Put the rope behind the vertical pole, holding an end of the rope in each hand*
2   *Swap the ends of the rope from one hand to the other so that the rope crosses over itself in front of the pole, with the rope that ends in your left hand lying on top and the one that ends in your right lying underneath at the point at which they cross (in knot-making terms, this is called taking the 'working end' of the rope across the 'standing end')*
3   *Take the 'working end' (in this case, the rope in your left hand) and wrap it around the pole again, below the first loop. As you bring it round to the front of the pole, bring it behind the point at which the two ends cross and out to the left between the two loops*
4   *Pull on the two ends of the rope to tighten the knot*

## Sheet bend

This knot is used to join two pieces of rope together. It works well if the two pieces you are joining are of slightly different thicknesses, but if they are very different you can make the knot more secure by turning it into a double sheet bend.

1   Bend the end of one rope back on itself (if one of the ropes is thicker, then use it here)
2   Hold this first rope so that the bend forms a loop, leaving the two ends parallel (not crossing them over)
3   Take the end of the second rope (this is the working end) and thread it up through the loop
4   Now take the working end behind the neck of the loop and up the other side, where you should bring it over the side of the loop, under itself and over the top of the loop
5   Hold your first rope again, so that you have both ends of its loop in your hand, then take the long end (or standing end) of the second rope in your other hand and pull gently but firmly to make the knot secure

To make a double sheet bend, follow the first four instructions above (so the knot is formed but not tightened), then pass the second (thinner) rope around the neck of the loop again (tucking it up under itself when you get back to the front) before pulling the knot tight.

## Reef knot

The reef knot is probably one of the best-known knots of all. Use it to tie superior parcels, and forget about granny knots (an inferior sort of knot, similar to the reef knot but unsymmetrical, and apt to slip or jam). Remember 'left over right, right over left' and you will always know how to tie a reef knot.

1   Place your string so that it lies under your parcel, then hold the ends up, one in each hand
2   Lay the string in your left hand over the string in your right hand, then pass it behind and up through the loop, as you would when you are tying shoelaces (this is the 'left over right' bit)
4   Next, cross the two ends over again, forming an X, but this time lay the string in your right hand over the string in your left. Then pass it behind and up through the new loop (this is the 'right over left' bit)
5   Pull the loose ends to tighten

## MORE KNOTS

A number of books and websites describe many more of the thousands of knots that exist. There is also an International Guild of Knot Tyers, whose website can be found at www.igkt.net. They produce a quarterly newsletter, 'Knotting Matters', and also host an online forum for knotty discussions.

# Navigating by the Stars

## NAVIGATING AT NIGHT WITHOUT A COMPASS

Before the introduction of the compass and long before the use of global positioning systems, man was able to navigate at night by using the stars. Through knowledge of the night sky, it is possible (on any clear night at least) to find the points of the compass, and with the addition of charts and an instrument such as a quadrant, sailors can also pinpoint their latitude. Modern technology has led to a decline in the craft of navigating by the stars, but such simple skills are still known to save lives, and can be enjoyable to learn for the most or least adventurous.

## ANCIENT MARINERS

*To the mariners of old these constellations were of essential importance. The polar star, in particular, was their great guide, when leaving sight of land they ventured to embark upon unknown seas. The magnetic compass has enabled the mariners of the present day to steer their course over the pathless ocean with unerring certainty, even in the darkest night; and astronomical science has furnished them with other means of determining their position on the earth's surface; yet the polar star may still be regarded as the great celestial compass of the northern half of the world.*
Robert Sullivan, *Geography Generalized* (1859)

For thousands of years it has been known that in the night sky of the northern hemisphere north is indicated by the Pole Star, or Polaris. (With a little celestial knowledge, it is nearly as easy – and obviously just as important – to find south in the southern hemisphere, as described below.)

The Pole Star travels in a tight circle above the north pole, and so remains a relatively fixed point in the sky, making it invaluable in navigational terms. Early navigators could also estimate how far north they were by the position of the Pole Star in the sky – the further north the higher it appears, the further south the lower, until you reach the equator and it disappears from view.

While this worked for very rough estimation, later seafarers needed not only to know where north was (and from that, where east, south and west were) but also to gain a more accurate idea of their position in latitude (ie angular distance from the equator). This was achieved by measuring the angle of the Pole Star above the horizon, then converting this to a latitude position.

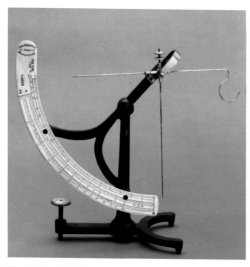

An instrument commonly employed for this was the quadrant – a quarter-circle, carved from wood, with the degrees from 0 to 90 marked around its curved edge, sights at each end of one straight edge and a plumb line hanging from the point where the two straight edges met. The sights were lined up on the Pole Star, and the plumb line hung down and indicated the angle of altitude. Christopher Columbus used a quadrant during his voyage to the New World in 1492, and the instrument later evolved into the sextant. The astrolabe performed the same function as the quadrant. Often made of brass, this was circular, with degrees marked around the edge. Both instruments were difficult to use, particularly on a swaying ship, and they were hopeless in thick fog. However, they were useful additional checks in ensuring the accuracy of a ship's course during the night.

*Quadrant*
© *National Museums Scotland Licensor*
*www.scran.ac.uk*

## STAR LIGHT, STAR BRIGHT

To learn the craft of celestial navigation on land, you need to practise identifying the necessary stars in the sky (initially this can be done with the help of a book and a torch in a suitably dark spot away from sources of light pollution). If you decide that you feel confident enough to have a go at navigating by the stars, be careful about stumbling around at night – don't try it near cliffs or on a night with no moon.

### Northern hemisphere

The Pole Star or North Star, which indicates north, is the final star in the constellation Ursa Minor (also known as the Little Bear or the Little Dipper). The key constellations you will need to learn in order to identify it in the night sky are Ursa Major (also known as the Plough, the Great Bear or the Big Dipper), and, for times when that is not visible, Cassiopeia. Ursa Minor lies between these two.

Ursa Major is often thought of as resembling a pot with a long handle. A simple way to find the Pole Star from this is to look at the side of the 'pot' opposite the handle. This side is made up of two stars. Imagine a line going through these two stars and extending beyond it for five times the distance between them. The end of this line should put you at or very near the Pole

*How to find the Pole Star using the Plough*
*© Robin Scagell / Galaxy*

Star (be warned, the Pole Star is not that bright, so you may overlook it at first, especially if there is any light pollution). If you prefer things to be more technical, the stars on this side of the pot are called Merak and Dubhe.

To find the Pole Star when Ursa Major is not visible, look for Cassiopeia. This constellation is shaped like a squashed letter W, and you can find Polaris by coming straight out of the first V of the W.

Once you know you are facing the Pole Star, you are also facing north.

## Southern hemisphere

To find south in the southern hemisphere is slightly more tricky as there is no one star to guide you. Instead, you need to find the Southern Cross, then two stars next to this called Rigil Kentaurus and Hadar (these are known as the pointers). Imagine a line that comes from between the pointers, and another line that extends from the long arm of the Southern Cross. The two imaginary lines will cross above south.

*How to find south
using the Southern
Cross*
© Robin Scagell / Galaxy

*Decorative Crafts*

# Making Corn Dollies and Harvest Knots

## STRAW CRAFT

Figures made from straw, known variously as kern dolls, kern babies, corn maidens or harvest queens, have long been associated with harvest customs. More recently known as corn dollies and harvest knots, these decorations are made by plaiting or tying straw into numerous designs, from the simpler 'countryman's favour' to much more elaborate designs such as the 'Marches fan'.

## MYSTERIOUS HISTORY

While it is known that harvest figures have been made for centuries throughout the British Isles, their exact function remains unclear. Large figures were sometimes triumphantly paraded on a pole when the last of the harvest was won, or sent to neighbouring farms to mock those who had not completed their work. Other, smaller figures were made from the final sheaf of the harvest, and were kept in the farmhouse or barn until they were replaced in the following year, or were used to decorate the church at the time of the harvest festival.

It is often said that the figures are a direct link to pagan festivities of corn spirits and fertility. Legend has it that either Ceres, the Roman goddess of agriculture and corn, or some other corn spirit would hide in the last corn left standing in the field, but had to be beaten back into the ground to keep it fertile for the next year. This might have been the basis for the tradition of weaving the last of the crop into dollies, with the corn spirit trapped inside the hollow spaces of the doll, ready to be ploughed back into the land in the following year, thus ensuring continued fertility and a good crop. Unfortunately for those who enjoy the colourful elements of such theories, they have been discredited by modern folklorists, and more research is needed before we can fully understand the true significance of these attractive ornaments.

It is known that simpler pieces, called harvest knots or countryman's favours, were given by young men to the women they were courting at harvest time, and were worn as brooches. The simplest of these is a lover's knot of three pieces of straw plaited together, with the ears of grain left on for decoration.

## LOST CRAFT REVIVED

The craft of corn-dolly making had all but died out in Britain by the early part of the 20th century, but was revived in the 1940s, 1950s and 1960s by organizations like the Women's Institute and individuals such as Minnie Lambeth, who wrote the first manuals to instruct new enthusiasts on mastering the techniques involved. It has been suggested that the term 'corn dolly' is of mid-20th-century origin.

Modern corn dollies and harvest knots are woven to almost any shape and design. Horseshoes, cornucopias, neck or sheaf dollies, drop dollies, fans and lover's knots are all popular, often decorated with blue or red ribbons. A corn dolly, once made, can last for fifty years if it is well cared for – and kept away from mice. Some regional designs exist, including the Norfolk lantern, the Essex terret, the Cambridgeshire handbell and the Okehampton mare.

## GOING ABOUT IT

*A degree of proficiency can be achieved quite quickly by some whilst others never can master the art.*

J E Manners, *Country Crafts Today* (1974)

Any straw can be employed to make corn dollies and harvest knots, but – while rye, oats, barley and even grass have been used – wheat is the most popular choice. Some straw-crafters bemoan modern wheat varieties and current farming practices, claiming that in combination they do not always produce suitable straw. The straw must be undamaged and of a good length between the wheat ear and the first joint, as this is the portion that is used. It must also be hollow. Wheat gathered by a combine harvester is generally unsuitable, as are the short, pithy varieties now often grown commercially. Among straw-crafters, preferred wheat types are Squareheads Master, Eclipse, Flamingo and Maris Widgeon.

To start work, trim the straw just above the top joint, and strip away the leaf sheaf to leave a clean stem. Choose a stem with a good ear if the design you are following requires it to be left on. Unless the straw has come straight from the field, you will need to make it workable by dampening it. Soak it briefly in water until it is pliable – the older the straw the longer this takes, but beware overwetting it, and don't wet more straw then you need, as straw left damp may become mildewed.

## A SIMPLE DOLLY

For a simple dolly, also known as a neck dolly or sheaf dolly, five straws are plaited to create a naturally spiralling shape with ears at one end. First a core is formed, fat in the middle and tapering at the ends. Tie together a bundle of around seven straws, using cotton or raffia, with their ears downwards, then add headless straws of graduating lengths to the bundle until the tapering core is formed.

When you are happy with the core, choose five good working straws for the weaving – headless, undamaged, of a good colour and of similar widths so the finished product will look neat. Tie these five, equally spaced around the bundle, just above the ears (which are now held upwards). Mentally number the straws from one to five, then carefully bend them downwards, so they stick out at right angles to the core.

Take straw one and lay it over straws two and three so that it lies between straws three and four. Turn the work clockwise through a quarter turn, and then lay straw three over one and four so that it lies between four and five. Another quarter turn clockwise, and take four over three and

Traditional English
corn dolly
*Matthew Ward © Dorling Kindersley*

five. Another turn, and take five over four and two. Another turn, and take five under and then over five to lie between one and three. Remembering the quarter turns, weave as follows: lay one over two and three, three over one and four, four over three and five, five over four and two, two over five and one. If a straw breaks, add a new one by sliding the thick end of a new straw over the broken end – remember that we need hollow straws.

This basic shape forms part of many designs, and is a good place to start. Although all the numbers seem daunting, they are easy to follow when you have the work in your hands. Should you feel concerned that you might be one who will never 'master the art' then it might be best to start with art straws, which can satisfactorily be used to create many corn-dolly shapes, and are a good way to practise. They are also good for the beginner because they do not need dampening. This means you can take a break, rather than working the piece from beginning to end in one go. Also, you cannot snap them.

*Making a corn dolly*
*© Paul Felix Photography / Alamy*

## DEVELOPING THE CRAFT

Members of the Guild of Straw Craftsmen (www.strawcraftsmen.co.uk) run courses, as do other experts, and City & Guilds Straw Work courses are available in some locations. There are a number of books, both in and out of print, which give detailed instructions on the craft of corn-dolly making, including *The Complete Book of Straw Craft and Straw Dollies: Techniques and Projects* (1987) by Doris Johnson and Alec Coker, and *Discovering Corn Dollies* (1974) by Minnie Lambeth.

Few people are in the enviable position of being able to grow their own straw, but an Internet search will locate a number of specialist shops that supply the raw materials for corn-dolly making, although many experts believe that hand-cutting your own straw is the best course of action.

Following negotiation (and payment), a local farmer will often allow you to cut your own straw, should you think the variety suitable. This is best done just before the crop is fully ripe, while it is still a little green. If cut in this state, it will still dry to the desired golden colour, but the grain will be less likely to drop when your decoration is finished. Beware cutting when the crop is too green though, as it might dry and wither.

# Making
## Bobbin Lace

## BOBBIN LACE

Bobbin lace, also known as pillow lace or sometimes bone lace, is made by
plaiting and twisting numerous threads, wound on bobbins (the making
of which is described on p306), around pins which are stuck into a pillow
(hence one of its alternative names). It developed in the mid-16th century
as a separate tradition to needlepoint lace (essentially a type of fine
embroidery, worked with a single needle and thread). Different styles of
lace developed in different countries and regions, and were often named
after the area in which they originated – for example, Honiton lace and
Bedfordshire lace in Britain, Mechlin lace from Belgium, and Lille lace
from France – but each style was made with the same basic techniques,
and using a pillow and bobbins.

## LACE MAKING

*Lace is not woven, and of course it requires in the operation neither warp nor woof.
It is made of silk, of thread, or cotton, which is wound on little bobbins made of bone
or ivory, about the thickness of a skewer ... The pattern to which the lace is made,
is drawn on paper or parchment, pricked with pin-holes, and then put on the pad
or cushion which the woman holds on her knees. All the ends of the thread are first
fastened together, and the Lace-Maker twists them variously over and under one
another round the pins, which are stuck into holes in the pattern: these pins they
remove from one part to another, as their work goes on; and by these means, are
produced the multiplicity of eyes, or openings, which give to lace the desired figures.*
John Souter, *The Book of English Trades* (1818)

The first stage in lace making is pricking out the pattern, traditionally into pieces of parchment. The pattern is then attached to a pillow, with pins stuck into the holes of the first part of the pattern. The pillows were traditionally stuffed very hard with straw to keep the pins in place. Each stitch involves two pairs of bobbins (depending on the size and design of the work being laced, many dozens of bobbins can be involved), which are manipulated to twist the thread around the pins to suit the design. When one part is finished, the pins are moved to the next part of the pattern; in this way a continuous length of lace can be produced.

## THE LACE-MAKERS

*Lace-making I do call a dead penny indeed; the poor women who live by it, look like walking spectres. I have been assured by a family who were all brought up to lace-making, that the whole of their diet consisted of potatoes and tea—that they never rose from their pillow even to take a meal ... and that by this close and ruinous application, they earned barely enough for this wretched supply of food, and just a Sundays' gown once in two years or so ... I do not, of course, recommend lace-making to eke out the income of the cottager's wife.*

Esther Copley, *Cottage Comforts* (1834)

Devonshire lace-
maker, 1878
© *Illustrated London News /*
*Mary Evans*

Although it originated in Nottingham in the late 18th century, machine-made lace did not take over from handmade bobbin lace until the late 19th century. Before this time, lace-makers (who were predominantly women) often worked together, not only for the companionship this brought, but also for reasons of economy – in the winter especially it was important that they could share light. The lace-makers often worked around candle stools – these held a candle at the centre, which was surrounded by condenser globes (glass globes filled with water, which acted as lenses and got the most from the candlelight). While lace making was a useful opportunity for women to earn money, the rewards were often poor – the more intricate and skilled the work, the better the remuneration, but also the longer it took to make.

## LACE SCHOOLS

The early to mid-19th century was the heyday of the lace schools, which developed from the charitable tradition of teaching poor girls how to make bobbin lace in order to augment the family income. Some reading and writing were also taught, but the children worked hardest on lace-making skills, and were often exploited. Once they had become proficient at lace making, their lace was sold, and while they did receive a small wage, they worked for very long hours, and were often severely punished if their work was not up to standard. Many lace-school children repeated 'tells' as they worked – chants which not only relieved the monotony of long hours at the lace pillow, but which also kept up the momentum of the work so that more lace was produced.

## LACE TODAY

The art of bobbin lace making is today most often practised by highly skilled hobbyists, who work with pillow and bobbins in the same way as the earlier lace-makers (although the straw pillow is now often replaced with a polystyrene cushion, and the bobbins are sometimes plastic). If you want to learn more about lace making, the Lace Guild (www.laceguild.demon.co.uk) is one place to start, and a number of lace-making courses are available.

# Tatting

## TATTING

Tatting is a kind of knotted lace. It is made by hand, originally using a small shuttle. The lace is created by a series of knots and loops, and was traditionally used in lace edging, such as that added to doilies, and in making collars.

## SHUTTLE TATTING

*The needlework called Tatting in England,* Frivolité *in French, and* Frivolitäten *in German, is a work which seems, from all accounts, to have been in favour several generations ago ... Tatting differs entirely from crochet, and is composed of stitches forming knots. It is intended as an imitation of point lace, and is especially used for trimming under-linen, on account of its strength. To make stitches or knots a small instrument is used, called a* shuttle. *This shuttle consists of two oval pieces, flat on one side and convex on the other, and is made of wood or ivory.*

Isabella Beeton, *Beeton's Book of Needlework* (1870)

The craft of tatting emerged in the early 19th century (perhaps as a development of knotting, a decorative craft popular in the 1700s, which also used a shuttle, although a larger one). Shuttles were originally made of wood or steel, although more decorative and expensive shuttles were carved from tortoiseshell or ivory.

The shuttle is normally less than 7.5 centimetres (3 inches) long. The tatter loads thread on to the shuttle, then wraps the thread around one hand and manipulates the shuttle with the other. The shuttle is woven in and out of the work, creating a series of knots and loops. Where the shuttle is fitted with a hook (used when joining elements of tatted work together), no other equipment is needed; if the shuttle has no hook, a separate crochet hook is used. Although tatting looks complicated to the uninitiated, it is really made up of only one type of knot. However, many experienced tatters advocate learning the craft from an expert rather than from a book.

## NEEDLE TATTING

*I have been much solicited for some time past to introduce the work [tatting] in England, but have delayed doing so until I could simplify the mode of working, and endeavour to render it suitable to the taste of the English lady: for I considered that the old system required more time in completion than the most elaborate design in crochet. To obviate the difficulties ... I have substituted a 'Netting Needle,' for the 'Shuttle.'*
Mlle Riego de la Branchardiere, *The Tatting Book* (1850)

Border made from tatting
© V & A Images, Victoria & Albert Museum

The art of tatting using a needle was introduced in the mid-19th century, and is considered by some to be an easier method of working. There is no shuttle to wind, and stitches are formed on the needle, giving them a uniform size. Modern tatting needles are long and blunt, and come in a variety of thicknesses to suit the thread being used.

## TATTING TODAY

After a decline in popularity in the mid-20th century, tatting is again a popular pastime, and early shuttles have become collectors' items. For more information on tatting you might want to contact the Ring of Tatters (www.ringoftatters.org.uk). Many tatting patterns can be found online.

*Smocking*

## SMOCKING

Smocking is a needlework technique in which a section of material is gathered into tight pleats that are held together with various ornamental stitches. This gives not only shape but also ornamentation to clothing, and a certain amount of elasticity. In Britain, smocking is mostly associated with the practical smocked overgarments once worn by rural workers.

## SMOCKS

Smocks were popular in the 18th century and the early part of the 19th, falling out of fashion by the late 1800s (although smocks were still worn by some into the 20th century). They were worn by a wide variety of workers, including shepherds, gardeners and stonemasons, although they are usually associated with farm workers.

A smock is an essentially practical garment, cut and stitched to a relatively simple pattern, with the addition of smocking adding shape to the finished garment. The most common kind of smock was the reversible smock, identically smocked on both back and front (and around the cuffs) and with no discernible front or back, while coat-type smocks (full length, and with buttons from top to bottom) and shirt-type smocks (with some buttons, but still pulled on over the head) were also worn. Smocks were usually made from heavyweight cotton or linen, and while they were primarily used as a form of overall, it is thought that many workers would have owned two, one of which was reserved for 'Sunday best', or for wearing on celebratory days. These smocks often had more elaborate stitching than the everyday versions, and it is thought that the wearing of these smocks outlasted the use of the simple overall type.

## HOW TO SMOCK

The first stage in smocking is to sew several rows of stitches across the area that is going to be gathered, leaving the end of the thread used in each row loose at one side of the material. These loose threads are then gently pulled to create evenly spaced gathers, before being secured by a knot or by tying them around a pin. Next, the gathers are held in place with various decorative stitches, one of the most popular being the honeycomb stitch. Finally, the threads which were used for gathering are pulled free, and the smocking is complete.

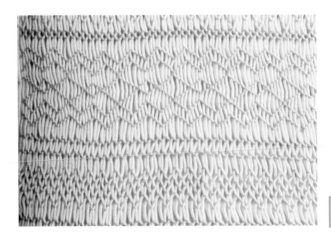

*Smocking stitches*
© *Jacqui Hurst / Alamy*

# *Sewing Samplers*

## SAMPLERS

A sampler is an embroidered panel displaying a variety of stitches.

## EARLY SAMPLERS

Samplers are thought to have been sewn since the 15th century. Early samplers were practical pieces sewn by women as a way of recording various stitches, which could be referred to later (early pattern books were rare and expensive). When a woman saw a new stitch or pattern that she liked, she would copy an example of it onto her sampler – an increasingly crowded piece of material, as cloth was expensive and no patch of it would have been left blank while there were more examples of stitches to be gathered. These samplers were treasured for the variety of stitches they displayed and the knowledge they preserved, and were often passed down through the generations.

## ALPHABETS AND SCRIPTURE

By the middle of the 17th century, samplers commonly included alphabets and borders, and often included the name of the maker and the date. Sewing was an important part of a girl's education (for girls of the wealthier classes sewing was a necessary accomplishment, while for poorer girls sewing might lead to employment – maids, for example, would be expected to be skilled at sewing). By the 18th century, samplers were made both at home and in sewing schools and Sunday schools. As well as decorative designs and motifs, they increasingly included quotations from scripture or pious verses, thereby combining moral education and reading and writing with the teaching of needlework skills. These samplers displayed skill, and proof of a girl's needleworking abilities, rather than acting as a record of stitches for constant reference.

## PLAIN SEWING

In the second half of the 19th century, there was a move away from decorative embroidered samplers to 'plain sewing' samplers, produced in schools throughout the country. These included practical rather than decorative needlework, showing darning, hemming or gathering, and perhaps some simple embroidery.

## SAMPLING SAMPLERS

Most surviving samplers are from the 19th century, and these, and more especially earlier examples, are now collectors' items. A number of museums have textile collections which include samplers, such as the Victoria and Albert Museum in London, which holds the earliest

*Jane Bostocke sampler, 1598*
*© V & A Images, Victoria & Albert Museum*

British dated sampler known to have survived. It was worked by Jane Bostocke in 1598, and seems to show the transition from the early practical samplers to the later ones which displayed the sewer's skill, and includes an inscription which commemorates the birth of a child.

Samplers are still stitched today, but as purely decorative items. Some needleworkers reproduce historic samplers, while others create modern designs. Many patterns are available, both in books and online.

# Making Pomanders and Pot Pourri

## POMANDERS AND POT POURRI

Pomanders and pot pourri are both methods of perfuming the air. Pomanders are the older of the two: from medieval times onwards, aromatic substances were made into a ball, and carried or worn (by the wealthy at least) in a small perforated globe or box, often made from gold or silver, as a supposed protection from diseases thought to be carried in foul-smelling air. Pot pourri is of a later origin, although it probably evolved from an early tradition of mixing fresh herbs to scent homes and ward off 'evil' smells. Recipes for pot pourri as we know it today – made from dried flowers as well as herbs – became popular in the 1800s.

## MAKING A POMANDER

*To make Pomanders, take two penny-worth of Labdanum, two penny-worth of Storax liquid, one penny-worth of* Calamus Aromaticus, *as much Balm, half a quarter of a pound of fine wax, of Cloves and Mace two penny-worth ... and of Musk four grains: beat all these exceedingly together, till they come to a perfect substance, then mould it in any fashion you please, and dry it.*

Gervase Markham, *The English House-Wife* (1675)

Although Markham gave the 17th-century housewife instructions for making a pomander by mixing aromatic substances, modern pomanders generally follow an alternative tradition of pomander making, involving studding a citrus fruit with cloves. To make an orange pomander, which can be hung in a room or wardrobe, you will need an orange, some cloves, masking tape, ribbon, orris root powder (made from the roots of Mediterranean irises, and sold in some health food shops) and ground cinnamon.

First, use the tape to divide the surface of the orange into four equal segments. Next, insert cloves into the exposed orange, either in a pattern or to cover the orange completely (if necessary, pierce holes in the skin with a small nail first, and remember to leave a small space around each clove, as the orange will shrink when it is dried). Then mix the cinnamon and orris root powder, and place them in a paper bag, adding the orange and rolling it around to cover it with the spice mix. Put the orange (still in the paper bag) somewhere warm and dry. The orange must dry out completely, which will probably take at least three weeks. If it shows any signs of mouldiness discard it and start again. When it has dried completely, remove the tape, replace it with ribbon, and the pomander will be ready to perfume a room.

*Making a pomander*
*Dave King © Dorling Kindersley*

## MIXING POT POURRI

*A quicker sort of pot-pourri.—Take three handfuls of orange-flowers, three of clove-gillyflowers, three of damask-roses, one of knotted marjoram, one of lemon-thyme, six bay leaves, a handful of rosemary, one of myrtle, half of mint, one of lavender, the rind of a lemon, and a quarter of an ounce of cloves. Chop all, and put them in layers, with pounded bay-salt between, up to the tip of the jar. If all the ingredients cannot be obtained at once, put them in as you get them; always throwing in salt with every new article.*

Sarah Hale, *The New Household Receipt-Book* (1854)

*Drying lavender*
© Romain Bayle / Alamy

Pot pourri can be made from any combination of dried herbs, flowers, bark, seeds, fruit and berries. Flowers and leaves are dried by tying them in small bunches, and hanging them upside down somewhere dry and airy. Essential oils are often used to give the mixture extra fragrance, or to renew its fragrance once it has become stale.

# *Making*
## *Tussie-mussies*

## TUSSIE-MUSSIES

A tussie-mussie, or tuzzy-muzzy, is a small posy of flowers and herbs. The tradition of tussie-mussie making dates back to the Elizabethan period, when small posies of flowers and herbs were made and carried for their fragrance, and for the stimulating effect that such fragrance was said to have on the brain. Fragrant herbs were also thought to protect people from the 'bad air' believed to cause disease, most notably the plague.

By Victorian times, tussie-mussies were widely popular, but they were no longer simply attractive and pleasantly scented posies of flowers – by this time the study of the 'language of flowers' (ie the meanings signified by different varieties of flower) was highly evolved, and every young woman of even modest means knew what could be read into the flowers presented to her by a beau. Tussie-mussies are still made today, but more for their cheerful colours and their scent than to pass secret messages.

## THE LANGUAGE OF FLOWERS

*Why do flowers enter and shed their perfume over every scene of our life, from the cradle to the grave? Why are flowers made to utter all voices of joy and sorrow in all varying scenes, from the chaplet that adorns the bride to the votive wreath that blooms over the tomb? It is for no other reason than that flowers have in themselves a real and natural significance. They have a positive relation to man, his sentiments,*

*passions and feelings. They correspond to actual emotions. They have their mission—*
*a mission of love and mercy. They have their language, and from the remotest ages*
*this language has found its interpreters.*

Henrietta Dumont, *The Language of Flowers:*
*The Floral Offering: a token of affection and esteem;*
*comprising the language and poetry of flowers* (1852)

While Shakespeare's Ophelia speaks of rosemary for remembrance and
pansies for thoughts, it was not until the 19th century that the language of
flowers was fully reported. In 1818, Louise Cortambert published *Le Langage*

*des fleurs* (under the pseudonym
Charlotte de la Tour). An English
translation appeared in 1834, and
apparently started a trend for
books on the language of flowers
that lasted for several decades, with
numerous books on the subject
being published in both Britain
and America. Unfortunately, these
books often contradicted each
other, as do modern lists on this
topic – does a daffodil represent
'regret', 'self-love', 'unrequited love'
or 'regard'; and does lavender signify
'love', 'forgiveness' or 'mistrust'?

## MAKING A TUSSIE-MUSSIE

Tussie-mussie of herbs
and flowers
Dave King © Dorling
Kindersley

Whether choosing flowers and herbs based on seasonality and colour, or
using flowers associated with a particular meaning, a tussie-mussie is one
of the simplest and most satisfying floral arrangements to make. First, a
central flower is selected (often a rose, for 'love'). Then the central flower
is encircled with a herb such as rosemary or some stems of foliage. A very
simple tussie-mussie stops there, while the type of tussie-mussie most
often made today continues with wider and wider circles of flowers and
then foliage, before it is tied to keep everything in place.

# Carving Welsh Love Spoons

## LOVE SPOONS

Love spoons are particularly associated with Wales, although the tradition is not entirely confined to there. They were originally produced by carving or whittling wood, and were given as love tokens by suitors – they showed off skill, expressed seriousness of intent and indicated ability to provide. They are now popular collectors' items and are often given as wedding, anniversary, birthday or baby gifts.

*Welsh love spoons*
*© Les Evans / Photolibrary Wales*

## SPOONING

Welsh love spoons have been whittled or carved since the 17th century. Carved or whittled decorative spoons evolved from the basic, practical wooden 'cawl', or spoon. Highly decorated spoons were whittled by young men, from a single piece of wood, to be presented to their intended bride. The practice was particularly common among sailors who were away from home for months or even years – this is reflected in many of the traditional designs, which incorporate chains, anchors and other nautical symbols.

Producing love spoons required a great deal of skill and patience. Designs became increasingly intricate as the whittlers worked to show the strength of their love and, perhaps more importantly, their skill and potential for providing for a family. Today, the carving of love spoons is a lucrative craft industry, and many are made with at least some input from power tools. These days most people find it easier to express their love by buying a spoon rather than carving one.

## SAYING IT WITH SPOONS

Over the years, Welsh love spoons developed their own symbolism. Some of the popular symbols and their supposed meanings are given below, although it is unlikely that there was as much consistency of meaning as is now suggested.

*Carving lovespoons*
© *Neil McAllister / Alamy*

> Horseshoe – good luck
> Cross – faith
> Bell – marriage
> Heart – love (a double heart symbolized mutual love and a
>   heart-shaped bowl symbolized a life full of love)
> Knot (sometimes of rigging rope) – everlasting love
> Anchor – heart anchored at home
> Ship's wheel or cartwheel – an intention to work hard
> Twisted vines – love that will grow
> Flowers – growing affection, or a request to court

Some carvers made double-bowled spoons, or pairs of spoons joined by carved chains, again symbolising mutual love. Perhaps the most impressive design was the carved, freely moving ball inside a cage, which showed that the maker's heart had been captured.

## SPREAD THE LOVE

Sycamore and beech are the most suitable species for making spoons, although being of a decorative rather than a practical nature, the choice of wood for love spoons is not so important. Where possible, start the carving while the wood is still green (freshly cut). The first stage in making a love spoon involves marking out the basic shape. The bowl can then be hollowed out with a rounded gouge or curved knife. Next, the basic shape can be cut out using a saw. After this, the style of carving and choice of tools will depend on the chosen pattern. In general, it is best to take away too little with each chisel or knife cut than too much, and to work in towards the final shape in small stages.

The National Museums of Wales are a good starting point for finding out more about Welsh culture. The oldest known example of a Welsh love spoon, thought to date from the 1660s, is at St Fagans National History Museum in Cardiff (www.museumwales.ac.uk). A simple Internet search will also reveal many examples of craftspeople and companies selling love spoons, or patterns and instructions for making your own.

# Whittling

## WHITTLING

Carving and whittling are often used interchangeably to describe cutting and shaping objects out of wood, bone, horn, amber or other hard, carvable substances. However, whittling strictly involves cutting, shaving and shaping with only a knife, and is traditionally carried out using found wood, while carving often employs a range of specialist tools, including chisels, shaves, gouges, saws, axes and mallets, and specially selected materials.

## HOBO ART

Whittling and carving are ancient arts. Objects have been carved using available tools since prehistoric times. By the Middle Ages, the carving of figures, sculptures and decorative work had become a craft of artisans. However, many of the techniques and tools of carving were also employed in general woodcraft, green woodworking and the manufacture of a wide range of practical items, including barrels, wheels and furniture. The art of whittling is often thought of as something of a poor cousin to these crafts – a hobby carried out by country-dwellers and seamen with time on their hands. Indeed, in the USA it is sometimes described as one of the hobo arts. However, whittling has been employed in the manufacture of incredibly intricate items, including the famous 'ball in a cage' or open-link chains that were once used to adorn items such as Welsh love spoons, or were made simply to show off the craftsman's skill. The lifestyles and spare time that once created the ideal conditions for whittling are now long gone for most people. However, there are now a growing number of hobby whittlers on both sides of the Atlantic.

## WHITTLING AWAY THE HOURS

The beauty of whittling as a craft is that it can be done by anyone with a small piece of wood and a knife. Any light small-bladed knife can be used, but specialist whittling knives are also available, with thicker handles to make them more comfortable for extended use and to allow for greater precision. The primary consideration is that the knife is sharp – strange as it sounds, you are less likely to injure yourself with a sharp knife that moves easily through the wood. Having said that, there are still obvious dangers in whittling – so take care, make small, gentle cuts and work away from the body (and hand) as much as possible.

Whittling should not be carried out in a hurry. It requires patience and, like fishing, many whittlers practise the art for the process as much as for the outcome. Peeling the bark from a stick and sharpening it to a point by careful shaving, or making simple shapes from soft wood, are good ways to practise the basic skills. As a general rule, take off very little with each cut, working in towards the finished shape in stages. It is also a good idea to look at the direction of the grain in the wood – it is easier to shave with it than across it. Green (freshly cut) wood is generally easier to work with than seasoned, dry or treated wood. A number of books of patterns and whittling ideas are available, but you may prefer to take your ideas from the shape and grain of the wood itself.

*Working Scrimshaw*

## SCRIMMING

'Scrimshaw' was originally used to refer to any of a range of handicrafts and tool-making and time-wasting activities practised by sailors on long voyages. The origin is obscure, although there is an (unsubstantiated) suggestion that it might come from the Breton Celtic phrase 'cham charch' meaning 'useless work' (many whalers were from Brittany in France). Eventually, 'scrimshaw' was used more specifically to refer to the work created by etching and inking designs into whalebone, whale teeth and walrus tusks. A practitioner of scrimming (making scrimshaw work, also known as scrimshonting or scrimshonging) was called a scrimshander. Today, scrimshaw is used to refer to engraving on a variety of hard materials, including animal bone, horn, ivory, shells and man-made alternatives.

## A WHALE OF A TIME

From the beginning of European whaling, at the time of the Vikings, sailors carved small items out of whalebone, whale teeth and walrus tusks. Later, these substances came to be used as cheaper alternatives to ivory. Their decoration was also common among the Inuit, who inevitably exchanged products and techniques with European and North American sailors.

Scrimshaw work as it is now understood (involving the etching of designs into, or the carving of small figures and objects from, hard whaling by-products) was first produced on board commercial whaling vessels in the early 19th century. Prior to this, whittling and the manufacture of hand tools and other implements from found materials had taken place on board ships for many centuries. However, whaling voyages often lasted for years, and the time between whale sightings could amount to months, creating a lot of spare time – ideal conditions for the growth of the art. By the time it reached its peak, sperm whale teeth, baleen and whalebone were of little or no commercial value and were therefore readily available to whalers – teeth were particularly good because they could be polished to a high gloss before etching. Walrus tusks were also used when they could be obtained from indigenous hunters.

The designs were etched using metal needles and other sharp tools that came to hand. Once the design had been etched, lamp black was used to colour the indentations. More elaborate, multicoloured designs were sometimes produced using any available coloured inks, pigments or home-made dyes.

At the height of scrimshaw production in the mid-19th century, a vast range of items were being produced.

*... lively sketches of whales and whaling-scenes, graven by the fishermen themselves on Sperm Whale-teeth, or ladies' busks wrought out of the Right Whale-bone, and other like skrimshander articles, as the whalemen call the numerous little ingenious contrivances they elaborately carve out of the rough material, in their hours of ocean leisure.*
Herman Melville, *Moby Dick* (1851)

Scrimshaw on a whale's tooth, showing a late 18th or early 19th century man-o'-war
© Angus Council Licensor www.scran.ac.uk

Traditional scrimshaw died out with the reduction in whaling and its eventual ban. Due to the complex legal status of ivory and whale products, modern craft scrimshaw is mainly carried out on alternatives such as bone or horn, and man-made substances including plexiglass and micarta.

## SCRIM IT YOURSELF

Trading in whale or elephant ivory is, of course, illegal, except in very particular circumstances. But it is possible to practise the techniques of scrimshaw on synthetic alternatives, or, as a starting point, you could try animal bones available from pet shops. Cut the bone to shape and carefully sand it, using increasingly fine glasspaper and then a polishing compound. Waxing the finished bone will help to prevent the ink from spreading when you add it.

Marks can be made in the surface to build up your design, using hard needles or fine drill bits. There are two basic techniques: pushing the needle in to make dots (the harder you push, the larger the dot), and holding the needle at an angle and dragging it to scratch lines. Any ink can be used to fill in the picture. Apply the ink using a cotton bud, wiping away the excess from the surface with a cloth. When you have finished, wax the final piece again.

# Bone, Antler and Horn Working

## BONE, ANTLER AND HORN WORK

Bone, antler and horn work are often grouped together. Many of the techniques employed are similar and, in the past, all three materials were used side by side. However, there are distinct differences in the working possibilities they provide and in their durability. Horn is a softer substance than bone, consisting of keratin (the same substance that makes up hair, nails, feathers and hooves). Cows, sheep and goats would have been the main sources of horn for working. Deer antlers are not horn but a form of bone, and as such are harder, less plastic and more durable than horn. Antler and bone can be worked and used in the same way.

## ANCIENT PLASTICS

Bone and horn are among the earliest substances used by man to make tools. By the early Middle Ages, both were being used to manufacture a vast range of products. However, horn breaks down much more quickly than bone or antler, so only a very limited number of early horn artefacts have survived. Conversely, there is a significant amount of bone work dating from the Viking period and before.

## HORN OF PLENTY

The image of the medieval drinking horn or musical horn has now become something of a cliché. Although horns would certainly have been used for these ceremonial purposes, the fact that horn can be softened by heating meant that it could be used for a far greater range of practical purposes: it could be formed into plate, cut and shaped and made into a number of products for which we now use plastic. In addition to this, horn becomes almost transparent if thinned and oiled, meaning that it could be used to make the panels of 'lanthorns', or lanterns.

By the later Middle Ages, horn working was an established trade with distinct jobs – horn pressing to make plate, and horn moulding, turning and carving. As well as spoons and combs, horn could be made into small containers, window panes, helmet plates, knife handles and decorative or protective tips and panels to be added to wooden tools and weapons.

Horn is perhaps best known in modern times for its use in dressing sticks and shepherds' crooks. However, from the 17th to the 19th century the craft developed into something akin to the modern plastics industry: horn-rimmed spectacles became more and more popular; hornbooks were used to teach reading (a text was placed on a wooden board and covered with a transparent horn plate to protect it); horn was carved or moulded into ornaments, jewellery and seals; and it was made into lanterns, powder horns, mass-produced combs, shoehorns, buttons, cups and cutlery, and much more.

Horn tumblers,
Shetland
© Shetland Museum Licensor
www.scran.ac.uk

The development of man-made plastics and other metal-alloy alternatives, improvements in mechanization, the decline of tanning and changes in farm husbandry (reducing the supply of the basic material) all led to the almost total disappearance of commercial horn working by the early 20th century. However, it is still practised by a few as a small-scale craft.

## BARE BONES

Bone items have survived from the early Middle Ages, and earlier, in greater quantity than horn. Working with bone to make small items such as needles, jewellery, tools and whistles or pipes was, and still is, found in pre-industrial cultures throughout the world. A by-product of hunting or farming for food and clothing, the basic material is strong, carvable and durable. Antler is similar in its properties, although slightly stronger, and has the added benefit that it is shed annually by stags and so can be found in a ready-to-use state.

The Vikings and their contemporaries used bone to make board game pieces, dice, combs, needles, whistles, knife handles and a range of decorative items. Larger items were made from whalebone when it was available – the material that was later used in the craft of scrimshawing. By the end of the Middle Ages, bone had developed a new industrial use, being the basis for the manufacture of glue and the 'size' used in the paper-making process.

## TAKE THE BULL BY THE HORNS

*Carved-bone snuff spoon*
© *National Museums Scotland Licensor www.scran.ac.uk*

The first stage of working with bone or horn is obtaining your raw material. Historically, bone would have been cleaned by burying or similar exposure to the natural action of invertebrates. Today, if you don't want to boil and scrape the bones yourself, cleaned bones can be obtained from pet shops. Horn might be more difficult to come by. Both bone and horn will require you to remove the soft inner material and carefully scrape and scour away anything that might rot. Because this can be difficult and time-consuming, it is best not to make anything that is to be used for food or drink until you have become more confident. If it begins to smell, you haven't cleaned it well enough!

The basic tools required are few, and are much the same as those that would have been used by the Vikings. A fine-toothed saw, a sharp knife, a sharp needle, small files, glasspaper or emery cloth and, if desired, a hand drill and chisels of the type used for carving wood can be used. Dry bone is brittle and hard to carve – if necessary, soak it in water for a few days; this will make it easier to work. Horn can be reshaped by heating it. The safest way to do this is by putting it in water and boiling it (probably for two hours or more), because there is no danger of its reaching its melting point. The period for which it remains plastic is short, and you will probably still need to use pliers or similar to help you bend it. Obviously, care will be required in handling it while it is hot.

## Working with bone

Bone can be sawn and then carved like wood. Small hollow bones could be used to make whistles. Discs cut from a bone can be used to make board-game pieces and thicker pieces of bone can be cut to make dice. The range of items, as with whittled or carved wood, is limited only by your imagination (and developing skills). If you attempt a comb, antler would be a better choice as it will produce stronger teeth.

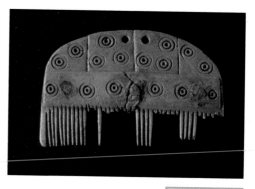

*Antler comb, Orkney*
*© Orkney Islands Council*
*Licensor www.scran.ac.uk*

## Working with horn

Horn can be turned and carved in a similar way to wood. The solid tip is probably best for this. The rest of the horn can be cut open and flattened, using heat, to make plate to work with. From there, by heating, pressing and bending it can be made into a variety of items, including spoons and combs.

# Making Whistles

## MAKING A WHISTLE

At its most basic, a whistle is a simple piece of equipment designed to produce a loud 'whistling' sound when air is forced through a hole. Such a sound can also be produced by blowing air through pursed lips or through the teeth, by blowing through a small opening made between the thumbs into a closed chamber made by cupping the hands together, or by blowing across the opening to a closed chamber, such as a bottle.

Devices designed to increase the volume of the sound, or even tune the sound to notes, can be separated into two basic types: those where the hole into which you blow also produces the sound, and those with a separate mouthpiece and sound hole. Each can be further subdivided – they can have a 'closed' chamber to produce a single note (the standard whistle as used by referees and PE teachers falls into this category), a 'closed' chamber with several holes that can be covered to produce a range of notes (such as an ocarina), a closed chamber that can be altered in length to change the note (as in a swanee whistle), or an open-ended tube with holes along it (flutes, where you blow across the sound hole, or 'fipple' flutes – which include penny whistles and recorders – with a separate mouthpiece, or fipple, and a sound hole).

## WHISTLE-STOP TOUR

Simple single-note whistles, fashioned from wood, bone and clay, have been used for thousands of years. They allow communication over long distances, can signal emergencies, and can be used to salute important people, play simple music, keep time for rowing, issue commands in noisy environments and keep wayward sportspeople in line. One of the major benefits of the single-note, two-hole whistle is that there is no requirement to learn a particular blowing technique, as the device takes care of this; if you blow hard enough in one end it will consistently make the same loud whistle.

Wooden whistles, bone whistles, twig whistles or clay whistles were used by shepherds and other country-dwellers for many centuries. Whistles were certainly also in use for military purposes by the time of the Crusades. By the second half of the 19th century, metal whistles were being mass-produced for the navy and the new police forces on both sides of the Atlantic.

Perhaps the most important developments in modern whistle making took place following the first use of a whistle at a football match – generally cited as a match at Nottingham Forest in 1878. In 1883 Joseph Hudson of the Acme Whistle Company in Birmingham, the company that produced this first referees' whistle, developed the police whistle. A year later the first pea-whistle, the Acme Thunderer, was made – the now ubiquitous referees' and teachers' whistle, with a pea inside the chamber to repeatedly block and unblock the sound hole and thus produce a distinctive warbling sound.

## WHISTLE UP A TUNE

The aerodynamics involved in producing a whistling sound are extremely complex. In simple terms (leaving aside tuned, open-ended woodwind musical instruments), the whistling sound in the examples discussed here is made when the high-speed flow produced by forcing air through the small mouthpiece is split at the sound hole. The upper portion forms vortices above the sound hole, causing the air to vibrate and therefore making a sound. The lower portion forms swirls of air inside the chamber, which are also forced out through the hole, reinforcing particular frequencies of sound produced above the hole through the effect of resonance.

### *Wooden (or bone) whistle*

To make a simple wooden whistle (a similar technique can be used for bone), take a short piece of stick (making sure you don't choose a poisonous species). Drill out the centre from one end (or remove the soft pith if using bamboo or similar), making sure you don't go all the way through. Then cut a notch into the stick, about 2–3 centimetres (1 inch) from the drilled end (using a perpendicular cut and a 45-degree cut to meet it, so that it will split the airflow as it comes in from the end) to reach the sound chamber you have made. When you have done this, make a wooden plug to fit into the open end, shaving one side of the plug flat, so that when it is pushed in it will leave a narrow hole to blow into – this should be at the top of your whistle in line with the sound-hole notch. If you wish, you can then shape the sound hole.

## Stick whistle

If you use a 'green' (freshly cut) stick that still has its bark on, you can cut the notch first, then loosen the bark by tapping all round it and slide it off. Keeping the bark moist in water while you work, cut away a piece from the top of the inner twig (it mustn't reach right to the end) to make a sound chamber, meeting with the perpendicular edge of the original notch cut. Shave a little wood off the top at the mouthpiece end so that it will leave a small opening to blow into when the bark is replaced, and slide the bark gently back into position.

## Clay whistle

The whole whistle arrangement can be made using clay, the basic principle for making the sound being the same. First, make a small clay pot, then squeeze the top edges together and join them by moistening and pinching. This will make an airtight chamber. Use a tool to punch through a sound hole, at an angle so that it will split the air blown in from the mouthpiece. Finally, make a hole to blow into (this must be aligned carefully with the sound hole so that the airflow can be directed accurately – some experimentation will be required) and shape your mouthpiece.

Now, blow away! Your neighbours will love it.

# Canal Boat Painting

## CANAL ART

The canal boats of 19th-century British waterways, and many of the practical items on board, were adorned on almost every available surface with a particular style of art. This folk art form grew and flourished along the canals of the English Midlands during the 'canal age' of the 19th and early 20th centuries.

## LIFE ON THE WATER

*The boatman lavishes all his taste, all his rude, uncultivated love for the fine arts, upon the external and internal ornaments of his floating home. His chosen colours are red, yellow, and blue: all so bright that, when newly laid on and appearing under the rays of a mid-day sun, they are too much for the unprotected eye of the unaccustomed stranger. The two sides of the cabin, seen from the bank and the towing-path, present a couple of landscapes, in which there is a lake, a castle, a sailing-boat, and a range of mountains, painted after the style of the great teaboard school of art.*

John Hollingshead, *Odd Journeys in and out of London* (1860)

As the canal network grew towards the end of the 18th century, a new way of life was born. In the early days canal boats would have had an employed, working crew, with the boatmen and their families living on the bank. However, competition from the railways and rising costs of living forced the boatmen of the Midlands to take their families to live on board the narrow boats. Within a generation, the cultures of boatpeople and land dwellers had diverged dramatically, with the boatpeople tending to retain traditional clothing, crafts and customs, and leaving those ashore to embrace 'progress'.

Whether it was through a desire to improve living conditions in the cramped narrow boats, to make the most of limited space and resources or simply to defy the stereotypical 'dirty and uneducated' label applied to them by much of the wider society (which often used derogatory terms such as 'water gypsies'), the people who lived on the canals developed a style of ostentatious decoration that became a proud statement of their membership of the canal club.

*Traditionally decorated narrowboat*
© *Lesley Pegrum / Alamy*

Initially, the decorative paintwork was applied by the boatmen themselves but it later became an intrinsic part of boat building – some of the more accomplished painters even made it their exclusive profession. It wasn't just the boats alone that were decorated: some portable items, such as the water can, bucket and dipper, as well as the horse's harness when boats were still horse-drawn, would be covered in bright, elaborate designs.

The tradition continued until the decline of commercial carrying on the canals in the first half of the 20th century. However, as the canal network was revitalized in the second half of the century, becoming a holiday attraction, new life was breathed into the painting tradition of the canals. Today, the style is employed for a range of portable items, pictures and gifts, as well as being found aboard the boats themselves.

## ROSES AND CASTLES

There are three main stages to canal boat painting. First, the separate areas of the boat are picked out in blocks of bright colour. This is often extended to dividing rectangular spaces with diagonals and adding coloured diamond patterns. This might then be finished off with the addition of borders, scrollwork and any number of patterns and symbols. A tradition of painting a pattern of figures such as diamonds or circles at the bow of the boat stems from the need for often-illiterate boatmen on the Birmingham canals to identify which company owned a particular boat – each fleet would have its own distinctive arrangement.

*Roses and castles*
© *Tom Bowett / Alamy*

The boat's name and owner's name and details are then added on a large, elaborate sign in beautifully executed hand-painted lettering, to comply with waterways regulations and advertise the boat owner's services, again demonstrating the link between the decorative and practical aspects of canal boat painting.

Finally, certain parts of the boat and its equipment and utensils are decorated in the 'roses and castles' style. Often described as naïve, this artistic style is famous for its stylistic floral decoration and romantic scenes depicting castles and grand houses more reminiscent of the Rhine than Runcorn. The painting will often be carried out quickly, producing representations in bright colours, rather than exact depictions, and building up a charming but slightly gaudy illusion of opulence.

# Making Stained Glass

## MAKING STAINED GLASS

Stained glass making as a craft grew with the rapid expansion in constructing churches and cathedrals from the 10th century onwards. Windows were made by creating a picture or pattern using pieces of coloured glass. Further detail was added by painting with enamels or other substances, then firing to 'stain' the glass. Lead strips held the separate pieces together. An alternative method of manufacture involved painting colours on to the surface of a single plain piece of glass and then firing it to fix the picture in place.

## A COLOURFUL HISTORY

Glass had been coloured by the addition of metallic mineral salts ever since the manufacturing process was first discovered over 4,000 years ago. The ancient Egyptians, Phoenicians, Greeks and Romans and, later, medieval Islamic cultures all used coloured glass in the manufacture of a range of vessels, jewellery and mosaics. There is some evidence that coloured glass was being used in mosques and churches in the early Middle Ages, but the use of stained glass to make the great windows of churches can only be traced back (with any certainty) to the 10th century.

As the years passed, the styles, themes and architectural settings for the windows became ever more elaborate and grand. Many had to be supported by huge iron frames. In the 15th century the accurate depiction of scenes and characters became more common, and a number of stains (particularly silver stain) were in use for painting on to the surface of the glass in order to colour, shade and pick out detail.

Most of the medieval examples of stained glass windows in Britain were destroyed during the Reformation, or later under Oliver Cromwell. But a number of examples remain elsewhere in Europe. During the 19th century there was something of a revival in its manufacture, which began to be conducted on an industrial scale to fulfil a renewed desire for ecclesiastical stained glass.

Since then, the production of a range of stained glass has become a popular art form and it can be seen in homes as well as churches, in the form of lampshades, windows, pictures and a whole range of other decorative items.

*Stained glass window, Canterbury Cathedral*
*© Tibor Bognar / Alamy*

## PUTTING THE PIECES TOGETHER

The basic process for making a stained glass panel has changed very little since it was described by the German monk Theophilus in his *De Diversis Artibus* ('The Various Arts') in around 1125.

Starting with a template of the space to be filled, a full-size 'cartoon' of the whole image is drawn – the glass colours and finer detail to be painted on may also be added. This cartoon is then cut up to make templates for the individual pieces of glass. The pieces of coloured glass are selected and cut into shape. Detail and stained shading is added to the inner surface of the glass by painting on mixtures of metallic oxides and ground glass. Each piece of glass is then fired to fix the stain before the picture is fitted together on a board, with the pieces of glass held slightly apart using nails.

Finally, lead strips, with an H-shaped cross-section, are cut and soldered into position between the glass pieces to hold them in place. Glazing cement is applied to fill in any gaps, preventing water ingress and movement of the glass pieces.

## FURTHER THROUGH THE WINDOW

Impressive examples of ecclesiastical stained glass can be seen in most cathedrals, including a number of interesting modern windows. More about the history, making and preservation of stained glass, and the opportunities available for training in the skills, can be found out from the British Society of Master Glass Painters (www.bsmgp.org.uk). Kits and materials for having a go yourself (on a somewhat smaller scale) can be obtained from a number of craft suppliers.

# Glass-blowing

## BLOWING GLASS

In its most basic form, glass can be made by heating silica (from sand or quartz), soda (naturally occurring as natron) or potash (from burnt seaweed or other vegetation) and a little lime (from limestone or chalk) to a very high temperature using a furnace. Glass-blowing is a technique for shaping glass that exploits its high viscosity and plastic properties when molten. By adjusting the proportion of soda, the material can be made stiff enough to allow air to be blown carefully into the molten blob through a blowpipe, inflating it to form a bubble.

## LOOKING INTO THE PAST

Naturally occurring glass (formed through volcanic action) was carved, chipped and fashioned into simple items by prehistoric peoples. However, the first manufacture of glass and the exploitation of its properties when heated are usually attributed to the Phoenicians or the ancient Egyptians in about 3500 BC. Initially, the glass was pressed and shaped to form solid objects, fused to make mosaics, or moulded around cores formed from sand, dung or clay to make crude vessels. However, by the first century BC in the area that is now Syria, small containers were being made by blowing into molten glass through a glass tube. The method was rapidly developed and spread throughout the Roman Empire. Glass tubes were replaced by clay pipes and eventually metal tubes. Glass was blown both freely and into moulds to make a vast range of items. Shaping and decoration became more complex and lavish.

*Glass-blowing*

With the decline and contraction of the Roman Empire, there was a corresponding decline in the level of production and quality of blown glass in Europe. However, the production of high-quality glass continued to an extent in the eastern Mediterranean and the Islamic world. During the Middle Ages the skills were gradually transferred, through trade, back to Europe, and Venice became a renowned centre for the craft of glass-making, famous for the production of clear 'cristallo' glass.

## FOREST GLASS

Medieval glass-making elsewhere in Europe mainly took the form of 'forest glass', manufactured in small timber 'glass houses' in the forest (near to the source of fuel needed to feed the hungry furnaces). Using a large fire-clay furnace, with a fire at the bottom and shelves running around the inside, washed raw ingredients were dried and then mixed together and heated for 24 hours. The mixture was then placed in pots in the hottest part of the furnace to melt it. A blowpipe could then be dipped into the molten mixture and

*Traditional glass-blowing*
© Paul Felix Photography / Alamy

turned to pick up a lump of glass, which was then rolled on a flat, polished surface to form a 'paraison', into which air was then blown. A number of tools were used to shape the bubble of glass, including various shears and tongs, and a rod called a 'pontil', which would stick to the outside of the glass bubble, allowing it to be manipulated and 'cracked off' the pipe so that the neck of the vessel could be shaped or other parts attached. All the while, the object being worked on would be repeatedly returned to the heat of the furnace to keep it malleable. Once the object was made, it was cooled in an annealing oven – if glass is cooled too quickly it breaks.

Glass-blowing could even be used to make window glass. Initially, this was done by flattening the sphere of molten glass out on a surface, making a disc with a 'crown' at the centre where the pontil had been attached. Later, a technique was developed in which a cylinder was formed, cut open and laid flat.

In the early part of the 17th century there was a rapid change in the nature of glass-making in Britain. A ban on the felling of timber for glass furnaces, in favour of shipbuilding and the iron industry, brought an end to forest glass-making. Coal became the fuel of choice and glass-making moved to the towns and cities. There were a number of developments during the Industrial Revolution, including the discovery of the technique for producing lead crystal, improvements in the use of moulds and, later, the machine method for making plate glass.

## A WINDOW ON MODERN GLASS CRAFT

The art of blowing glass survived industrialization through the demand for 'art glass' and high-quality decorative items. However, until the revival of studio glass-making in the 1960s, manufacture still took place mainly within factories. In recent years there has been a growth of interest in craft glass-making, and demonstrations of the process can be seen in a number of craft studios, museums and factory outlets. The International Guild of Glass Artists (www.igga.org) or the Glass Association (www.glassassociation.org.uk) are good starting points for finding out where to see handmade glass or where to learn more about the techniques of glass-making.